The Chocolate Elephant

The Chocolate Elephant

by

Gwendoline Page

Previous books by the same author:

Coconuts and Coral
Growing Pains – A Teenager's War
We Kept The Secret
They Listened In Secret

ISBN 9780900616 776

Printed and published by
Geo. R. Reeve Ltd., 9-11 Town Green, Wymondham, Norfolk

ACKNOWLEDGEMENTS

Aunt Kate's Day by Day Book Pub.by John Leng & Co Ltd. 1937
Articles in Saga Magazine by Roy Johnstone
Chambers Biographical Dictionary
People and Places Collins Dictionary
The Guiness Book of Aircraft David Mondey & Michael J.H. Taylor
The Blessings of a Good Thick Skirt Mary Russell
Hertfordshire Record Office (Hals)
Aviation, The Pioneer Years Mackworth-Praed B.
The Vimy Flies Again Peter MacMillan
The Age of Illusion Ronald Blythe
National Geographic
Articles in Eastern Daily Press Steve Snelling
Malcolm Perkins
Friends Robert Harris
        Rene Pritchard
        William Knights
        Christopher Watts
        Joyce Gorvin

CONTENTS

CONTENTS (continued)

CONTENTS (continued)

INTRODUCTION

Each one of us has a bank of personal memories known only to ourself, our own experience of episodes in our lives, our thoughts, feelings, sensations of significant or insignificant happenings to ourselves, or as onlookers to others. All these memories are fleeting things for when the time comes for us to leave this world, the memories go with us and are lost forever. That is unless they are recorded in some way.

In time past such memories were handed down from generation to generation by word of mouth, but then there was the risk that they would be changed in the telling. As in the game of Chinese Whispers, when a sentence told to the first player is whispered along a line of players and usually ends with the last player's reception bearing little resemblance to the original sentence, having been misheard along the way.

In modern times there are many other ways to record our personal recollections, by tape recorder, video camera, or the many and forever increasing forms of computers. But even these technological marvels become obsolete after a time and without the right machine such forms of recollections can be lost again.

It seems to me that the written word which can be picked up and deciphered by most people, as it has been through the centuries is the only true way to know how those who came before us viewed their time. The diaries of people like Samuel Pepys in the seventeenth century; A soldier from the Peninsular War; A Rector of a parish in the Georgian era; or letters written by travellers to those at home; Love letters written to those apart; these are the recollections which give a true picture of the life of such times which are not corrupted by others mishearing, or misunderstanding, but with care can be preserved for all time.

I do not claim that the memories of which I write can compare with those I mention above, but added to those of others of the same period, they may help to unfold a picture in the minds of those who follow, of life in this period between two devastating World Wars.

Here are gathered some of my memories along with those of other people, plus some recorded facts of the more important occurrences in those two decades to show what was happening in the wider world outside our small village. Many of those recorded facts were to affect all our lives greatly in the following decade. Even fifty or sixty years on repercussions of the time are still with us and affect many people in the view they take of present day events. Therefore it is necessary to have a knowledge of previous history to understand such attitudes.

Those memories I write are not of important personages, but of ordinary people who had to live their lives in the light of decisions made by the politicians, scientists, and inventors of the time whose ideas affected everybody. But do not dismay, for this is not a tome of disillusion, only a lighthearted look back at life as we knew it with many happy memories to balance the scales.

My thanks go to those kind friends who shared their memories with me allowing me to peep into their childhood, or reminded me of events and people I had almost forgotten and correcting me on other points of which I was unclear. Thank you all. I have gained a great deal of pleasure in listening to you apart from useful information. I hope that you will enjoy the result of our combined efforts.

Gwendoline Page

Children's Games

CHAPTER 1

Memory is a strange thing, especially as one reaches those more mature years of retirement. On occasion it takes French leave and names, which have been familiar for years, suddenly desert one. Simple activities taken part in only a day or two before, such as the meal you ate, the job you did (or intended to do) fade from memory and yet events which happened to you more than half a century ago are recalled with extreme clarity. Some of those events may have been of great importance, but not all. Many recollections are of insignificant happenings often lasting only a few moments in time, but remain permanently imprinted in the mind. Perhaps the clearest of these memories come from childhood. Such a one is my memory of the Chocolate Elephant.

My parent's shop in Risborough Road, Cheriton

THE CHOCOLATE ELEPHANT

It must have taken place when I was about twenty months old, certainly not much older than that as my brother was born when I was two and I have no recollection of him being around at the time. My parents owned a shop in Risborough Road in Cheriton, near Folkestone where they sold toys, sweets, fancy goods and stationery among other things. We, my father, mother and I, lived in the premises attached to the shop. A photograph taken at that time shows my father standing in the shop doorway, the windows full of toys and books with bundles of wooden hoops hanging each side of the door. Bowling hoops was a happy pastime for children and like whipping tops and marbles (or alleys) seemed to come in season. On the left hand side of father's shop was a furnishing store and on the right an off license.

From the actual shop itself it was a step down into our living room. In the centre of the room was a circular table where we had our meals. When standing on my toes, my eyes were just about on a level with the table top. One day when both my parents were busy elsewhere, my father in the shop and mother with some domestic duty, I wandered into the living room and standing on tip toe, holding the table edge to support myself, I looked over the surface of the table. There on the cloth stood an elephant, a chocolate elephant to be precise. Being partial to chocolate, even at that tender age, I looked at it for some time, thinking how wonderful it would be to taste. Perhaps I could try just a little piece? My hand moved towards this tempting morsel just within my reach and closed around it. Releasing my grip on the table I gazed at the chocolate elephant in my hand. The smell of the chocolate was beyond resistance and before long the elephant had lost his trunk which was dissolving in my mouth.

I think it was probably at this stage that I realized that what I had done was very naughty. My parents would not be pleased. It was too late to go back now and the chocolate was still so tempting. Crawling under the table I hid myself behind the draping tablecloth and devoured the rest of the elephant. I was licking the last of the chocolate from my fingers, when I heard my name being called by my mother. Knowing that what I had done was wrong, I did not respond, but kept very still and quiet. Mother continued to call. I could hear doors being opened and closed all over the house. Eventually my father was called in to help in the search. In my hiding place I listened, but did not move.

From under the table I saw their legs moving around the room. Finally mother lifted the tablecloth and bent to look under the table.

"She's here" she cried relief in her voice. Father came to look as well and I gazed back at them without speaking. I had expected them to be angry, for I was still suffering with guilt from my naughtiness, but they were so glad to find me that I had kisses and cuddles instead and the chocolate elephant was never once mentioned!

The Chocolate Elephant

Although we moved from Cheriton when I was just over three years of age and my brother still under two, other memories of that home remain with me; sitting on the back door step and picking burrs out of the cat's fur is one of them. Others are in connection with the Army Camp stationed on the hill nearby. Every Sunday afternoon in the fine weather, the band gave a concert to the local population who gathered around the band stand to enjoy their musical efforts. I loved the music and could not keep my feet still, but danced every moment they played, much to everybody's tolerant amusement. Strangely enough there were times when I was scared by the band. This was on Sunday mornings when the band led the soldiers in their church parade. Watching from the bedroom window over the shop, which looked out upon the main street of Cheriton, we could first hear then see the military band approaching, playing their lively march tunes, accompanied by various young boys doing their best to emulate the marching soldiers. Dressed in their smart uniforms and led by the bandmaster with his long, gold baton which he flung into the air before skillfully catching it again, the band made their way along the road coming closer every minute to where we watched at the window, the polished instruments shining in the morning light and the men neatly in step caused my heart to beat with excitement;— that is until the drummers appeared. The small drums with their rat-a-tat-tat I enjoyed, but when the big drum with its booming bass note, the drummer in his leopard skin apron, wheeling his big drum sticks in the air came into view, I was terrified! Leaving the window I dived into my parents' bed and hid under the blankets until the drummer had passed by. Why I should be so scared seems unreasonable, but I have a feeling that it was something to do with the leopard skin apron. My behaviour certainly surprised my parents. I can still see their amazed faces as they saw me dive into the bed.

High Street, Cheriton

Father sometimes had occasion to visit the army camp and I remember one time when he took Alan and I with him. I don't know if there were always cavalry regiments at Cheriton, but there was certainly a cavalry regiment there at this time. My father had been chatting to some soldiers at the stables where they were grooming their horses. All of a sudden this tall soldier in his khaki uniform looked down at me and said, "Would you like to sit on my horse?"

I must have nodded, for the next thing I remember was being lifted high in the air and being placed on the back of this huge brown creature with a distinctive smell. Everything developed quite a different aspect from up there. I was actually looking down on my father and the tall soldier and the ground seemed a mighty long way off! My brother received a similar ascent from another soldier on another horse, but he was probably too young to remember it.

MARINE CRESCENT & HARBOUR FROM THE LEAS, FOLKESTONE.

Another pleasure we enjoyed in the seaside town of Folkestone were the lifts taking passengers up and down the cliffs. There were three lifts altogether at various points on the cliff; one at The Leas, another at Sandgate Point and a third at another point which I have forgotten. It was a great sensation to sit in the cars and watch the beach as it appeared to come closer and closer. Of course the wonderful thing about the upward ride was that it removed the effort of climbing up a very long flight of steps, bringing passengers to the top of the cliffs with ease and comfort, while remaining cool and complete of breath.

THE CHOCOLATE ELEPHANT

Talking films were a new phenomena in the late 1920s. The first 'movies' were seen in the United States of America in 1894, but did not come to general viewing in Britain until the early part of the twentieth century. One film company I remember called themselves 'Twentieth Century Films'. Rudolph Valantino was the great 'heart throb' in the 1920s and the film in which he starred 'The Sheik' caused a sensation when it opened in New York in 1921. The first 'talkie' film came out in 1927, 'The Jazz Singer' when Al Jolson was heard singing on screen. My parents were keen to see such a film at the local cinema. Perhaps there was no willing baby sitter at the time, for I went along with them, my very first experience of movie films. The darkened cinema, the large audience, but most of all the huge black and white images of the moving, talking, figures, was overwhelming to my young mind. Also bearing in mind the fact that it was probably long past my normal bedtime, my eyes closed and I was soon fast asleep, so remember no more of my introduction to the movies or 'pictures' as it was then called.

The very first of all talking feature films to be made in Britain was in 1929. It was called 'The Clue of the New Pin' and a young John Gielgud played the part of the villain of the story. About the same time cartoon films came into being and the character 'Tin Tin' appeared for the first time in the January of that year. Colour and sound cartoon films came much later. Walt Disney's 'Snow White and the Seven Dwarfs' was first premiered in the United States in December of 1937. It was a full length film and caused a great sensation. Most children must have been taken to see it. Most loved it, although I can remember a few tears from frightened, very young children when the wicked queen appeared on the screen. Children were not used to visions of the wicked or ugly monsters which appear on the screens to thrill, or terrify them, as are seen in the later years of the century.

There must have been another occasion when I accompanied my parents to see a Jessie Matthews film for I remember a scene took place in a railway carriage and involved a lost ticket, but what the name of the film was I can't remember. Jessie Matthews who was born on November 3rd 1907 was a most popular actress famous for her singing, dancing and the romantic leads she played in comedy films. In later years she took part in radio programmes taking the title role in 'Mrs. Dale's Diary', a long running serial

My Father's shop, 129 Shenley Road, Boreham Wood. We lived above the shop

'soap' programme on BBC Radio.

I remember as a young child hearing the name 'Fatty Arbuckle' being spoken, often by children referring to a rather plump companion, but for many years I did not understand the reference. Eventually in much later years I discovered that Fatty Arbuckle was a more than plump silent film comedian, who in 1921 was tried for rape and manslaughter and found not guilty by 10-2 jury.

He was retried and again found not guilty, but his career had been ruined.

When I was three or three and a half and my brother two years younger, my parents decided to leave Cheriton and move to Boreham Wood in Hertfordshire. The big industry there was the film business, although often referred to as Elstree Studios, they were actually situated in Boreham Wood. My parents opened a newsagents in a small parade of shops alongside the large studios of British International Pictures Ltd. The shop was much larger than that in Cheriton and sold, not only newspapers, cigarettes and sweets, but toys, and fancy goods. It also provided a library. In those days we had no public library in the village, so customers use to borrow the books for a fee of 2d. a time.

Many of the actors from the studios came into the shop for papers or cigarettes, both Claude and Jack Hulbert, well known comedy actors, among them. Gracie Fields the Lancashire mill girl, who started her long career on stage and films by singing in a Rochdale cinema, married Monty Banks the film director who worked in those studios When he died in 1950 his funeral cortage passed from the studios along the main road of the village, while my husband and I watched from the window of our living room above the shop. For at that time as a newly married couple, we were living in my childhood home.

Elstree Studios, Boreham Wood

Anna Neagle and Herbert Wilcox lived in a nearby village close to the studios and many other actors and actresses bought or rented houses in our village and Elstree. A well known Chinese actress, Anna May Wong and Betty Balflore were among those one might see in the village. I once met Richard Tauber, the tenor singer, well remembered as the singer of the song 'You Are My Heart's Delight'. My father asked me to take a newspaper to his house where he lived with Diana Napier, on the hill in Allum Lane, near to the village of Elstree. The great man took the paper himself patted me on the head saying "Thank you my child" in his attractive Austrian accent, before I shyly turned and ran to the car where my father waited. I was about five or six at the time. Father often took orders for papers and delivered them to the studios himself. He frequently took me with him and so from an early age I became accustomed to the interiors of the vast studio floors, the façade sets, glaring lights and large cameras. Among the skilled workers were the plasterers who fashioned many marvels from their plaster mix, earning good money for those days. This was the hay-day of the film industry when all the studios were working to capacity with stars like Jack Buchanan, Mary Ellis and many others.

When 'Glamourous Nights' was being made with Mary Ellis as the singing star, with my father I was watching a scene being taken when a young lady was led off the set in tears. The strong lights had given her a severe headache. Often scenes had to be shot many times before the director was satisfied, which was frustrating for everyone. I was asked by one of the commissioners (we would call them security guards these days) if I would like to be a film star when I grew up. My answer was a decided "No". However, one girl from our village did become a film star. Dagma Winter was the daughter of our local doctor. She went to the convent school and I remember her travelling home on the bus from Barnet at the same time as myself, but this of course was in the 1930s and early 1940s. She made her name as actress Dana Winter in films, went to Hollywood and became a star.

I had one experience of working for a film. The studio required a number of children to sing for the film 'Henry Hall's Birthday Party'. The man asked to provide the choir was lodging with someone my mother knew. He simply rounded up the children in the road starting with the two children of his landlady and some of their friends and myself, aged five at the time, and took us all to the studio where we were taught the song which went something like this:

"We wish you many happy returns of the day
Many happy returns of the day.
Full of prosperity, as you could ever be . . ."

After over fifty years my memory runs out and the last lines are forgotten.

Henry Hall, a popular dance band leader was conductor of the BBC Radio Dance Band for many years into the 1940s. Whether or not it really was his birthday I do not know, but certainly the film was made. The children collected together to sing this particular song were of all ages, boys and girls. Among the group was one small boy who was completely tuneless and the musician trying to teach us how to sing in the one morning was becoming quite desperate. A film of children being driven along in open cars or coaches was shown while we sang and our voices were to be attached to this piece of film. We ourselves never appeared on the screen, only our voices were heard. When we had all become at least word perfect a director came along to listen. The musician explained the difficulty he was having with the little boy whose voice came out at least an octave below all others. After the director had heard us sing the piece he decided to leave the voice of the small boy as it was, as it sounded more authentic that way. So it was that after several hours of work when we were almost hoarse from repeating the tune over and over again, we were each given five shillings and told we could go home.

Many local people were co-opted in as film extras when they were needed. Mother, my brother Alan and myself found ourselves in this position on Elstree Station one day. The film crew were taking some shots for the Tom Wall's film "Rookery Nook". Alan and I were still very young. Apparently Mother was asked to get a hankie out and pretend to help me blow my nose. What it did for the film I can't say! I don't ever remember seeing it. We grew quite used to strange requests like this.

One of the first film studios in Boreham Wood was the Ideal Studio. A small studio it was situated in Essex Road off Clarendon Road. It later became Leslie Fuller's Studio and then the Rock Studios. In its early days it compared with Denham Studios. Mrs Pritchard writes to me of her memories and recalls the time she and one of her sisters were taken there and dressed in long dresses and pantaloons to take part in a film. They were two and three years old at the time. Of course there were many star struck people who longed to become film stars, imagining it to be a glamorous kind of life. They used to queue at the studios in the hope of being taken on as film extras, hoping they would get the 'big break' and become a star. Some were lucky, but many were turned away.

While the film industry prospered more studios were built in Boreham Wood. By 1930 twenty five million people went to the cinema, or 'pictures' each week. Things continued to go well until television appeared on the scene. The Leslie Fuller studios could be entered from Clarendon Road or from Eldon Avenue. Many comedy films were made there. The building is now used by BBC television for documentary films and provides the settings for 'Eastenders' television series. The Gate Studios were close to Elstree Station. In Elstree Way more large buildings were erected for the film industry. All these studios provided employment for local people and brought many visitors to the area.

Other employment in Boreham Wood was found at the Keystone Stocking Factory. Many young girls leaving the elementary school at fourteen found their first jobs here, others went into shop work. The photographic firm of Dufay-Chromex Ltd. also provided employment as did the firm of Wellington and Ward situated off Shenley Road before them. In Drayton Road was the Challenge Rubber Works also giving local employment. Other people might find a job with the local council or the cinema. In later years after World War Two, an industrial area grew up along the Elstree Way and Manor Way which included light engineering works, Adhesive Tapes and other light industries.

There were still one or two farms in the area and plenty of countryside before 1939. On the hill at the top of Allum Lane was a farm where the pig sty was alongside the footpath close to the main road. When we were small our Sunday walk used to include a visit to the pigs to scratch their backs with a stick. Many years later I took my own daughters on this same walk to the pigs, although I doubt that they were the same pigs, but their pig sty was not changed.

There were bluebell woods and fields where we could play and climb trees without fear and near the railway was an area of parkland with ponds to dip for tadpoles, newts and sticklebacks. When of school age we would ride our bicycles and meet our friends there. Memory of these days always seems to be full of space to roam without restriction, or worry of possible dangers. Certainly we had no fear of strangers or adults, although we did have a healthy respect for older people and if we were forbidden a certain area we did not disobey, at least this worked for the majority of children.

The way to this parkland of open fields was across a metal railway bridge. A great delight was to stand on this bridge waving to the engine driver and then become enveloped in the smoke puffing from the engine funnel as it passed under us. We thought it great fun. When I was around twelve years of age, I used to take my neighbours' two little girls in their pram to this same railway bridge to see the trains go by. It was not until one of these little girls was in her forties that she told me that she had been scared of these puffing giants! At the time I had picked up no indication of this, but thought she enjoyed seeing them. At this rather late stage I apologized for causing her distress.

As mentioned earlier, we lived above my parents business. A steep staircase led up from the back door in the shop yard to a landing on the first floor where our kitchen, bathroom, dining room and living room were situated. The stairs continued upwards to a second floor where there were four bedrooms. My bedroom looked over the back yard and a small area of garden beyond the access road to the back of the parade, entered from Whitehouse Avenue, which was a road of mixed private dwellings, a number of which were probably rented out.

From the first floor a flat roof jutted out beneath the dining room and kitchen windows. Under this was the office next to the shop. This office had a barred window. I have a strong vision of this window after one particular incident.

Mother had hired a young woman about eighteen years of age to act as nursemaid to Alan and I when my mother was helping my father in the business. Mother was responsible for the confectionary side of things and often had to meet the travellers representing the various sweet manufacturers such as Sharps, Rowntrees, Cadbury, Nestle and Mackintosh when she placed orders for fresh stock. Josie looked after us during the day and took us for walks when required. Things went reasonably well for some time, until one day she lost her temper with me. I was no doubt playing up a little and refusing to get off the floor. She grabbed my arm roughly to pull me up and in so doing broke my arm. This of course caused great distress all round and I believe it must have been after this episode that Josie was sacked.

Some little time later she took her revenge. Father came down one morning to find that the shop had been broken into and a large number of packets of cigarettes had been stolen. I remember coming downstairs after hearing strange voices and finding several policemen examining the back of the shop showing particular regard to the barred window. All around strewn on the ground and leading to the gate, lay a trail of picture cigarette cards. A card depicting a picture of a famous personality or item of interest was enclosed with every packet of cigarettes in those days and small boys delighted in collecting them, positively encouraging their fathers to smoke. A game played with the cards was to stand some of them against a wall and then try to knock them over by flicking them with the rest of the cards, thrown one at a time. Not a great many women smoked in the 1930s, at least not in public as it was considered 'not nice' for a lady to do so.

When the police made their various enquiries and put the facts together, it transpired that Josie and her boy friend had been responsible for the break in and theft. Thinking over the happening many years later, I find myself wondering why they bothered to strew the cards around the yard, for to do so they must have stopped to open the packets which meant that risk of discovery must have been that much greater.

There were other burglaries in the 1930s, but rarely carried out with any violence. The machine dispensing cigarettes, costing something like 6d for five Woodbines, or 1 shilling for ten, was taken several times and rediscovered in a nearby field, broken open, with cigarettes and coins removed. The damage done to the machine probably cost more than the thieves gained. The Police usually knew who was most likely to be responsible for these thefts and they were mostly caught and punished, but as I say violence was not a feature of most of these crimes then.

It must have been before, or just after Josie's time with us, that I decided to take Alan for a short walk in his pram one day. The handle of the pram was just within comfortable reach for me and we wandered down the service lane behind the shop into Whitehouse Avenue. We had not gone far when a lady asked me to stop. She produced a camera and took a photo of us both. Not having seen many such contraptions before, Alan and I both stared with suspicious curiosity. The lady asked where we lived and what our names were. I indicated our home. She may have suggested we returned, I don't remember. I do know that later she presented Mother with a copy of the photograph. Mother was horrified when she saw what a grubby pair we looked. We probably should not have been out at all. If that was the case, we had been well and truly caught out.

CHAPTER 2

As children we caught our usual share of infectious diseases which seemed to do the general rounds; measles; German measles; whooping cough; chicken pox and mumps. It was usually around the age of five, the age at which children started school that the first signs of such diseases appeared. Because I had friends who were going to the local council school in Furzehill Road, I was very keen to start school there. I envied my friend and thought school must be a wonderful place.

On my first morning I remember being taken into a large room full of children sitting in rows, two to a desk. The desks had wooden lids that lifted exposing a cavity where items could be placed and the seats were wooden benches fixed to the desk with iron pieces. The teacher stood before the class, consisting of probably around fifty children, beside a large blackboard and easel. I was told to sit in one of the desks in the front row along with a few other children, none of whom were known to me. I remembered feeling completely bewildered and overwhelmed and was not at all happy, but did not cry. My other memories include playing with boxes of letters and making basket patterns on squared paper, one square with vertical lines the next with horizontal lines, until the piece of paper was completely covered. This kept the new pupils occupied and allowed the teacher to give attention to the more advanced infants in her large class. She had however, at some time managed to teach me how to write my name, for I remember one day finding a piece of chalk and writing 'Gwen' on the doors of a garage near our home, something I had never done before. It was a sudden urge to try out my new skill which caused this activity and was my very first attempt at writing on my own. Later on that same day, without telling my mother what I had done I checked on my prowess.

"Mummy, do you spell Gwen 'G.W.E.N.?"

"That's right dear" said my mother sounding pleased, and my

chest fairly swelled at the success of my achievement.

Most elementary schools had fairly basic toilet arrangements for their pupils usually consisting of outside brick buildings, the doors of the cubicles shielded from the elements and the view by a brick wall. One needed to be pretty desperate to relieve oneself in the biting winds of winter! Town or city schools were mostly provided with flush plumbing, but in the countryside many schools still had only earth closets up into the 1950s. In many of these country schools holidays were arranged to suit the farming seasons, so that children would be available to help with the potato harvest at the end of September for instance.

Mother treated most of our ailments with simple homely remedies. If we looked a little off colour, we were given beaten raw egg to drink. A spotty skin and lack of sunny disposition was treated with drinks of infused stinging nettle tea, 'to clear the blood' Mother said. It was not popular with her patients! Constipation brought forth the bottle of Syrup of Figs; coughs required spoonfuls of sulphur and black treacle. The treacle was fine, but the yellow sulphur powder tasted disgusting. The name Fryers Balsam comes to mind in connection with this remedy. Coughs and chest complaints also required Camphorated Oil to be rubbed onto our chests before going to bed each night and sometimes a piece of red flannel was placed on our chest and buttoned under our pyjamas to give added warmth. I can still recall the smell of the oil that was not unpleasant and the aroma certainly helped to make breathing easier if suffering blocked tubes. A sore throat could be eased by tying a sock around the neck. These days I prefer to use a silk scarf! An outbreak of boils, large suppurating spots, often appearing on the neck or back, were treated with bread poultices, Brewers yeast or Kaolin. When first applied to the boil, the heat of the poultices made one wince, but they were successful in withdrawing the puss. Suppurating spots of impetigo were painted with Gentian Violet. Tummy problems or indigestion called for a teaspoon full of Milk of Magnesia, a milky looking fluid that left a dry taste on the tongue. A daily dose of Cod Liver Oil and Malt was a regular thing which we enjoyed as it had almost a toffee taste, at least that is how we came to think of it over the years. Castor Oil was not so popular and was given for constipation. It was not one of my mother's remedies, but some parents believed that a visit to the gas works was a cure for children's coughs and colds. This was when gas was extracted from the burning of coal, producing a pungent odour.

Cuts and grazes were painted with iodine that stung when applied and brought tears to the eyes at times. We had no easy plaster pieces to cover wounds, but pieces of lint and bandages of torn strips of cotton sheeting served instead. Knees suffered many grazes, especially with boys who all wore short trousers until the age of thirteen or fourteen, and many wounded warriors walked around stiffly with bound knees. The problem was that it was difficult to keep the bandage firmly fixed over a continually moving knee joint. More often than not, the bandage became loose and dangled down the leg impeding games such as running, football and other activities. A cut such as one I inflicted upon myself by falling on the sharp edge of a tin toy that opened up my wrist, was far more serious. It was close to an artery and bled badly. Mother bound it tightly and put me into the push chair and walked a mile or more to our doctor's surgery in Radlett Road. Dr. Neil took one look and then got out the needle and thread and put in several stitches. I probably howled like mad, but I don't actually remember. I do know that the white scar will stay with me all my life.

Measles, whooping cough, mumps, chicken pox and other such diseases were treated at home. Parents usually hoped that all the children in the family caught them around the same time and early on in childhood, as it was generally thought that catching these infectious diseases once, immunised them against any further outbreaks. They also believed that it was less serious at that time than later in life. However my father told me that he had suffered measles three times in his life and I believe that I have had it twice, so the belief does not always apply. The gas works and the smell of hot tar were believed to alleviate whooping cough. So should workmen be repairing the road with their barrels of tar and steam engine while an outbreak of whooping cough was in progress, they were quite likely to find a number of parents with suffering children standing by!

Much more serious infectious diseases were scarlet fever and diphtheria. Diphtheria, which was the scourge of earlier years, was being brought under control by the 1930s, but outbreaks of scarlet fever were fairly frequent. Mavis, a friend I often played with was struck down with scarlet fever, a very nasty disease causing the skin to go bright red and peel. I was forbidden to go to her house to play and was told Mavis was not well. The next day the ambulance arrived and Mavis was carried from the house on a stretcher. She was wrapped in a red blanket and was very still. When I asked Mother where they were taking my friend, I was told, "To the isolation hospital".

Mother then explained that Mavis had scarlet fever and was very ill. She would have to stay in hospital for two to three weeks. I was most concerned for my friend, for the sight of her wrapped in the red blanket had frightened me. Perhaps it was the red blanket that caused me to be so scared, for we had been taught that the colour red signified danger. It was not until Mavis was well and safely home once more that my fears were allayed.

Luckily Alan and I did not suffer scarlet fever, although not long after starting school I caught a severe attack of measles and was quite ill. Mother put me to bed in a darkened room to protect my eyes and my body became a mass of red spots. In my fever I can remember feeling that I was smothering in a mound of feathers and then a little later the bed on which I lay felt as hard as rock. Mother bathed my face with a cool cloth and tried to bring down my temperature. When the fever passed and the spots were all out I was kept in bed and given plenty of drinks. In those days, if one child in the family had an infectious or contagious complaint, all the children of the family were kept in quarantine and not allowed back to school until all signs of spots had disappeared, usually ten to fourteen days.

When the attack of measles was over for both myself and my brother, I returned to school only to catch whooping cough almost immediately. Another bad attack and another longer stay at home caused my parents concern and once I was clear of the whooping cough, it was decided that Mother should take Alan and I to Margate, Kent for some healthy sea air. A friend of Mother's and her small son accompanied us and we went off in happy anticipation of a week at the seaside. We had not been there many days when I began to get dreadful earache. A visit to the local doctor was made, who suggested syringing the ear. This did no good at all and I remember being as much frightened by the syringe as by the pain I was suffering. A return visit to the doctor at Margate offered no solution, but he said it would be best to go back home and see our own family doctor. So cutting the anticipated holiday short, we did as he suggested. As soon as we arrived home I was taken to Dr. Neil who examined me and immediately rang up the Ear, Throat and Nose Hospital in London. That same afternoon I was taken to London where an operation was performed for mastoid.

Lying on the operating table I kicked and screamed for my Mother until the nurse put a mask over my face and I became unconscious under the ether. Children were treated like any other patient and nothing was explained to them beforehand. We were plunged into a bewildering and frightening new world, separated from our parents, who were only allowed to visit us twice a week, and with no understanding of what was happening.

The operation was successful or I should not be writing now, but I had to remain in hospital for six weeks. For the first few weeks I was in a large ward full of children from babies to twelve years of age. It was not a happy time. The child in the next bed was in a worse position than myself, possibly a year younger, she was of a foreign family and spoke no English. Two unkind older boys made fun of her and the nurses seemed not to notice. These boys bossed the other children and I was rather scared of them. On visiting days, the father of the little girl came and brought fruit for her to eat, often giving some fruit to me at the same time. He had a nice smile and I thought him very kind.

When my parents came, they too brought fruit or chocolate, but unless it was eaten while they were there, I had no chance of enjoying it. As soon as the visitors left, nurses came and collected all food given to their patients. We were told it was taken to share out amongst the whole ward as a dessert to the next meal. If it was not the fruit salad, our dessert was invariably tapioca pudding. I am sure it was good for us, but I have never eaten it since then!

No doubt the other small children missed their parents and home as much as I did. In my high sided cot I was confined most of the time to my bed. Just for a short time each day a nurse would let down the side of the cot and I and others would be allowed to walk in the ward for a while, although I do not remember moving far from my bed. I do remember feeling very lonely and unhappy and one day was sitting in my bed crying. All I wanted was a little affection and when the nurse came towards me I put out my arms for a little cuddle. Instead, I was taken to the bathroom and dumped on the lavatory seat. Then nurse turned around, walked out of the door shutting it behind her and promptly forgot me. I was still sitting there an hour or two later, when my parents arrived to visit me. It was not until my parents asked where I was that I was rescued from my imprisonment. Mother and Father were certainly not any happier about this episode than I was and complained. I do not remember any other child under going such punishment. The regime was very strict, but obviously although the medical care was excellent, understanding of children's fears and need for affection was lacking.

One day a little deaf and dumb girl arrived in the ward. She was taken around by the sister of the ward and was made to understand that she could choose any bed she wished. She chose mine. In a short time all my belongings were packed into a bag and they and myself were transported through the long corridors of the hospital to a lift and down to the ground floor of the building into a small side ward just off the women's ward. This must have taken place during the fourth week of my stay there. I wondered what was happening, but was not upset as curiosity had taken the place of fright. The little girl did me a great favour by choosing my bed, for my stay in that side ward was much happier than it had been in the large children's ward. I was in a single bed, not a cot and my companion in the room was a pleasant seventeen year old girl. I had toys to play with and the doctor sometimes came in to talk and join me in play.

Every morning some ladies from the women's ward came to carry me around their ward in order to say "Good morning" to everybody. One nurse allowed me to accompany her when she made up the beds and taught me how to make tidy sheets with 'hospital corners'. I began to enjoy my stay and my parents must have been relieved to find me so much happier. My stay should have been longer, but Mother wanted me home. It was decided that I could go home as long as I continued to have a daily dressing for the operation wound from our family doctor. So after six weeks in hospital I made my round of the ladies ward to say goodbye to everyone there before leaving for home. It was wonderful to be back in familiar surroundings with my parents and brother, but the memories of that hospital have not faded after more than sixty years.

Marie Curie, the Polish born French physicist, along with her husband Pierre Curie, had discovered radium in 1898. Her work on radioactivity made a method of X-ray possible and advanced the diagnosis and treatment of patients in hospitals. Before she died in 1934 on July 4th she had twice been a Nobel Prize winner. Sadly her discovery was also the cause of her death as she died of overexposure to radiation. Another step forward was made in helping new born babies to survive when in October 1934 a baby was kept alive with the aid of an 'oxygen bed'.

The chance to avoid a life of continual child bearing came with the opening in 1921 of the first birth control clinic in London run by Doctor Marie Stopes. Her ideas were radical for the time and were by no means approved by everyone, but many women were grateful that they had a possible chance to limit their families. The very first country to legalise abortion was Iceland. Unwanted pregnancies otherwise were dealt with by back street operations frequently putting the women's lives in considerable danger.

A great medical discovery had been made in January of 1922, when insulin was first used successfully in the treatment of diabetes and gave hope to many sufferers of the disease. Further steps forward in medicine were made when Alexander Flemming, the Scottish bacteriologist discovered Penicillin in 1928, although it did not come into general use until several years later during the Second World War. He shared the Nobel Prize for Physiology and Medicine in 1945 with E.B.Chain and H. Florey for their work on Penicillin. It was looked upon as the miracle cure of the time, responsible for saving many lives.

In 1930 when I was five years old I had to make my first visit to the dentist. A tooth had been causing me trouble and the dentist decided it must be removed. This required the use of gas. When gas was used it had to be administered by an anaesthetist and its effects often left the patient feeling a little whoosy and confused. The dentist's surgery was in one of the terraced houses by the garage in the centre of the village. Mother brought out the push chair to wheel me to the surgery, a distance of a quarter of a mile or so, past the parish church, past Beaty's the photographer and across the main road to where the dentist's chair awaited me. It was not a pleasant prospect and I was definitely not looking forward to the experience. However between them, Mother, dentist and anaesthetist had me in the chair and a mask over my face. The next thing I knew was being woken to find the taste of blood in my mouth and a tooth missing. Instead of being in my mouth, I could see the gory object on the dentist's table. All this was rather vague at the time as the effect of the gas had not yet completely dispersed. Hence the need for the push chair, for my legs were incapable of walking even the short distance home.

It was while I was still in the children's ward in hospital, that my parents came to visit me one day dressed in black. My father wore a dark suit and black tie and coat. Mother had on a black dress, coat stockings and shoes and wore a black hat. I was puzzled by this change of dress and asked the reason why. Mother then explained that my granddad had died and she was dressed in black as she was in mourning for him. This of course was explained in a simple fashion suitable for the understanding of a five year old child. It was quite usual in those days when someone in the family died for all adults in the family group to dress entirely in black, foregoing any other coloured garment for some weeks after the relative's death.

My mother's father, I remember as an elderly man with a long, flowing, white beard which tickled when I kissed him, who sat in a tall armchair with his thick walking stick beside him, its handle hooked over the arm of his chair. I remember him as a kindly man with a twinkle in his eye, who when I was small, jogged me up and down on his foot to a rhyme, to my great delight. Unfortunately, we only saw him and Granny about twice a year as they lived in Horley in Surrey, which was some distance from our home. When my parents bought a car and Mother learnt to drive our visits became more frequent.

I have a vision of Mother's first driving lesson. Uncle Harry, my mother's brother-in-law had been a driver in the First World War and it was he who taught my mother to drive the little Austin car my parents had bought. On the day of her first lesson, I stood at the back gate and watched as with a grinding of gears, Mother let in the clutch, put her foot on the accelerator and moved off down the road frog hopping all the way. In time progress was made and she was able to drive with confidence. This would have been around 1930 when no driving test was required. It was not until 1934, that the British Road Traffic Act introduced the driving test for motorists. If one could afford a car and learn to drive, that was it, one was free to travel almost anywhere. In fact Mother continued to drive until she was in her eighties and never once took a driving test. The same applied to my father, although he died at a much earlier age of sixty-eight.

My parent's Standard 8 car

Having a car made a great difference to the family. Outings and picnics to beauty spots in the south of Britain on the infrequent times the family were able to be together, meant visits to bluebell woods where red squirrels played among the tree branches and areas where primroses and violets grew wild. Sometimes when on a visit to Granny we stopped at Leith Hill and explored the tower or Box Hill, when after climbing to the top, we then enjoyed a roll down its grassy slopes to the bottom of the hill, once again avoiding the little blueberry bushes on the way. Of course, in Autumn when the berries were ripe with the bloom on them they were delicious to eat, then we gave up the idea of rolling past and enjoyed a repast instead. Should there be a plentiful supply they were gathered and put in a paper bag to flavour a fruit pie Mother would make when we got to Granny. I also have memories of another outing made to Richmond Park. It turned out to be rather more exciting than my parents had anticipated. Father had stopped the car in a grassy area with a few trees surrounding it, in order to give we children a chance to stretch our legs and have a last game of catch before making the return home. We had dismounted from the car and were enjoying our play, when a large stag appeared on the scene. He began to paw the ground and lower his head and seemed to be making my four year old sister his target. My father noticed his actions and started to run towards us just as the stag made his move towards us with lowered head. Dad ran between the stag and my sister, distracting the creature and at the same time calling to me to get her to the car quickly. The confused stag changed his target and chased after my father who dodged round and round the trees until either the stag got dizzy or just tired of the whole game and gave up the chase. Somewhat puffed Dad returned to the car, when we quickly left the area and made our way home before any other unfriendly stags appeared. I assume it must have been the rutting season as the deer in the park had always seemed fairly peaceful before.

Later, when Father had a full time manager to run the business, we were able to go even further afield on holidays to the West Country, where the banks of Devon lanes were smothered in pale yellow primroses in Spring and where, when it rained the lanes flowed red with the water spilling from the soil off the fields. It was here in the West Country where Mother's grandparents, aunts, uncles and cousins had or still lived. At other times we went to the East Coast of England, Norfolk in particular.

My sister was born when I was six, but before then we had moved from above the shop to a detached house in Grosvenor Road. It was near enough for my parents to keep an eye on the business that was now doing very well. Apart from the manager, Father had several lady assistants and so had far more free time to join us on our outings. On fine days at the weekend we might go to Dunstable Downs to watch the gliders flying. Teams of men on ropes launched the gliders from suitable positions on the high hillsides when the winds were favourable and the craft would go soaring into the air, following the thermal currents like a great silent bird, before coming to rest on the field at the foot of the downs. Later cars were used to launch the gliders.

Dunstable Downs was also popular with children on a day over the Easter holiday weekend, when it became the scene of the old tradition of orange rolling. The tradition probably originated in earlier times with egg rolling, a custom which took place in various parts of the country, but when we three children made our attempt it was just as well it was oranges and not eggs that were used. Children took up positions on the hillside, looking upwards towards the summit of the hill where the adults stood with bags of oranges in their hands. These people proceeded to roll oranges down the hillside whilst the children attempted to catch them. It was actually much harder than it looked and we found it difficult to grab one of these fast rolling orange balls without losing our balance on the steep slope, but we all managed to obtain at least one and felt well satisfied with such success.

In the sunny childhood days of the 1930s, the sandy east coast of Norfolk was a favourite holiday place for our family. The popular resort of Great Yarmouth became our summer destination for several years until the outbreak of World War Two in 1939, in fact we were there that very August, just before war was declared.

Off to the seaside

Usually my father drove us, bulging suitcases packed securely in the boot of the car, along with buckets and spades, in the old Standard Eight car that had replaced the small Austin. AYH 485 was its number I remember. As we neared the Norfolk coast, there was great competition between my brother, sister and I as to who should be the first to glimpse the sea. Our excitement was infectious, amusing our parents. On arrival at the boarding house in one of the roads behind the sea front, Father unloaded the suitcases while we could barely restrain ourselves in our eagerness

35

to grab our buckets and spades and race to the beach. Father spent the day with us before driving back to look after the business, leaving Mother to cope with the family of excited children for the forthcoming week.

At the seaside. Great Yarmouth, 1936

Great Yarmouth had much to offer. Plenty of golden sand, especially when the tide was out, then we could feel the ridges of the hard wet sand, left by the ripples of the waves under our feet. As soon as we felt brave enough to chance the water, dressed in our one-piece woolly type bathing costumes, we made for the sea. First there was a dabbling of toes, then feet and ankles and eventually our knees and possibly up to our chests were submerged in salt water, when we splashed one another in delight, hardly noticing the chill of the North Sea. My little sister, Cindy could not join my brother and I in the deeper water, instead she raced the waves, or paddled on the sea's edge under Mother's watchful eyes from her strategically placed deck chair.

When it was time to leave the water, there were sandcastles to make and decorate with shells and seaweed. The town's landladies must have sighed in despair whenever they saw a child arrive with yet another bucket of shells and string of smelly seaweed to use as a weather vane.

Many other attractions took our interest. On the beach was the man who made wonderful models and pictures with damp sand, or the Punch and Judy show, where we sat on the sand in front of the red and white striped tent and watched Punch's wicked antics against Judy, the policeman and other characters, while the showman's dog, Toby wearing his frilled collar sat quietly on the corner of the shelf behind which the puppets appeared. The distinctive voice of the puppet Punch was clearly heard and appreciated by all the children as we joined in the shouts to warn him of the approaching crocodile.

In the days before everyone had television, we children were avid watchers of such 'live' theatre, Punch and Judy and the beach concert parties could always attract an attentive audience. Yarmouth Marina also provided live entertainment. The Marina was not a boat anchorage or mooring, but a circular open topped building within which was a stage and deckchair seating for an audience. Here many talent shows were held and the strains of 'South of the Border' the most popular song of the time could be heard issuing forth from numerous would-be singer stars of all ages. I shall always associate that particular song with the Marina at Great Yarmouth.

Something else, or rather someone else to watch out for was Lobby Ludd. Lobby Ludd was a character in a daily newspaper competition, (I believe the paper concerned was the Daily Mirror) whose picture was printed in the paper and who visited various resorts along the coast. He would be dressed as in the Newspaper and be carrying a copy of the newspaper. If you recognised him the correct form was to go to him with your own newspaper in your hand (The Daily Mirror of course!) and say "You are Lobby Ludd, I claim the prize"

Many poor men, bearing a similar appearance to the photograph, were accosted by complete strangers in search of a prize.

Another newspaper, the Daily Mail ran sand competitions for the best sand castles or pictures made by children. An area of the beach was selected and then children could apply to join in the competition and be allocated a place in the area. I don't remember joining the competition, but I remember seeing all the children hard at work at their own particular piece of art. Boat Swings and donkey rides were some of the more active entertainment. All the donkeys had their name on their harness and we had our favourite steeds. Along the front esplanade were (are possibly still) gardens with water ways on which small boats could be rowed or paddled. At night this area of gardens and water ways was lit by hundreds of coloured lights and became a veritable fairy land in children's eyes.

Alan and I at Great Yarmouth, 1932 or 1933

Some of our carefully saved pocket money (two pennies a week) went on ice cream and sweets, other pennies were spent on the slot machines on the pier, playing with balls on the Bagatelle game, or manipulating the crane to try and win some sweets, game or chocolate. I don't ever remember being successful at this as the prize always dropped out of the claws of the crane before it reached the outlet, but we kept on hoping and only gave up when we had run out of the necessary pennies. We would have liked to try 'What the butler saw' but Mother banned that particular machine, which caused us to be even more intrigued!

Among the shops close to the sea front was the shop where the sweet Yarmouth rock was made. Inside the shop were metal, sunken, sloping counters of large proportions where huge chunks of bright pink, or clean white, sweet rock were made into wide slabs. This was then cut and rolled from one enormous roll, backwards and forwards on the metal counter, until the roll became longer and slimmer and was finally cut into manageable sticks, when it was sliced off and a photo of Great Yarmouth was slapped onto it. It was then wrapped in cellophane paper and put on sale in the trays and baskets in front of the shop. While still in the slab stage, before the point of rolling had been reached, long letters in red rock were shaped to make the name of the town. These were placed in order on a layer of white rock over pink, so that on the base was a layer of red, then a layer of white, on these rested the long pink letters and then came another layer of white, which when all was rolled became the centre. Up until that day it had been a source of puzzlement to me, as to how, no matter how long I sucked my sticky stick of rock, the letters naming the town were always there. It may not have been the best thing for our teeth, but the traditional stick of seaside rock was one of the expected bonuses of a seaside holiday and we never went home without one.

Special days were when we got up very early to go out with the fishermen in their boat. We watched as they hauled in their lines which had large hooks every yard or so and we actually saw the large fish that got away! Another large fish that did not get away was a Ray fish at least four feet long and two to three feet across. It was the first time we had ever seen such a fish. The fishermen spread it on the sand for us to see clearly. With the boats, there were trips to the sandbanks to see the basking seals. Occasionally one would pop its head out of the sea close to the boat to take a look at us from its large brown eyes, its sleek head shiny with water and it whiskers drooping like 'Old Bill's' moustache.

A trip to the Lightship was another treat. The Lightship, painted red, was anchored permanently off the coast to warn shipping of the many sandbanks in the area and a boat trip out to her meant riding the swell of the waves and a clamber up the rope ladder on the ship's side. Aboard, the sailors gave us a conducted tour of the vessel, pointing out the large lantern shaped light on the high mast whose light flashed on and off at regular intervals to be seen for many miles both at sea and from shore.

On shore were the bloater houses where the herrings were hung up to smoke until they were sufficiently treated to be renamed 'bloaters'. We were of course presented with these for breakfast on several mornings and we always bought a box to take home. The fish market was another smelly yet great fascination for us. We watched as boxes and boxes of many kinds of fish, were quickly sold by the auctioneer, with his rapid patter to the buyers waiting around. It was not always necessary to go to the auction to buy fish. If one was up early enough, it could be bought straight from the fishermen as soon as their boat came in. That way one could not have had the fish any fresher. This is the way many landladies bought their guests' meals.

The docks where the fishing boats moored was a wonderful place, full of evocotive sights and smells, particularly when the fishing fleet was in. Great Yarmouth and Lowestoft were renowned for their herring fishing fleets, when large numbers of women arrived from Scotland to gut and clean the fish as soon as the huge baskets overflowing with the slippery, silver catch were brought ashore. Such scenes are now a thing of the past, for the fishing fleet of the present day is now sadly depleted.

With so many things to see and do, the days fled past and soon it was time for our father to return with the car to collect us all. Then one last day altogether before we left the seaside town of Great Yarmouth to return to our country village. Looking back, it is amazing how those holiday times always seemed so sunny.

One year friends joined us for our summer holiday. Mother did not often join us in the sea as she had my young sister to watch over, but this year as there were friends to share such duties she had made up her mind to take the opportunity for a swim. In preparation she had knitted herself a new bathing costume. All went well while she was in the water, but when she stood up to walk out of the sea, the knitting streached and everything sagged! She was so embarrassed! Modesty kept her in the water until her friend saw her predicament and waded to the rescue with a large towel. The costume was discarded and Mother never knitted another!

On returning from a holiday one evening in the car, we noticed a strange glow in the sky. As we drew nearer we could tell a large building was on fire. The closer we came we could see signs of frantic activity and hear sounds of crackling flames and smell the spreading smoke. Several fire engines and tenders were parked in the driveway of a large house and firemen were unrolling long hoses and directing them on to the fiercely burning building. Father stopped the car ordering the family to remain inside while he went to find out what was happening. When he returned a few minutes later we were told that it was the home of the 'Mustard King', Mr Coleman of Coleman's Mustard. I must admit that at that time in the 1930s the name did not make a great impression upon me. My brother, sister and I were much more interested in watching the firemen at work and exclaiming over all the fire engines to be seen at one time! However, since in later years I now live in Norfolk, I have a much closer acquaintance with the name of Coleman.

Not all families were as lucky as ours. Until 1938 when the Trades Unions first secured the rights to holidays with pay, wages were low and unemployment was high. Family holidays were beyond their means. A day at Southend or Brighten reached by the railway was as much as some people in London could hope for. Some London families combined work and play by going hop picking in Kent. The pickers were paid at the rate of so many bushels to the shilling. A bushel being a large hop pocket containing about 8 gallons. The tallyman recorded the amount from each picker and the workers were paid according to the amount picked. Whole families joined in the activity during late August and early September, from grandparents to the children to pick the crop, along with much good humoured bantering. At the end of the day, having picked the essential ingredient, the pickers filled the local pubs to sample the mature product of previous years pickings. Hop picking was a means of enjoying the countryside with the advantage of earning money at the same time. This way of life continued until after the Second World War when machines were introduced to do the job.

"HOP-PICKING. TALLYING OFF.

It was during the 1930s that holiday camps became a popular form of holiday for people on a tight budget. In the early days of their development the accommodation was in tents and simple meals were provided. Gradually, chalets replaced the tents and dining halls were provided for meals. Some games and keep fit classes were added to the improved facilities. Those taking advantage of this type of holiday were mostly from the working class in the cities, many of whom had never before taken a holiday apart from an odd day out. It was a completely new experience and for many children, their first introduction to the countryside. By 1938, when holidays with pay were introduced, the Holiday Camp had become a popular institution, with many more people able to take advantage of the opportunity for a break in the country, or by the seaside. One great bonus the camps had over the traditional boarding houses, was that you were not required to vacate one's room during the day, but could return to rest, read, or chat whenever you so desired. In general rules were kept to the minimum.

For those Londoners who were confined to the city, a resort on the River Thames at Hampton Court known as Palm Beach, became available in 1926, where bathing belles in modest costumes and rubber bathing hats could show off their charms. The River Thames became a playground for many small boys on hot summer days

London's Palm Beach, 1926

and the areas of water away from the busy shipping traffic became popular for small rowing boats and punts, particularly at weekends. Small boys who went bathing in the Serpentine at Hyde Park chanced the stern arm of the law, until George Lansbury, a member of the London County Council and the Labour Party, established an official bathing place there. It was known as Lansbury's Lido.

Illicit bathers at the Serpentine, Hyde Park, London, 1926

CHAPTER 3

Cars were not very numerous before the 1939 to 1945 World war. Most people had bicycles for transport to work and back. Butchers, grocers and others made their deliveries with the aid of delivery boys on tradesmen's bikes having a metal wire basket on the front in which to place the goods. There were plenty of these jobs then for youngsters just leaving school at the age of fourteen. Our family were considered by many to be 'well off', the car a great status symbol. I had never thought of it in this connection, but we certainly appreciated the freedom it gave us to travel over more of the countryside. Even so, there were times when it had its drawbacks.

Engines were not as powerful then and on coming to a long steep hill such as Reigate Hill, or even more so, Porlock Hill in Somerset, it was a time of tension when starting the climb. "Will we make it?" was the over riding thought. As the car progressed up the hill at a gradually slowing pace, with Father changing into third, second and eventually first gear, tension mounted and we three children leaned forward in our seats willing it to proceed. Encouraging it in its climb with "Come on Lizzie, you can do it, you can do it!" The relief when we finally reached the top and could let out our breath was tremendous and we all gave a great "Hooray". The easy run down the other side was joyful. Of course there were the other times when we did not make it and Lizzie's engine protested coming to a halt before reaching the summit. Then passengers had to dismount and either push the vehicle up the last few yards, or walk the rest of the hill while the driver waited for the engine to cool and then try again. It was quite usual to see one or two cars parked on the side of Porlock Hill with bonnets open and engines steaming. At the top of the hill water standpipes were placed to enable drivers to refill their radiators after the climb. Since there was little motor traffic in these years it caused no great hazard to other road users.

There were of course some unfortunate occurrences and people became alarmed at the number of fatal accidents caused by motor traffic, for the motor car had progressed in design and speed since the early inventions of pre World War One. There were 309 deaths in accidents in London in the three months of July, August and September of 1928. Cars still had running boards, but windscreen wipers had been invented in 1921 along with indicators for showing which way the driver intended to turn. Small, bright, orange, flag-like arms rose from the side of the vehicle, usually on a level with the windows when a turn was to be made. Although not all cars were fitted with such modern innovations and in many cases it was still necessary for the driver to wind down his window and signal with his arm. To signal that he wished to turn right was simple, he held his arm straight out. To signal for the left, he made a circular movement with his hand. I heard of a story of a driver who had recently returned from several years of living in West Africa, where to indicate that one wished to turn left, it was common to bang on the roof of the car. Forgetting where he was, and wishing to turn left at a police directed junction, habit took over and he banged on the roof. The policeman looking slightly puzzled came over to him saying "Where do you wish to go sir? Right, left, or straight up to heaven?"

Contrary to general belief, Motorways are not a recent invention. The first purpose built motorway was opened in Germany in the September of 1921. In England the traffic policeman came ten years later and were first introduced in 1931 in the Road Traffic Act, along with compulsory third party insurance. It was about this time that the cost of petrol was raised by two pence in the government budget to one shilling and four pence a gallon (the equivalent of 7p). In September of 1925 white lines were painted on roads to separate traffic on dangerous bends and intersections in an attempt to reduce accidents. In 1935 a speed limit of thirty miles per hour was imposed in towns. Belesha Beacon crossings were introduced to aid pedestrians to cross the road. They took their name from the then Minister of Transport, Mr. Hore-Belesha. The Highway Code was introduced in 1931, four years before the driving test. It was "a code of good manners to all courteous and considerate persons".

A note of interest, I discovered that 'breathalisers' for motorists is not an idea of the 1990s, but in Indianapolis, U.S.A. the first 'drunkometer' was introduced in December 1938. It was another fifty years before a similar test was introduced in Britain, but a four month sentence was imposed by parliament in November 1925 for drink-driving offences.

On our journey to our Granny in Horley, Surrey, we passed Croydon Aerodrome. In the early 1930s it was still an unusual sight to see an aeroplane pass overhead and when one was heard we children rushed into the garden to watch it make its progress through the sky. They were all bi-planes of a somewhat boxy shape and cumbersome appearance as they made their stately journey through the atmosphere with throbbing engines. We were therefore delighted when Father made Croydon Aerodrome a rest stop and we were able to have a close up view of these new monsters.

There was at this time only a low picket fence between us and the runway where passengers for the continent, probably Paris or Brussels boarded or alighted. The planes with their wide double wings joined by tall, crossed struts were guided by the pilot of the landing aircraft whom we could see, sitting in the nose of the aircraft, through the large, high window. The propellers of the two engines slowly came to a stop and the ground crew moved forward for the necessary preparations. The body of the plane was almost rectangular, slimming a little to its tail end. Passengers in their seats were visible through the windows that lined the sides. In the early air liners of around 1925, the seats were often of basket work chairs, but passengers on some aircraft could enjoy the luxury of a film show as they travelled. We watched as steps were wheeled up, the door opened and the lucky passengers walked down and across to the airport buildings. Filled with envy we longed for the excitement of a chance to fly in one of these great modern machines. We often made models of aeroplanes using a long rectangular cigarette carton for the body and another from which we cut the wings. Added rectangular windows, struts and tailpiece made a simple model of which we could be proud.

There was a small airfield at Elstree near the reservoir where smaller single engine aircraft could be seen, again with double wings, but with the propeller attached to the nose of the aircraft and the pilot in his leather helmet and goggles sitting in the open cockpit. We frequently saw the pilot quite clearly as one flew low over the village. Those who could not afford the luxury of a long journey had the opportunity to try out the new sport in short 'joy rides' for the cost of five shillings, given by pilots from some of these small airfields.

Ever since the American brothers Wilbur and Orville Wright, who had previously run a bicycle repair shop and a printing press, had built and made the first machine powered flight in their Kitty Hawk on 17th December 1903, men had been attempting to defy gravity and take to the air. In 1909 on the 25th July, the Frenchman, Louis Bleriot had succeeded in flying across the English Channel. For this wonderful feat the composer Radolphe Berger composed a celebratory march. By the time of Bleriot's death on 1st August 1936 vast distance had been conquered. During World War One, light aircraft were used for reconnaissance over enemy lines and then adapted for fighting with mounted machine guns. The Royal Air Force was formed from the Royal Air Corps on 1st April 1918 and two years later on 5th February 1920 the R.A.F. College at Cranwell was founded.

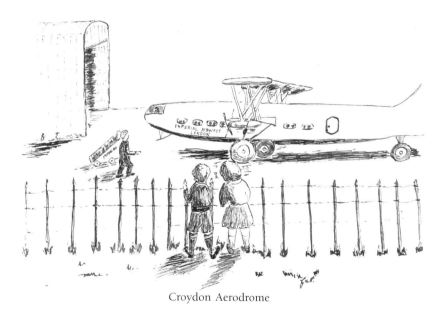

Croydon Aerodrome

After 1918 men returned to considering more peaceful uses for such flying machines and in 1919 Ross and Keith Smith, two Australian brothers, made the first flight from England to Australia, flying a Vickers Vimy aircraft powered by two Rolls Royce engines, making seventeen stops on the way. It was so cold in the cockpit that their sandwiches froze. Ross Smith had been a First World War flying ace, gaining many decorations for his bravery, and when the Prime Minister of Australia, W.M.Hughes offered a prize of £10,000 to the first Australians to fly from England to Australia in 30 days or less, Ross and his brother took up the challenge. With Keith acting as Navigator and with two air mechanics they took off on November 12th 1919 having very little in the way of equipment. Most of their journey took them over lands forming part of the British Empire, over Egypt, India through to Australia. After their successful and safe arrival in Darwin having made the journey in twenty-eight days, Ross Smith wrote

"Hardships and perils were forgotten in the excitement of the present. We shook hands, our hearts swelling with those emotions invoked by achievement and the glamour of the moment. It was and will be, the supreme hour of our lives."

Both brothers were knighted for this feat. Unfortunately, only three years later Ross was killed in a trial flight of a Vickers Viking amphibian plane in which he planned to make a round the world flight with his brother.

Also in 1919 on 25th August a daily service by air between London and Paris began. Two months before this on 15th June the British aviators John William Alcock and Arthur Whitten Brown had completed the first non-stop trans-Atlantic flight, also using a Vimy aircraft. Both men were later knighted. After this records for 'firsts' became fast and furious. Commander Richard E. Byrd of the American Navy, flew over the North Pole in 1926 with Floyd Bennett and over the South Pole, in a Ford 4-AT Trimotor named Floyd Bennett in November 1929, with his crew of pilot Bernt Balchen, radio operator Harold June and Survey man Ashley McKinly. They were the first men to make this flight. With three others Commander Byrd flew from New York to France in 1927.

Charles Lindbergh an American aviator, made the first solo non-stop flight across the Atlantic from America, in his aeroplane 'Spirit of St. Louis', beginning in New York on 20th May 1927 and arriving in Paris the next day, the 21st of May, 33.5 hours in all. Lindbergh and his wife suffered a great tragedy in 1932 when their baby son was kidnapped and found dead two months later.

The Russians formed their state Aeroflot airline on 8th February 1923. Aircraft were used for humane purposes when in 1928 the

Australian Flying Doctor Service was launched in Queensland. On 30th March 1929 the first England to India air service was started by Imperial Airways. A train journey from Basle, Switzerland to Genoa, Italy was necessary on this route, as Italy forbade the flight of British aircraft over their territory for several years. Two members of the Royal Air Force Squadron Leader A.G. Jones and Flight Lieutenant N.H.Jenkins made the first non-stop flight to India from Great Britain flying from Cranwell in Lincolnshire to Karachi on 24th-26th April 1929, using a Fairey Long Range Monoplane. Two more members of the Royal Air Force, Squadron Leader O.R.Gayford and Flight Lieutenant G.E.Nicholetts, also in a Fairey Long Range Monoplane, made the first non-stop flight from England to South Africa on 6-8th February 1933. Total distance covered 5309 miles in 57 hours 25 minutes setting a new world distance record.

Australians Charles Kingsford Smith and C.T.P. Ulm in their aircraft 'Southern Cross' made the first air crossing of the Tasman Sea, Flying from Sydney, Australia to Christchurch, New Zealand in September 10-11th 1928. In the June of the same year they had made the first flight across the Pacific, flying from California to Brisbane in ten days. They were also the first to make an aerial circumnavigation of the globe in 1929-30. Sir Charles Kingsford Smith accompanied by Captain P.G.Taylor made the first flight from Australia to the United States in the Lockheed Altair 'Lady Southern Cross' from 22nd October to 4th November 1934 via Fiji and Hawaii. Sir Charles disappeared over the Bay of Bengal while making another flight attempt on 11th November 1935.

Aviator Douglas Corrigan became a folk hero earning himself the nickname of Douglas 'Wrong-Way' Corrigan, when in 1938 he took off from New York supposedly bound for California after aviation officials had refused to grant a request to grant an exit permit for a solo trans-Atlantic flight, on the grounds that his rather rickety plane was unsafe for such a journey. Twenty-eight days later he landed in Dublin saying his compass had frozen. This story he stuck to for the rest of his life. He died at eighty-eight years of age. The eccentric U.S.A. multi-millionaire Howard Hughes designed his own plane and in 1935 achieved his first aviation record by flying at 352.46mph. He managed several more records before he withdrew into his self-imposed seclusion, becoming a recluse for the rest of his life.

Not to be left out of things, women also took to the air. The first woman to gain a pilot's licence was French woman Madame la Baronne de Laroche in 1909. An American woman, Harriet Quimby flew across the English Channel in 1912, Sophie Pierce, who later became Lady Heath, was twenty eight years of age, when in 1928 she became the first woman to fly solo from the Cape of Good Hope in South Africa to Cairo, Egypt in an Avron Avon 111 aircraft. Always careful of her appearance, she even managed to change from her flying gear to silk stockings, white gloves, fur trimmed coat, cloche hat and a necklace before leaving the cockpit to meet the photographers and reporters. After a short stay she continued her flight to London. Women flying over the Sudan had to be escorted by a man due to unrest among the natives of that country. Lieutenant Bentley escorting Sophie Pierce, lost sight of her and each flew on alone, meeting again in Cairo. Lieutenant Bentley had the previous year become the first person to fly solo from England to Cape Town. About the same time as Sophie Pierce was making her flight, another woman Lady Mary Bailey was travelling in the opposite direction on a first solo round trip between England and South Africa to be made by a woman, completing the journey in 1929. Sophie Pierce (Heath), who encouraged women to take their place in athletics and had herself been the British Javelin Champion of 1923, survived her flights in the air, but sadly died in 1938 from injuries received when she fell down the flight of stairs on a London bus.

British woman Amy Johnson became the first woman to fly solo from England to Australia in 1930. News reels showed her arrival at Darwin on 23rd May in the open cockpit of her dark green De Havilland DH60G Gipsy Moth, 'Jason,' to a great reception from the population. She was 27 years old at the time. Her plane 'Jason' can now be seen hanging from the ceiling in the London Science Museum. In November of 1932 she flew to South Africa in a Puss Moth in the then remarkable time of four days and six hours. In 1936 she flew the journey from London to Cape Town and back in another record breaking flight, arriving in England on 15th May. Amy Johnson was a complicated character from childhood on throughout her life. She found herself unable to settle at any of the many schools she attended, staying for only short periods before running away or being removed. She found it difficult to make any friends. She became more at ease when she took up flying, for which she had a natural talent. She was an excellent mechanic and was accepted by most of the male flyers as a good 'mate' or 'chum'. Amy married Jim Mollison a Scottish aviator who had made the first west bound solo flight across the Atlantic, flying from Ireland to Canada in 1932. They married in the same year and made several flights together, but the marriage did not last and in 1938 they were divorced.

Amy Johnson was followed by the American Amelia Earhart who flew the Atlantic solo on 18th June 1932 in a red Lockheed Vega, starting from Harbour Grace in Newfoundland. She had many problems on the way, including a failed altimeter, broken manifold and icing on the wings if she flew too high. On the other hand, if she flew too low she was blinded by sea fog. After fifteen hours she landed in a field in Derry, Ireland, to the surprise of the grazing cattle. Others had already tried to achive this record, but perished in the attempt. Amelia Earhart was also the first woman to fly solo from Honolulu, Hawaii to Oakland, California in the United States in January 1935 in a Lockheed Vega. She was later lost during an attempt at a round the world flight in July 1937 in a Lockheed Electra while trying to find Howard Island in the middle of the Pacific. In 1933 a Mrs Bonney, from Brisbane, flew solo from Australia to England, having a number of mishaps on the way.

In 1934 on 23rd May, New Zealand air woman, Jean Batten, who had sold her piano to pay for flying lessons, made another record solo flight. She flew a DeHavilland DH60M Moth from Lympne in Kent to Darwin, Australia, taking 14 days, 22 hours and 30 minutes, beating Amy Johnson's time by more than four days. She had bought her open cockpit Tiger Moth plane for £260 in order to make her record breaking flight. Jean Batten went on to make the first solo air crossing of the South Atlantic in November 1935, flying a Percival Gull from Lympne to Port Natal, Brazil and lived to die of old age in New Zealand, where a memorial at Auckland Airport commemorates her expolits. The first person to fly solo across the Atlantic to Newfoundland was a woman. Beryl Markham was her name. The beginning of a new career for women and a sign of the things to come, was made when in 1930 nurse Ellen Church, flying with Boeing Transport and eleven passengers between San Francisco, California and Cheyenne, Wyoming, became the first airline stewardess.

For some like the Duchess of Bedford, who took up flying at the age of sixty one, the plane became a useful means of travelling to attend social engagements, flying to Aintree for the Horse racing, or Putney for the Boat Race, as well as journeys abroad. The Duchess who had her own personal pilot, Flight Lieutenant Ralph Chevalier Preston to take control of the plane when flying, leaving her free to do her knitting which she liked to take with her. In moments of crisis she would continue to knit, relying on her pilot to get them out of danger. They survived several mishaps and forced landings, until one day in 1937 when the Duchess was seventy two years of age, the lady took off flying solo from Woburn Abbey in an effort to complete 200 hours of solo flying. It was a routine flight and not expected to take longer than a couple of hours, instead she simply disappeared for ever. It is most likely that she lost her bearings and crashed in the Wash or the North sea off the Norfolk coast as wreckage from the plane was washed ashore along the Norfolk-Suffolk coast some days later. A sad end to an adventurous lady.

Women were not exactly welcomed into aviation. In 1924 the International Commission for Civil Aviation decided 'that women shall be excluded from any employment in the operative crew of aircraft engaged in public transport.' Such attitudes continued up until the Second World War, when women proved their competence in many areas of what had been until then, a male domain.

Aviation had become so popular that in November 1932 a gigantic clock with a dial of over sixteen feet and its white figures on black background illuminated at night, was installed on the ground at Heston Airport in Middlesex for the benefit of aviators. In 1933 a British aircraft flew over Mount Everest. In 1934 an International Air Race to Australia, the idea of Australian philanthropist Sir MacPherson Robertson to commemorate the centenary of the State of Victoria, took place starting from Mildenhall in Suffolk. De Havilland designed a plane, the DH88 Comet, at their factories in Edgeware in Middlesex and Hatfield in Hertfordshire. It was the first aircraft to have a low wing and retractable undercarriage and was made almost entirely in wood. Painted red and white, it had a crew of two and was named 'Grosvenor House'. The Comet won the speed prize travelling 12,300 miles in 70 hours 54 minutes and 18 seconds. The pilots were C.W.A. Scott and Tim Campbell Black.

Illuminated clock (over 16ft in diameter)
for aviators at Heston Airport, Middlesex, 1932

Jersey Airways started a service between the island and Plymouth in the 1930s. The first plane landed on West Park Beach in 1933 and was charged harbour dues. Amy Johnson's Gipsy Moth and a new form of aircraft, the Autogyro took part in the St.Brelades Air Show held in Jersey. From St. Peter Airport in the Channel Islands, an air service to Exeter and St. Dinard began, although of course most people still braved the rather rough sea crossing. A weekly air mail service between Britain and Australia was started on 8th December 1934. The mail reaching Brisbane in about two weeks. The first passenger service on the same route began on 13th April 1935. It was inaugurated by Imperial Airways and the Quantas Empire Airways. The journey took twelve and half days to cover the 12,754 miles and the one way fare cost £195. Gatwick Airport was opened on June 6th 1936. At that time it consisted of a runway and a collection of tents in which the companies using the airport conducted their business. There were few facilities for the comfort of waiting passengers or for the staff attending them.

Flying was not without its casualties of course, for those in the air and also those on the ground. The first international airport in Britain was opened at Cricklewood, London in 1919. Handley-Page Transport ran flights to Paris and Brussels, until December 14th

1920 when there was a crash in which four people were killed. One passenger was missing and could not be accounted for at the time. He turned up later in Paris having no memory of the actual crash. It seemed that he had been thrown clear and knocked out. When he came to he could only remember that he had to be in Paris, so he made his way there by underground train and ferry boat. After this crash Cricklewood airport was closed and the flights moved to Croydon. On Christmas Eve of 1924 eight people were killed when an Imperial Airways plane based at Croydon aerodrome crashed into a housing estate in London. In 1935 the death was reported of Wily Post another American pioneer aviator who was killed in a crash on 15th August. In 1933 he had been the first man to fly solo around the world in seven days, 18 hours and 49 minutes.

Amphibious aircraft, flying boats or sea planes, as we children called them when we saw them flying over with their large floats like water skis instead of wheels, were also being developed through this period. One of the early pioneers of this type of aircraft being Glen Curtiss of the United States of America who died in 1930 on 23rd July. In 1914 Glen Curtiss had lost a patent suit in the United States courts on airplanes in favour of the Wright brothers. In Britain Southampton was an area where much of this development took place, and Southampton was the name given to a twin engined flying boat used by the RAF from 1925 to 1936. In 1937 Imperial Airways opened a flying boat service carrying passengers and mail from Cairo to the Cape. These flying boats were built in Rochester, Kent by the three Short Bros. Firm and launched down the Medway before taking up service in Africa. The amphibious aircraft required long stretches of water for successful take off and the River Nile provided just what was needed. Starting at Cairo they made their first stop Aswan, flying low to give their passengers a good view of the pyramids. On then to Khartoum in the Sudan to a small place named Gorden's Tree, named after the General who met his end at the hands of the Mahdi's followers in 1885. The route then continued along the course of the White Nile to Juba and from there to Lake Victoria where passengers disembarked for Nairobi. The great advantage of this route was that the whole journey was through British Administrated territory. From Lake Victoria the flight went across to the Indian Ocean and the island of Zanzibar and on to the Portuguese Isle of Mocambique before making its final leg of the journey to the Cape of Good Hope.

Just before the outbreak of the Second World War, a British Trans-Atlantic airmail service was inaugurated on 5th August 1939. In the June of the same year Pan American Airline started the first scheduled trans-Atlantic service with a flying boat carrying nineteen passengers. During the Second World War a number of women aviators who were unable to join the Allied Air Forces as fighting flying crew, played a most useful part in ferrying aircraft across the Atlantic and other areas. It was in doing this vital work that Amy Johnson was lost, disappearing into the mist of some murky weather on 5th January 1941 never to be seen again.

Helicopters and the small autogyros are familiar craft of our skies today, although considered fairly recent. However, the first successful flight of an autogyro was carried out by its Spanish inventor Juan de la Cierva, in the January of 1923. On the 28th June 1930 Frank Whittle patented the jet engine, but it did not come into use until many years later. The first flight made by a jet-propelled engine was made just before the Second World War by a Heinkel 178 aircraft in August of 1939.

Alongside the conventional aeroplane, experiments had been going on with dirigible aircraft, powered balloon flight. Germany had developed these huge balloon type aircraft called Zeppelins, using them to bomb Britain during the First World War. My mother remembered these monster balloons coming over England and the fear they engendered. When living in Billericay, Essex I was told that that area had also been visited by the Zeppelins in World War One, one of them being shot down and falling on farmland there. Great Yarmouth in Norfolk was another town that suffered Zeppelin attentions. After the 1914-1918 war experiments continued in Germany, also in Britain and the United States of America, not always successfully as the U.S. Dirigibe 'Shenandoah' broke apart at Caldwell, Ohio on 3rd September 1925. In England 49 Members of Parliament were taken for a flight from Pulham Market Air Station over Norwich and the Norfolk coast in R36 having a safe landing on their return. Pulham St. Mary airfield was completed in 1916 and the small airships operated from there on patrols over the North Sea were known as 'Pulham Pigs'. In 1925 one of these Pulham Pigs R33 was torn from her mooring tower by strong winds and blown across the North Sea. It was recovered later and brought back to Pulham due mainly to the courage and initiative of George William Hunt Known as 'Sky' Hunt he was one of the early pioneers of airships, who organised the repair of the torn fabric in the midst of a gale over the North Sea, enabling Airship R33 to return to its base. The outer envelope of the airships was made of linen and the outsides of the gas bags were made of pure silk. Some girls were lucky enough to have dresses made from pieces of this material if they were fortunate in knowing one of the workers, in much the same way as discarded parachute silk supplied other young women with sets of undies during clothes rationing in the Second World War!

The R100 was built by the Airship Guarantee Company at Howden in Yorkshire. This was a privately owned company, a subsidiary of Vickers. R101 was designed and built by the Government Airship Establishment at Cardington in the late 1920s according to one report, but Norfolk people tell me that R101 was actually built at the riverside workshops of Boulton and Paul (a photograph appeared in the Eastern Daily Press showing workmen making components for R101 at the Riverside Works). The parts were then sent to Cardington where they were assembled, and its first flight took place over Norwich. However, the German 'Graf Zeppelin' completed the first trans-Atlantic flight on 15th October 1928 and went on to complete the circumnavigation of the world on 29th August 1929. R100 crossed the Atlantic to Montreal on 29-30th July 1930 after its first trials on 16th December 1929, to be followed the next day by a crossing of the Atlantic by R101. On the 5th October 1930 came the dreadful disaster of British Airship R101 when it crashed at Beauvais, France while on route to India. Out of 54 passengers and crew, only six people survived. The victims were buried in St. Mary's Churchyard, Cardington, where inside the church building there is a plaque to their memory. The Church has now become a museum.

A further disaster occurred in 1937 when on May 6th the Hindenburg, the world's largest airship was destroyed in New Jersey, USA and 35 people lost their lives. The Hindenburg appeared to be coming in to moor at its tower, when it suddenly burst into flames. I can remember seeing the newsreel film taken at the time, watching people running in panic from the blazing monster, compared in size with ants alongside a large marrow. These terrific disasters in which a large number of people died, dampened men's enthusiasm for this type of aircraft and R100 was sold for scrap. The British Airship Station was moved to Cardington, Bedfordshire in 1948. The 805 feet long Hindenburg, adorned by Swastika emblems had been seen flying across the north Norfolk coast in the June of 1936. It had flown several times over England taking a different route each time, and after the war in 1946 photographs of British towns and factories were found at German airfields marked 'Hindenburg'. Was the Hindenburg spying for Hitler?

Being reluctantly dragged away from the aircraft at Croyden by our parents, we continued our journey to Horley with the car running smoothly down Reigate Hill, the town and countryside spread out in the valley below us. Still full of our experience with the aerodrome, it was easy to imagine that we were coming in to land in our own private aeroplane.

Watching an airship fly over

CHAPTER 4

Granny's home was a solid Victorian detached house, in front of which stood a very large cypress tree. A flower border around the tree was full of pink and mauve asters. A few yards away stood a monkey puzzle tree. A very strange tree indeed. Its trunk stood stiff and tall and its unyielding branches gave no shelter to the birds that avoided its prickly covering. To me it was not a real tree but rather some artificial form of decoration. I did not like it. This peculiar tree stood in front of another building beside the house in which first my grandfather and then my uncle displayed the headstones for graves, for both my grandfather and his son were undertakers. As children we were quite used to seeing my uncle and his assistants working on coffins, planed and polished with great care, for they were craftsmen at their trade. The insides of the coffin were lined with soft, shining, white satin, well shone brass handles were attached to the outside and the oak polished to perfection. Linseed oil was the prevalent aroma around the workshops, not an unpleasant smell, rather exotic in fact, it was mixed with that of sawdust, now a smell that takes me right back to my childhood and to my grandparents home. Another pervading smell from the work area behind the house was that of timber. I still love the scent that seeps from cut planks in a timber yard. Wood to make the coffins was stored on racks in order of size, under a roof of corrugated iron. To me wood has the warm friendly smell of natural things and when shaped and turned a comforting and sensual feel.

Beyond the wood yard lay the garden where fruit and vegetables were grown. There was no grass to play on, but a huge tank for rainwater stood high up behind the back of the workshops. The top was open, an invitation to sail small boats on it which was hard to resist. With our cousins we held our own boat races here. Had our parents been aware of our activities I am sure a stop would have been put to our games, for as an adult I can see the dangers of which we children were unaware or ignored.

A wonderful sweet plum tree grew in the neighbour's garden, but its branches overhung Granny's back garden, and in the season it was too tempting to refuse, although I never remember taking more than one or two at the most of its delicious fruit. We as children were sometimes given a bowl and asked to pick red currants for Mother to make a pie for our mid-day meal. Granny had many of these bushes growing beside the house and the glistening red fruit hung like bright ear-rings from the bushes.

Inside, the house was rather dark due mainly to the old, dark furniture and Victorian style of decoration. Lighting was by gas light or oil lamps. The oil lamps with their tall glass chimneys and smoky wicks when not properly trimmed, gave a soft glow to the room. The filters or mantles in the glass bowls of the gas lights in the bedrooms and on the stairs popped and flickered throwing grotesque shadows on the walls making a scary journey up to bed. I was always glad to be undressed and in the big brass bedstead under the bed clothes and feather eiderdown when Mother turned down the gas and kissed us good night. When we were small and afraid of the dark, we would be given little night-lights beside our bed. Made of wax and wick, these were a low and safer form of candle, less likely to be knocked over. The mattresses on the big brass beds were filled with feathers, soft and warm and comforting. If it was extra chilly, a stone jar hot water bottle was placed in the bed to warm it. A chamber pot was placed under each person's bed, for no one wished to make the journey to the outside toilet in the darkness of the night. In time, her daughters persuaded Granny to give up the oil lamps and gas light to have electricity installed, but not without a struggle on Granny's part for she felt the electric light to be harsh on her eyes.

Granny was small in stature and always dressed in long black dresses relieved only by a black and white sprigged apron. Her grey hair was drawn back from her face and tied in a neat bun on the nape of her neck above the neck frill of her dress. Granny was very conscious of a large goitre on her neck. Because of this she disliked having her photograph taken. At that time an operation to remove the goitre was considered too dangerous. It was not until the 1950s that such an operation was considered safe to perform.

The large kitchen or scullery as it was called, housed a big copper in one corner. At the bottom was a hole in which a fire was lit to boil the water for the big wash and on one wall a stone sink and wooden draining board stood beneath a window. Apart from a large and heavy table, a gas cooker and a mangle, the kitchen seemed bare. Leading from this area was a large walk-in pantry in which all the bottled fruit and other preserved items of food were stored. As there were no refrigerators then, meat was usually kept in a wooden meat safe with a perforated metal door. Mostly food was bought fresh each day and it was the remainder of the cooked joint which was so stored, but not usually for more than two days at most, weather permitting, for if the flies had managed to get to it, it was soon full of maggots.

I can recall turning the handle of the mangle to squeeze the water out of the clothes, for we had our own mangle at home. Washing machines were not in general use until after 1945, although various forms of them had been invented before 1939. There was no bathroom in the house although the house itself was of substantial size. Our body washing had to be done at the china basin on the washstand in the bedroom with cold water from the big matching china jug, or in the kitchen at the stone sink with its cold water tap and large square bars of yellow 'Sunlight' soap. We brushed our teeth under the tap using our individual toothbrush (kept in a china Micky Mouse toothbrush holder, Micky Mouse for Alan and Minnie Mouse for me) and little round tin of Gibb's toothpaste, a hard pink powder in a blue tin, I believe. Hot water was only obtained by boiling a kettle full on the gas stove, or from the copper on wash day. Baths were taken in a large tin tub placed in the kitchen. The toilet was a flush toilet, but it was necessary to go out of the back door and in through the next wooden door in a brick addition to the kitchen area. Luckily we were mostly there in the warmer months of the year! When it was dark we took a little night light with us to see our way, its light made dancing shadows on the whitewashed walls, which caused our visit to be a rather hurried one. Many houses were still without flush toilets, instead they used dry closets usually situated at the bottom of the garden or back yard. They would be emptied by the men of the night soil carts, who came with their horse drawn vehicle in the quiet of the night. From my own experience I know that outside dry or peat closets existed in at least one village school in Essex up until the 1960s.

The parlour in the front of the house was used only on Sundays and special occasions and at all other times it was shaded by green Venetian blinds at the large sash window. In the parlour on a table in front of the window stood a large potted Aspidistra. Most homes in the early part of the century appeared to decorate their parlour with these large green leafed house plants, of which the entertainer Gracie Fields recorded in her song 'The Biggest Aspidistra in the World'. Not far from the Aspidistra and table, tucked into a recess by the fireplace, stood a tall organ. My cousin Ron who was several years older than myself, was a pianist and was granted permission to go into the parlour to play the organ. Even in his early teens he often played the organ for the Sunday services at the local chapel. All this in spite of having lost the last two fingers on his left hand in a childhood accident with a mowing machine.

Washing Day at Granny's house

All our cousins were boys, apart from the daughter of Mother's eldest sister who was nearer my mother's age than ours. Pranks were prevalent and I often found myself with an 'apple pie' bed, but I usually knew who the culprit was and returned the favour. I learnt to hold my own and became quite a tomboy.

Plush tablecloths with many tassels were popular in Victorian houses and Granny's was no exception. She also had the usual 'What Nots' and other pieces on the high over mantle with its mirror. I particularly remember the glass drop lustrers, one of which stood each side of the mantelpiece its dangling prisms catching rainbow tints of light. If I gave a prism a gentle jog it would send all the other prisms jingling, giving the tinkling sound of wind chimes. Of course I could not do this when the adults were around as it was strictly a 'no touch' area. On Sundays we were allowed into the parlour with the grown ups if we wished to read or possibly do a jigsaw puzzle, but other games met with disapproval from our strict chapel going aunt and also from Granny. There was no objection to games on any other day of the week.

Tradesmen called during the week with their deliveries; the baker with his two big baskets of bread rolls and cake. Granny always bought a Cottage Loaf. This was a fairly big circular loaf with a top knot, a little smaller than the base. Granny would part the loaf from its top knot and then slice each part separately as it was needed. The fresh, white and warm oval slices with their crusty outsides were thickly buttered, before being placed on a plate on the table for tea. They tasted delicious. I was known as a 'bread and butter girl' as I rarely wanted jam or honey spread upon my slice, but was perfectly happy to eat it just as it was. It was a rule in the family that we must always eat one or two slices of bread and butter before we were allowed any cake. The first time I tasted margarine was when I visited a friend at her home and was given what I assumed was a slice of bread and butter and jam. It tasted different to that which we ate at home. I mentioned it to my mother afterwards who said that it was probably margarine. I was five at the time and had not experienced many homes of other people and was inclined to assume that all others were like ours. It was some time later that I was informed by one of my friends that my parents were "well off"!

A favourite caller of ours was the muffin man who used to come down the road with his tray of pale, thick, round muffins covered with a clean cloth. He wore a flat cap on his head on which the tray was supported and in his free hand he carried a brass bell which he rang every so often before giving his street cry of "Muffins, muffins".

On hearing the bell housewives came out of their doors to buy his wares. He then took the tray from his head and placed the required number of muffins on the plate proffered by the customer. When toasted at an open fire on the end of a long toasting fork, then covered with butter which melted into every little hole, they were wonderful to taste and made a welcome tea time treat in the colder weather. I always associate the muffin man with autumn and winter, so he may not have hawked his wares during the warmer weather.

Toasting muffins by the fire

Since we mostly had open, coal fires in houses in my early years, the toasting fork then was a well used implement. If it was not muffins or crumpets, it was slices of thick bread which all had a completely different flavour to that which we now get out of the electric toaster. Toast spread with beef dripping was another delightful teatime treat. We children took it in turns to sit in front of the fire with a thick slice of white bread on the end of the toasting fork, the heat from the fire not only toasting our bread, but our faces as well. When one of us had become too flushed it was the turn of the next member to take his place. The bread of course had to be toasted on both sides and the fire needed to be well made up with a good red glow for the toasting to be successful. At home we also had a four bar electric fire for chilly days, but toast did not taste nearly so good when done this way.

A regular caller down the road was the milkman in his white coat and peaked cap. Who with his horse and cart made his way down the street, dispensing fresh milk from his large metal churn. The horse knew each customer's house, stopping outside without any command from the milkman. Then either the milkman came to the door, or the customer took their jug to the cart where a pint or quart (two pints), or whatever quantity was required was measured out with a long ladle or dip. The lid was put on the churn and the horse moved off to the next customer. It was not until the late 1930s that the first electric milk floats were seen. The milkman made three deliveries each day. The breakfast round in the early morning, the lunchtime 'pudding' round as some called it, and the tea round in the afternoon. People used more milk in their staple diet when such items as porridge, milk puddings, custards and milk drinks were general to all families. Milk was reasonably cheap costing 1d halfpenny to 2d in old money going up to 3d-4d in winter, but coming down again in summer after the cows had calved. It was still possible to buy milk straight from the farm, warm from the cows with the added bonus of being able to watch the cows being milked, during the 1920s and early 1930s in Boreham Wood, providing you took your own jug or can along. If the weather was thundery, women boiled their milk to stop it turning sour overnight.

The Milkman

A charabanc similar to Uncle Harry's

In our own village, supplies of coal were delivered by horse and cart. The coal could be ordered by the sack and many housewives counted the number of sacks as the coal man delivered them to make quite sure she received the correct number. Small amounts of one or two hundred weight could be ordered at a time. Granny was kept supplied by her son-in-law, our Uncle Harry who owned his own coal business and was more up to date with motorised transport. He also ran a Charabanc, a large open topped bus with a folding canvas roof, which was hired for outings by local groups. During the 1930s coaches became a popular means of travel and many new services were started. As well as the former, Uncle Harry had one or two large vans. These were part of his house removal business.

Visits to his home were intriguing due to the large yard behind it. This not only housed all his transport in large sheds, but was also where great mounds of shiny black coal were stored and where his workmen returned with blackened hands and faces and clothes ridden with coal dust after a day's work. When delivering coal the men often wore flat caps with the peak turned backwards and over this a sack with one corner folded into the other to make a long hood which helped to protect their head and back as they carried the one hundredweight sacks of coal. I actually enjoyed the smell of the coal almost as much as the smell of timber. Uncle Harry and Aunt Rose along with two of my cousins lived in the street parallel to that of my grandmother. There was an ally way connecting the two streets making a convenient short cut when Aunt Rose visited her mother. All were strict chapel going people, but Uncle Harry had a roguish twinkle in his eye at times and was popular with the children.

Uncle Ern was also friendly towards us, not minding when we went to watch him working on the coffins in the workshop, answering our questions and taking time to explain his work. We could not say the same for his wife who seemed to cut herself off from all members of the family. She was Irish and how she came to be married to our Uncle was a mystery to we children. Although living only two doors away from our grandmother, we were never once allowed into her home, and when sent to her with messages from Uncle Ern or Granny, we were always kept at the door, not a foot was allowed over the doorstep. She dressed completely in black as far as I recall and not once can I ever remember seeing a smile upon her face. Aunt Cath had no children of her own and was certainly not interested in any nieces or nephews.

When our stay at Granny's coincided with a Sunday we joined them all at the morning service at the Congregational Church close by. If we were still there during the afternoon the grandchildren attended the Sunday School along with our cousin Roy. Our older cousin Ron played the organ for the service and the congregation of the usually full church sang with gusto. As with many of the non-conformist churches, the sermon could be fiery and long winded. My parents had met while singing in the church choir and had been married in this same church, so were familiar with a number of the families there. It was usual then for people to wear their better clothes to church, their 'Sunday Best' as it was called. Those clothes normally worn during the week being put to one side until Monday came round again. As far as children went it meant being on one's best behaviour and not getting Sunday clothes crumpled or dirty, somewhat of a strain on the younger generation. Female members of the congregation were expected to wear hats and gloves, it was frowned upon if a ladies head was not covered in deference to the House of God. Boys and men of course were required to remove headgear, not only in church, but also on entering any house. When in the street it was a common courtesy for men to tip their hats to ladies they knew and always to walk on the outside of the pavement to protect the ladies from possible splashes or dust from traffic. In dismounting from any vehicle, the gentleman would open the door and descend first in order to help the lady down. These caring customs were appreciated by the ladies who felt themselves valued. Young people were encouraged to give up their seat on buses and trains to members of the older generation, as gentlemen gave up their seats to ladies. I wonder how many such courtesies are performed today?

Mother told me that when she was a child, funerals were very elaborate affairs. Her father, for his business owned a black hearse carriage. The carriage was drawn by black horses wearing large plumes of black feathers on their heads. All the undertaking staff would be dressed in black frock coats and top hats and the coffin and hearse covered in floral tributes. Many poor people saved their hard earned pennies to take out an insurance to pay for an elaborate funeral and be sure of a 'good send off'. The horses were no longer in evidence, but had been replaced by a smart black motor hearse, all kept well polished and gleaming and I believe black bowler hats had replaced the top hats.

A heatwave in 1928 boosted the sale of men's straw hats

THE CHOCOLATE ELEPHANT

Hats were worn by most people in the 1930s, even schoolboys were expected to wear their caps, although I fear many had rough treatment. I can remember a light straw hat of which I was quite fond and wore from the age of four. It was of an open work straw pattern, creating attractive shadows through its small straw brim in the summer sunshine. It also had a garland of pretty, white, artificial daisies around its deep basin shaped crown. Warm, woollen, or felt or fur hats were worn during the winter months, by both small girls and ladies. Easter Sunday was the day on which the straw hats came out of their boxes and were worn through spring and summer until Michaelmas time in October.

Men's head gear varied from the flat caps of the workmen to Trilby hats, bowler hats and a few top hats for special and formal occasions with frock coats and dinner jackets. A heat wave in July of 1928 revived the traditional industry for the men's straw boater hat, manufactured in the hat industry at Luton. Ladies wide brimmed hats festooned with ostrich feathers had gone out of fashion after the First World War, and women's head gear changed from the popular cloche hats of the 1920s worn with low-waisted dresses of the time, to the small crowned, brimmed hats of the 1930s. The smartly dressed lady often wearing a fox fur over her shoulders with a fastening to hold it in place. As children we loved to feel the soft, russet coloured fur against our cheeks and stroke the long bushy tail of our mother's fur. At that time it was most women's ambition to own a fox fur or fur coat, for people then had not thought much about conservation. The supply of animals for providing such items seemed endless and few thought of what cruelty there might be in obtaining them.

Men wore shirts with separate, starched white collars fixed with collar studs which had a tendency to slip from fingers when trying to attach them to the collar, resulting in a hands and knees search for the elusive object. Men's suits could be bought from Montegue Burton for two guineas (two pounds two shillings) or for fifty shillings from the Fifty Shilling Tailors, a chain of tailoring shops. Rubberised Macs, short for Macintosh after the Scottish chemist, Charles Macintosh who invented the waterproof fabric, were worn to protect one from the rain. Sir Henry Wickham a pioneer rubber planter who had first brought rubber seeds from Brazil to start the rubber plantations in Ceylon (Sri Lanka) and Malaya (Malaysia) died in 1928 on 27th September, leaving behind a thriving and growing industry in these countries. Especially thick leather coats and leather helmets were manufactured for the gentleman motorists, for cars then had no comfortable heating systems.

Some men still wore spats over their shoes and socks and these had to be cleaned. One method was to use raw potato pulp. The cloth was sponged with the pulp and then hung to dry. When dry it was well brushed. Boots and shoes could be made waterproof by standing the leather soles in boiled linseed oil and rubbing the uppers with castor oil. The seams of the shoes could be closed with a copal varnish. To polish up damp shoes it was suggested that a drop of paraffin oil be added to the blacking. I can remember my brother rubbing up his rugby boots with dubbin, a very messy business.

A most uncomfortable part of a lady's clothing was the corset, its stiff lacing and inserted whalebone restricting both movement and breathing. It was not until after the 1950s that the corset finally disappeared from most ladies wardrobes, although fashion made a start towards its demise in the 1920s. Ladies stockings, (only dancers and theatrical people wore tights) were made of rayon, lisle, artificial silk or silk and all had seams down the back which sometimes were inclined to go awry and not stay as straight as one would wish. There was of course no nylon and other such man made materials for they had not then been invented. Nylon stockings were first on sale in the United States of America in October 1939, but we in Britain had to wait until after the war before we had them. Silk stockings were the most expensive, but much nicer to wear. All stockings required suspenders to hold them in place. These were attached to the corset or a suspender belt, an extra item of clothing for females. On more than one occasion a lady's suspender has given way causing her to clutch her thigh, resulting in an embarrassing situation. Some men, it seems, find the sight of a young lady's suspenders fascinating and titillating, but I believe the fascination decreases as the age of the lady concerned increases!

Mother told me she once had a most embarrassing moment when a suspender gave way when she was shopping in the High Street. She clasped her thigh and managed to reach the car where my father was waiting for her. She opened the door sat down and said "My suspender's gone!" Only to discover when she looked round that the driver behind the wheel was NOT my father, but a complete stranger! She had got in the wrong car! Covered in confusion she apologised and left the car as quickly as possible. As the driver appeared to be waiting for HIS wife, he no doubt understood the situation and probably enjoyed a quiet chuckle.

Children's clothing also differed to that worn by children of present day. When small we were dressed in an undergarment called combs or combinations. It combined vest and pants into one garment. Buttoned up in front with linen covered buttons, having short legs in the pant area, a slit was left in the under-part to allow for necessary toileting and the whole was made of a type of jersey stockinet material which fitted to the human form. Over this was worn a liberty bodice, white material with a fleecy lining, which fitted almost as a waistcoat and again buttoned in the front with linen covered buttons.

As one grew older combs were discarded and instead we wore vests and fleecy knickers in which there was a pocket to keep a handkerchief. If, without a pocket in dress or knickers, girls tucked their handkies in the elastic of their knicker leg which came some way down the thigh almost to the knee. Also worn in cold weather were black or ginger coloured stockings. Over vest, liberty bodice, and knickers came the petticoat and over the petticoat, a skirt and blouse or dress. When very small we usually wore an apron over our dresses. In the winter, the blouse was replaced by a woollen jumper. Again there were no man made fabrics, the jumpers would have been made of real wool.

Boys vests were buttoned up to the neck and had short sleeves. Over this they wore a shirt in the summer or a warm jumper in the cold weather, but no matter what the weather only short trousers were worn. A knitted tie, usually with horizontal stripes, arranged under the collar of the jumper completed this part of boy's wear. Trousers were secured by striped belts with snake-like metal buckles or by braces. The striped pattern seemed popular as long socks to the knees often had coloured stripes around the top, held up by garters. Boots rather than shoes were worn by boys, usually being lace up type in black or brown. Apart from the laced shoes, I remember having a pair of black patent leather ankle strap shoes and a pair of silver shoes worn expressly for parties when little girls often wore long frilled taffeta or satin dresses. The more frills there were the better we liked it. A dress that swirled out wide when we spun around was a great source of pride. A party was a very special occasion and we dressed appropriately, even to velvet cloak to protect us from the chill air.

Over all normal dress in inclement weather was worn an overcoat usually navy blue, but always of a dark or sombre colouring, or a navy gabardine raincoat and of course the round peaked cap for boys, or felt or velour hat for girls. When very small, to keep our legs warm in winter we wore soft gaiters fastened on our legs by a row of buttons stretching from foot to knee up the outside of the leg. They took ages to fasten. Leggings were another method of keeping children's legs warm in winter. Young children wore this trouser like piece of clothing with narrow legs made in a warm material often resembling tweed, fastened with more buttons.

Miss Shelton's Class at Deadons Hill School.

On my recovery from the mastoid operation my parents decided to send me to a private school in the hope that I might avoid any other distressing ailments. In due course my brother joined me. It was a small private school in Deacons Hill run by two ladies who were quite strict, but kind and just. They took pupils up to the age of ten or eleven. We all wore school uniform. In summer, cream coloured shantung dresses and Panama hats with brown hat band and school badge in its centre. Also, we had a brown blazer with badge on the breast pocket and a brown cardigan, worn on cool days. Winter uniform consisted, I believe, of cream coloured blouses and brown skirts and brown overcoat. The boy's colour scheme was the same for shirt and trousers and cap with badge.

There were only two classrooms and a larger room for physical activities and dancing. Outside was a pleasant playground, surrounded by trees and bushes where we had our games period and playtime. The teaching was formal. We sat in rows in single desks with separate chairs, as opposed to the combined desks and forms at the Council School. The atmosphere was also quite different, much quieter and more restrained. Rules of behaviour were adhered to, girls were expected to behave as young ladies and boys as young gentlemen. A story I was reminded of by my cousin Agnes, was of a time she was staying with our family and had volunteered to walk me to school one morning. The school was at least a mile and a half from our home and we were a little late in starting. Agnes said, " Come along Gwen or we shall be late, we must run."

It seems my reply was, "Young ladies do not run". And I steadfastly refused to do so. I was six years old at the time.

CHAPTER 5

My father's family lived in a large detached house in a quiet residential road in Pinner, Middlesex. My grandfather had retired on a very good pension from the Yorkshire Insurance Company where he had held a responsible position. My father's mother had died when I was only two months old and Grandpa had married for a second time. We knew his wife as Aunt Helen. Living with them was my father's younger brother, our Uncle Sidney. My father also had an unmarried sister who lived nearby with a lady companion and between them they ran a secretarial school.

From the time when I was four years of age and my brother two, we were taken to visit my father's family, usually for the day, Father driving us there in the car. When we were respectively six and four years old, we were taken for a much longer period. Alan and I were not sure of the reason, but made no protest as far as I can remember. Aunt Helen treated us with great kindness although she was a little at a loss in her understanding of children having had none of her own. She made us special dishes she thought we might like and tried her best to keep us occupied with games and activities, joining in when she could.

When I was asked what I should like to have for dessert one day I replied, "Bread pudding please".

It was a favourite of ours at home. Aunt Helen was not quite sure what I meant, so I tried to describe it saying, "It has bread, currants and sultanas in it."

After we had finished the main course, the maid brought in Aunt Helen's bread pudding, and Aunt Helen dished it out. She watched closely as Alan and I ate it and asked, "Is that like the bread pudding you have at home?" I shook my head. It was not like the bread pudding our mother made. It was actually much nicer! I wish now that I had told her so, but we were rather overawed in my Grandfather's home and on our best behaviour, having been brought up and reminded at times by my father that "children should be seen, but not heard" and also that "children do not talk at the meal table". I did not make any further remark, but perhaps the fact that the bread pudding was eaten with relish by both Alan and I, may have indicated that we very much approved.

Grandfather's house, 14 Woodhall Avenue, Pinner, Middlesex

Grandpa was an enthusiastic bee keeper and had several hives at the bottom of his large garden. He was a quiet and reserved person and I never once heard him raise his voice. We were his only grandchildren, but he was not demonstrative in his affection. He was willing to tutor us when it came to bee keeping and decked out in straw hats with voluminous veils tucked into the necks of our long sleeved shirts, blouses or coats, we were allowed to go with Grandpa to the hives to remove the honeycombs. One of us having the honour of carrying the smoke gun. Grandpa would lift off the lid of a hive and puff in some of the contents of the smoke gun in order to lull the bees. In time we were given the gun and allowed to do the puffing while Grandpa held the lid. Once the bees were reasonably tranquilized, Grandpa carefully lifted out one of the frames holding the honeycombs and examined it for honey. If it had plenty of honey, this was collected into a bowl, the sweet golden wax combs being carefully brushed free of any remaining bees, and the frame replaced. This was done carefully and calmly with each frame in turn before moving on to the next hive. As he worked he explained about the bees, how they worked for the Queen in their hive, gathering nectar from the flowers and turning it into honey. Some honey must always be left for the bees themselves and sometimes a form of sugared liquid was provided as an additional boost for them.

Helping Grandpa with the bees

Once the honeycombs had been collected, they were taken into the house and placed in a centrilfugal separator and spun. The separated golden, liquid honey was then stored in clean glass jars. It was at Grandpa's that Alan and I tasted a fresh honeycomb for the first time and found the sweet, sticky wax honeycombs entirely to our taste.

Close to the hives was a large mound of earth over which marrow plants grew. This was my first recollection of seeing the large green vegetables with the striped skins in their growing situation. A gardener helped Grandpa in looking after these and many other vegetables and plants in this, to children's eyes at least, very large garden, but we were always warned not to worry him when he was working and so never really got to know him.

On the other hand, Kemp, Aunt Helen's maid was friendly and did not mind if we went to talk to her in the kitchen or when she was cleaning the rooms. Kemp, for she was called by her surname only, was not a young woman and she suffered with a slight limp. When she served at meal times, she wore a uniform with lace edged apron and white head dress tied around her forehead and back of head, similar to that worn by the 'Nippy' waitresses at Lyon's Corner Houses. A different uniform was worn for cleaning purposes. She remained with my Grandfather and Aunt Helen for many years and I always made a point of going to her little room by the kitchen to chat with her whenever we visited them.

When it was time to prepare for bed, Grandpa always read us a story. It was our introduction to Brer Rabbit, Brer Fox and all the other characters in the Uncle Remus stories. I believe Grandpa enjoyed them as much as we did. We sat on stools by his feet as he reclined in his winged armchair and listened intently as he recounted the adventures of Brer Rabbit and the Tar Baby, and other exploits of this cunning bunny. Other stories came from Aesops Fables, The Fox and the Sour Grapes is another story I remember from that time spent with my Grandfather.

It was during this stay that Alan lost his curls. I had always had straight hair from the time I lost my baby waves when about two years of age, but Alan retained his curls for much longer and when we went to Pinner he still had long ringlets. Aunt Helen decided that they were really too long and took him to the hairdresser to have them cut off. When our parents came to collect us, complete with new baby sister, the first thing mother noticed was Alan's short hairdo. She was very upset and rather annoyed with Aunt Helen, although there were no harsh words between them. I don't think Alan regretted the loss of his curls at all for he was not obliged to under go as much brushing and combing as before. He could be off to play in half the time it had taken before he lost his locks.

One of my pleasures when visiting Aunt Helen was to tidy her needlework box. I spent a good hour or more sorting the coloured threads, needles, pins, buttons and winding up her tape measure. Aunt Helen left me to it with an amused smile, while I sat on the floor surrounded by the contents of the box, until one by one I had them all back in their proper places, once more neat and tidy.

Christmas day was sometimes spent at Pinner. The family went by car with either parent driving, taking our presents for Grandpa, Aunt Helen, Uncle Sidney and if they were there Aunt Dorothy and her friend, all in the boot. All was done to make us welcome with a traditional festive meal, after which, came the most exciting part for we children. In the drawing room was a large Christmas Tree alight with small candles which burned with a real flame and which were clipped on to the branches by metal clips under small rimmed holders that caught the hot wax drips. The silver tinsel draped around the tree picking up the light and glittering in the reflection of the flames. Other coloured decorations hung around the tree along with packages of interesting shape. On the top stood a beautiful silver fairy doll complete with gossamer wings and shining wand in the form of a star. Other larger packages were propped around the decorated tub in which the tree stood.

Uncle Sidney took charge of the proceedings. When all the adults were seated, he started to hand out the brightly wrapped packages. Each parcel was a surprise. One never asked outright for a particular article, although I suppose many hints could be given, but the greatest pleasure for us as children was the unexpected surprise that awaited us in each of the packages. There was one gift that Aunt Helen gave me each year apart from the many packages from the tree, and that was a new party dress made by herself. I remember one dress in particular for it was different to all others I had had. In swirly patterns of shades of blue it had tiny beads sewn into the almost transparent material and a full skirt that swirled as I turned, weighted as it was with the beads. It would be every little girl's delight. I thought it wonderful, but from the look in my mother's eye, I had the feeling that she did not think it very practical.

Our gifts were not usually expensive items as people did not generally spend the great amount of money on children's gifts as they are so inclined to do now. We were not over indulged with fancy toys, but those we had gave great pleasure and lasted for years. When all the gifts had been given and all the appropriate thanks had been said, the final event especial to me took place. Uncle Sidney climbed the stepladder to take the beautiful fairy from the top of the tree and presented her to me. This was the moment I had been waiting for. Fairy dolls in their beautiful silver dresses, a silver star in their hair, gossamer wings and silver wand, were many small girl's dream, and at fancy dress parties that is how many little girls loved to dress, all in white and silver with sparkling tinsel and silver shoes. There would probably be a bevy of them at every party, but every one of them felt imbued with her own special magic.

One heard much more of fairies then, than young children do now I think. We really believed in them. When a child's teeth started to fall out at the age of six or seven, the tooth was kept to put under the pillow at night, to be replaced by a silver sixpenny piece from the fairies by morning. There were more stories and poems for children involving fairies, all charming and uncomplicated, although bad fairies were also included. We had a magic world of make believe without the modern gory monsters of the present day television, films and picture books. There were the giants and dragons and other beasts such as the wolf in Red Riding Hood and the Three Pigs, or the beast in the Beauty and the beast, but even he was kindly. I believe we were lucky in the fact that our childhood was in a kinder, more gentle, world altogether.

At the end of the afternoon it was time for us all to leave, for children had fairly early bedtimes and we were all usually tucked in bed by seven to eight o'clock. It had been an exciting day and my parents did not want over tired or fractious children on the way home.

It was the custom that on Epiphany, 12th night, January 6th all Christmas decorations should be removed. This is a custom we still maintain. Also on this day, it was the custom, certainly still maintained in 1937, for the King to observe the day in the Royal Chapel with offerings of gold, frankincense and myrrh, commemorating the gifts of the Magi to the Infant Christ.

In the period after Christmas came the pantomimes. Opening on Boxing Day they continued through January in most big towns. Our parents usually took us to one of the London theatres that meant another adventurous journey on the train, underground railway or buses. They were of course steam trains and they arrived, puffing into the station to pull up with a great hissing and shushing of escaping steam and grinding brakes. In the open engine cab were the driver and fireman in blue overalls and peaked caps stained with the marks of coal and oil and sweating from the heat of the engine's fire. Once the passengers were in the carriages labelled 1st., or 3rd class, (we always went 3rd.class), porters checked that the doors were properly slammed shut. Then we watched from the window as the guard blew his whistle, waved his little green flag, and then we were off. With a great puffing and blowing, the train slowly moved out of the station, the chugging of its wheels gradually increasing in pace, the sound moving up the scale as the engine got into its rhythm. As we came to a tunnel the driver blew the engine's whistle and my father closed the windows to prevent the smoke filling the compartment. Sometimes the lights would be out and we were in darkness until the end of the tunnel was reached. All this was exciting for small children.

The Underground was also an experience with its moving escalators and automatic doors on the trains. We clung tightly to our parent's hands in this busy and crowded world. On reaching the theatre we were engulfed by the crowds of excited children with their parents or accompanying adults, squeezing their way into the foyer of the building, out of the winter's cold. While father collected our tickets from the box office, we gazed at the posters and photographs, listened to the high chatter of other children and the deeper voices of adults attempting to keep their charges within sight and control.

Father usually bought tickets for the dress circle that meant walking up a flight of stairs to enter the auditorium through double doors in which there were small oval glass windows. Here the attendant took our tickets and sold programmes if patrons had not already bought programmes in the foyer. Entering from these doors the whole vista of the theatre could be seen. From the semicircle of the dress circle with its tiers of seating, one looked down upon the stage and the seats of the stalls. On a level with the dress circle and to each side of the auditorium were the boxes like bay windows with velvet drapes where the more privileged sat in stately seclusion, closer to the action taking place on the wide stage. Above us in the high ceiling and around the walls, electric lights shone causing the golden painted swag and garland decorations to glow in response. If we were fortunate we had seats in the first row of the dress circle where we could look down upon the rapidly filling theatre. Going to the theatre was a special occasion for most people in the 1930s, when ladies wore their long evening dresses and jewels and men wore dinner jackets and black bow ties. Although such formal attire did not apply to children's matinees, people still took the trouble to look well dressed and fully presentable.

As time drew near to the commencement of the performance, the members of the orchestra began to take their places in the pit in front of the stage. One of the advantages of the circle seats was the bird's eye view it gave us of the musicians and their instruments, for this was one of the few times which enabled us to watch such instruments being played. With the arrival of the conductor, bowing to the applause of the audience before turning to face the orchestra and stage, there came a hush as the lights were lowered and conversation ceased. The conductor raised his baton, the musicians raised their instruments and the overture began. I loved the music and delighted in watching the manipulation of the shining wind instruments and the moving bows of the string's players as they rose and fell in harmony. Sometimes there was even a harp, when the nimble fingers of the harpist brought forth delightful tinkling notes descending like a gentle waterfall from the strings of this large instrument.

As the overture came to an end, the painted fire curtain was raised, then as the orchestra started the music for the first act, the heavy velvet curtains were lifted or parted and the show began. No matter what the story. Whether Aladdin, Dick Whittington, Cinderella, or some other fairy tale, it usually began with a crowd scene and chorus to get it off to a rousing start, before some of the principal actors walked onto the stage to be picked out by the spotlight and clapped by the watching audience.

We all delighted in the antics of the dame, a man dressed in outrageous female garb and taking the part of the mother, such as Widow Twanky in Aladdin, or in the case of the story of Cinderella, two men playing the parts of the ugly sisters. Of course, the principal boy was played by a woman, who showed her legs to advantage in sleek tights and short jacket. But, the principal girl, was portrayed by a lovely lady as was the Good Fairy. Costumes were colourful and gorgeous with plenty of shining sequins and tinsel. Other characters were most amusing, causing us to laugh and giggle at their foolery. At times the audience were invited to join in the repartee and scenes in which the 'baddies' were creeping up on the dame, brought frantic shouts from the children of "Behind you, behind you" in answer to the Dame's "I can't see anybody!". And so the show went on, with laughter, music and song always to come to the conclusion when the 'baddies' got their just deserts and the hero and heroine 'lived happily ever after' just the way a fairy story should be.

One year, instead of the pantomime, we were taken to see a performance of Sir James M. Barrie's story of Peter Pan, the boy who never grew up. It is believed that Sir James Barrie was inspired to write this story in memory of his beloved brother who tragically died while still a child. Sir James made a gift of the copyright fee of Peter Pan to the Great Ormond Street Children's Hospital in London. This play was the first occasion on which we had seen the actors flying above the stage. Our imagination was fired by the sight and we dreamed of emulating them to join the birds in their effortless flight. Of course our common sense told us this was not possible and our illusions came to earth when our parents explained that, the actors were aided by wires. Fifty to sixty years later some people more daring than I, have managed this almost effortless flying with hang gliders or similar contraptions, but they are still restricted by topography and thermal currents.

Little girls identified themselves with Wendy who tried to make a home for the 'lost boys and become a substitute mother. Little boys fancied themselves as Peter Pan fighting the wicked Captain Hook and of course when Tinker Bell was expiring, we all believed in fairies, and many children really did.

My father was a keen follower of the Gilbert and Sullivan operettas and as I grew in years I accompanied him to one or two performances of the D'Orly Carte Company. I may not have understood all the Victorian political implications of the plots, but I could enjoy the delightful music and excellent singing of the performers when every word of the lyric was audible to the audience. "Take a Pair of Sparkling Eyes" from the Gondoliers was one of my father's favourite songs, which he liked to hum to himself. At the end of every performance or film show, the National Anthem was played at which the audience stood to attention as a mark of respect until the end when the orchestra put down their instruments.

Leaving the theatre in the wintertime, we walked through the lamp lit streets of town. Many of the lamps were still lit by gaslight. I remember a song I used to play which went . . . 'There beneath the gas lights glitter

Stands a little fragile girl'.

A rather sad song as I recall. However, gaslights before the Second

World War were still numerous and these had to be lit manually. As evening approached, it was a regular sight to see the lamp lighter making his rounds with his long pole in his hands. With the hook on its end he opened the glass side of the lamp and pulled on the arm, which then released the gas to be lit by the pilot flame. One by one the lamps were set aglowing as he made his way down the road. The radiance of the lamps did not extend to any great distance, but provided a pool of light around each post. In late 1939 at the outbreak of war even these lights were extinguished and it was another five or six years before they were to shine again.

The lamp lighter continued to perform his occupation in certain areas of the country up until 1952 at least, for I well remember one coming along the road where we lived in Exmouth, Devon, while my children were young. There was a charming little song about the lamp lighter called 'The Lamp Lighter's Serenade'. The music was by Hoagy Carmichael, but the words escape me now.

The Lamp-lighter

The Music Halls were still playing to appreciative audiences and my husband has memories of sitting up in 'the gods' at the top of the theatre where the seats were hard wooden benches in tiers. Looking down from this great height could make one dizzy, but as long as one concentrated on the action on the stage and not on the great drop below, the dizziness could be overcome. The performers included comedians, singers, jugglers, conjurers and acrobats. Audience participation was encouraged in singing the songs as most people knew both music and words. Delivery boys whistled the catchy tunes as they rode their bicycles along the streets and at family parties the songs were heard sung again, as each member was encouraged to perform their 'party piece'.

Outside the Music Hall during the winter, men with burning braziers roasted sweet chestnuts in pans over the glowing coal. As well as being good to eat, they had the advantage of keeping the hands warm. Small boys even found a use for the shells, dropping them on the heads of those in the seats below them, along with the shells of the peanuts also bought from the vendors outside!

CHAPTER 6

A short time before my sister was born we moved from living over the shop to a detached house in a residential road opposite the parade of shops, still near enough for my parents to walk to their business. It must have been fairly soon after the move that Mother engaged a maid, Catherine, to help in the house. Catherine was accommodated in one of the rooms that we had recently vacated and one floor was let out as a flat.

Catherine was a north country girl from the Durham area. She must have been about twenty years of age, slight and fair in appearance. It took a little while to get used to her regional accent which was strange to our ears, but she was good tempered and tolerant of we children and we became very fond of her. My parents valued her sufficiently to leave her in charge of us when they took a short holiday, and we all managed very well together.

During the great depression of 1929 and the 1930s, there were many people from the north who journeyed south to look for work, among them were the Jarrow Marchers, unemployed men who in 1936 decided to bring their plight to the notice of the government and people of the south in an active and substantial fashion by marching all the way from Jarrow Town Hall in County Durham to London. A distance of three hundred miles. Jarrow, a town relying on its shipbuilding reputation for employment, had seven thousand unemployed. On the 5th October two hundred and seven men started the Jarrow Crusade March, hauling heavy oak chests holding petitions to Stanley Baldwin the Prime minister. Their Member of Parliament Ellen Wilkinson, short of stature, but strong of heart marched with them. Their ranks were joined by others on the way, until they numbered several hundred. People of many towns on their route helped by giving accommodation and food when they could and the shoemaking workers of Northampton and Leicester stayed up all night to repair the marchers sadly worn boots. But after all their efforts, the government remained stony hearted. Nothing was done to help Jarrow.

We began to hear more strange regional accents in our part of England. Up until that time people had not really travelled far, but had found work in their own areas close to their homes. The depression which started with the collapse of the New York Stock Exchange on 28th October 1929 and caused a world wide economic crisis, when over a few days millions of shares were wiped off the market as a panic of selling ensued. This crisis caused a change in many a way of life and those who could find no work in their own areas moved to other parts of Britain causing more of a mix of population. Documentary films showing how people lived in the industrial areas of the north of England and the mining areas of Wales, where wooden and leather clogs were still worn by workers in mills and mines, started to be made by a few innovative people. It was the first time that many people in the south of England became aware of the many difficulties and different mode of life that existed in these more distant regions. To those who came from the grime and smoke stained rows of terraced houses of the industrial north, the semidetached villas and gardens blooming with flowers and shrubs, surrounding the capital city in the south of the country, seemed a virtual Garden of Eden.

King Edward VIII talking to the unemployed during the depression, 1936

The building of the suburbs of the south spread rapidly during the 1930s and can be recognised by the architecture of that time. Before his abdication, Edward VIII made a tour of South Wales in 1936, talking to the unemployed miners and factory workers. Although they were probably glad of his recognition of their plight, the government in distant London did little to help the situation and practical help was hard to come by.

Mother still did most of the cooking, but Catherine took over the housework, washing and ironing. Our new house only recently built was not large, but much more convenient especially with a new baby in the family. There were no long flights of stairs, instead of a back yard, there was a front as well as a back garden where Mother could leave our baby sister to sleep in her pram and be able to keep an eye on us while we played there.

Downstairs we had a dining room, a drawing room or lounge as it was often called, a kitchen and a small bedroom that became my brother's room. Upstairs were two more bedrooms and a bathroom. Later my father added a conservatory to the side of the house. This became known as 'the glasshouse'. As the house was so new, there was no established garden, so Father had some hard work to produce a garden out of the tough clay soil, but eventually a lawn was laid and borders sewn and so the garden developed. There was plenty of opportunity for we children to indulge in making 'mud pies', a wonderful form of play mixing mud and water to a gooy mess and adding bits of carrot tops and other leaves in the pretence of cooking. Mother provided old containers for our pies and did not mind too much if some of the sticky mud ended elsewhere than in the container, for this form of play kept us all happily occupied for an hour or more.

As all the houses had been built around the same time, the neighbours were new to one another. There was a distinct reserve to begin with, but in time we were on speaking terms with most of them. However in the twenty or more years they were in that house, I never heard my parents address their neighbours in any but formal terms. Always Mr A… or Mrs B… using surnames and never Christian names. People only used first name terms for members of the family, or perhaps those friends with whom they went to school.

At the end of the road away from the main street was a recreation ground. We were very close to its main iron gates, only one other house between our house and the entrance. These gates were open every day except Sunday and provided a short cut to the main part of the village for the residents of the road. Unfortunately, they were closed on Sunday, the day we were required to go three times to Chapel, which meant a much longer walk for us. Once we were old enough to be allowed out on our own, Alan and I spent most of our free time in the recreation ground. Playing on the swings, round-about and see-saw, or climbing the monkey ladder, a metal frame structure with wooden ladder like bars from which one could swing, do somersaults or climb along the top, depending on one's ability or inclination. I believe an incident on the monkey ladder may have been responsible for giving me my fear of heights. Alan and I were playing on top one day and I was watching other children from my perch, when Alan asked me to move backwards a little further. I did so. "A bit more" he said, and without thinking or looking behind me I did so again…. And came tumbling off the end. Some workmen who were there came to my rescue as I was feeling rather stunned. They checked to see if I had any broken bones. Luckily apart from a few bruises I had escaped injury, but the fall reminded me to be more cautious of heights in the future. Apart from the swings and other attractions, the recreation ground provided a large area of grass for ball games. There were no trees, which perhaps was just as well or there may have been more falls.

Another source of pleasure on winter days, were the scrap books in which we pasted treasured pictures, cards, or other memorabilia. It was possible to buy sheets of coloured cut-outs for a few pence and taking these apart and adding them to our scrap books kept us happy and quiet for some time. We made up our own paste with flour and water, each having our own small jar in which to keep it, usually an empty fish or meat paste jar, along with small paint brush. I recall the awful smell it emitted if we had forgotten to wash it out and it had been left for some days, probably hidden under a pile of other paraphernalia. Painting and colouring was another activity for the inclement days and again we each had our own small paint-box of water colours and a box of crayons, sometimes wax crayons which snapped when pressed too hard, or were trodden underfoot to all the grown-ups annoyance. Coloured chalks for our blackboard could also make an unholy mess and bring forth trouble. In 1935 the game of Monopoly was invented by unemployed engineer Charles Darrow and became the world's most successful board game. It was certainly a great success with our family and friends, continuing for hours, often long past bedtime during holiday periods.

I joined the boys in playing football, cricket and other boisterous games for apart from my young sister there were no other girls in our road. Consequently I became a regular tomboy who could bowl as straight as any boy and take a tumble with the rest of them without tears. By this time I had left the 'ladylike' atmosphere of Deacons Hill private school, for at nine years of age I passed the entrance examination for fee paying pupils for the Girls' Grammar School at Barnet.

Queen Elizabeth's Girls' Grammar School was the more recent addition of a Grammar School founded for boys in 1578. Girls were only admitted in 1888. We were of course in separate buildings some distance from each other in the town. The boy's school being off Wood Street not far from Wellhouse Hospital and the girl's school being at the top of Barnet Hill. A number of pupils from Boreham Wood attended both schools and met up on the bus (306) which travelled in each day. The route of the bus was from Watford to New Barnet and Enfield. It stopped in the centre of our village to travel up Furzehill Road and past the Home and Rest for Horses. This meant a walk of about a quarter of a mile to the bus stop each morning, which sometimes became more of a run. The drivers and conductors of the buses grew to recognise us as regular passengers and if they saw us running would wait for us. Tickets for the term were bought in advance, so that we did not need to carry money, but presented our three penny ticket instead to the conductor who clipped it on his little machine strapped across his chest before returning it. On one occasion soon after starting at Queen Elizabeth's, I lost my ticket and dissolved into tears, but the kindly conductor gave me another ticket instead. When I told mother of the incident she gave me a small wrapped parcel of cigarettes to give to the conductor to thank him for his sympathy and kindness. Sometime later the ticket system on the bus must have changed, as I remember my friend and I saving a halfpenny on the fare by walking part of the way home with friends, who lived near the boy's school and spending the halfpenny saved on a bar of sticky toffee from the sweet shop.

Miss Fitt's class of 1936. Queen Elizabeth Girls' Grammar School, Barnet.
I am in the front row far right

Children's behaviour on buses was generally good as the conductor would not tolerate unruliness. Any misbehaviour was reported to the school, for we all wore school uniform that was easily recognised. Should pupils be reported, they would most certainly be called before the head teacher and receive a severe dressing down for bringing the name of the school into disrepute.

Apart from the elementary schools, uniform was the accepted dress for all schools. For those parents who could not afford new items, there was a second-hand exchange system run by the school, so that uniform was obtainable for all pupils. As children normally grow out rather than wear out their clothes, the system was acceptable to all. At Queen Elizabeth's our uniform for winter consisted of a navy gym slip, cut with a flared 'Princess Line' pattern skirt, rather than pleats. A blue striped long sleeved blouse with V shaped neck, which meant that we did not have to wear ties as many other girl's schools did. A navy cardigan, black woollen stockings and black laced shoes. A thick serge navy overcoat and brimmed velour hat with school hatband and badge completed the outdoor uniform. All pupils had to provide a shoe-bag in which were kept their gym shoes and indoor house shoes. These black, strapped, lighter shoes had to be put on before going to our classrooms, while our outdoor shoes were put into a wire cage under a wooden bench below our clothing pegs, each girl having her own peg marked with her name in the various cloakrooms for each class.

For physical education lesson on apparatus we wore singlets or vests and our navy blue knickers, white socks and of course our black, rubber, lace-up gym shoes. For outside games, we retained our blouses and gym-slips, black stockings and gym shoes. These, after an energetic game retained a strong, hot, rubbery smell for some time! For a game of hockey, we changed into strong hockey shoes.

The summer uniform was blue striped cotton dresses with white collars, buttoned at the front, and navy blazers with a red Tudor rose, the badge of the school on the breast pocket. Our velour hats were changed for off white panamas, again with brims, hat bands and elastic chin straps sewn in by our mothers.

All our teachers were female and single, for no married women were employed in teaching. Those younger members of staff who found themselves a husband were obliged to give up their profession and any chance of a career. Consequently those more mature members of staff were rather set in their ways and many were old fashioned in their dress. Our history mistress, Miss Jewel, belied her name by wearing long, rather drab clothes and never changing her hair style which was drawn back severely from her face with a centre parting and the long hair plaited and coiled around, then pinned over each ear like a pair of ear phones. She was however a popular though strict teacher, and never had any problems with pupils playing up as her lessons were always interesting.

Miss Sharp was our physical education and games teacher. I always enjoyed all her lessons, particularly the gym lesson at the end of term called 'Shipwreck' when all the apparatus was brought out and we had to make our way via upturned forms, or benches, bars, rails, ropes and vaulting equipment all round the room without touching the floor. Quite a challenge! Also of mature years, Miss Sharp always wore a very short pleated gym slip tied at the waist with a band, fringed at each end and thick black stockings. Like her pupils she wore thick navy blue knickers and was remarkably agile. Her hair style was a no nonsense short and straight, as were a number of other members of staff. Most of those who grew their hair long, pinned it in a bun at the nape of the neck. A younger games and gym mistress Miss Gunnery, joined the staff after I had been there a year or so. Her hair was short but very thick and wavy.

Every Christmas the school held a party for the pupils when we had a small feast in the classroom and then a dance in the hall. With Miss Green at the piano we formed long lines facing one another and danced the Roger de Coverly, swinging with our partner and skipping round and through the arched arms of the lines. The other dance we enjoyed was the polka, both lively dances taught to us by Miss Sharp. We all kept going until we were dizzy and out of breath or Miss Green wanted a rest from playing. It was a lot more fun than normal lessons!

The school day started with classroom registration and then the assembly of the whole school in the gymnasium that doubled as a hall. A separate hall was built in 1938 a few years after I joined the school. All girls sat cross legged on the polished wooden floor until the entry of the headmistress, (a Miss Griffiths in my first years at the school), when all rose to their feet. Hymns were sung, Miss Green, the music teacher accompanying us on the piano, prayers said and notices given out, before all classes filed out of the hall to return to their classrooms to begin lessons. On November 11th Armistice Day, the programme was a little different as about 10.45 we again filed into the hall and listened while Miss Griffiths reminded us of the meaning of Armistice Day. At the striking of Big Ben at 11o'clock we stood in silence for a full two minutes before singing a hymn and returning to our classroom.

At our morning break we were given a small bottle of milk, a third of a pint, which we drank with the aid of a straw before leaving the classroom. This was given out by the milk monitors who were also responsible for seeing that all empty bottles were returned to the crates. Having finished our milk we were free to go to the tuck shop and buy a sticky iced bun. These cost a halfpenny each and were always fresh, large, shaped like eclairs and delightful. I still remember the taste of them and how we looked forward to the break, wishing the lesson would pass quickly so that we might indulge in their sticky sweetness.

Each class at the beginning of each term chose their form captain and games captain. I was chosen once as form captain, but found it a rather thankless task as we were supposed to keep the class in order between lessons whilst waiting for the teacher of the next subject. Other duties were to assist the teacher when required.

Games lessons included netball and hockey during the winter. Tennis and rounders during the summer. As mentioned earlier, the school was built on a hill and the netball and tennis courts were in a terraced area. Some way below these, were the rounders and hockey pitches in a field close to the bottom of the hill. It was fine going down, but quite a hike back up again carrying all the equipment, having run oneself silly in the process of the game. The pitches themselves were not flat by any means and playing uphill was of course a lot harder than playing downhill. I nearly came to grief during a game of rounders, one day. Back stop, behind the batsman was my usual position, quite a dangerous spot where one had to avoid being hit by the batsman's bat and also the oncoming hard, white rounders ball. In this instance, the batsman had hit the ball straight up in the air between the bowler and myself. Watching the ball I ran forward up hill to catch it as it descended, only to collide with the bowler also watching the ball, coming downhill. Our heads met and I was knocked over and dazed, but was gratified when I came to, to find I held the ball in my hands, having caught the batsman out.

The singing lessons with Miss Green were most enjoyable. I had always enjoyed music and singing in particular. Sir John Barbarolli, the conductor of the famous Halle Orchestra once paid a visit to the school and spoke to us about music. It was not until some years later that I discovered how famous he was and heard and watched him at work with an orchestra. One year the staff put on a pantomime for the school written by one or two of their members. They really let themselves go, even to the extent of wearing tights in costume and often acting the fool. It was a time when we saw our teachers in a completely new light and all the school applauded heartily.

At the age of eleven in the Upper Third Form was when the girls who had won scholarships from the council elementary schools joined us. Some of these girls came from Boreham Wood and joined us on the bus journey. We all got along well together and in the village we all suffered the same taunts from the rougher element of the elementary school with their "Look at the Grammar School kids then" or Grammar School kid, Grammar School kid" shouted after us down the street. We put it down to jealousy and ignored them.

Once a year a photographer came to take the school photograph. All the pupils, about 200-300 were arranged in a large semicircle on the netball court and the camera was set up on a tripod. The head of the photographer then disappeared under his black cloth draped over the back of the camera and all had to remain absolutely still while he took the picture, moving slowly around the semicircle. The resulting picture was extremely long. I still have one rolled up among my souvenirs.

There was no swimming pool at our school and it was not until well into the 1930s that one was built at the boy's school. The Heads of both schools came to an arrangement where the pool could be used for lessons for the girls at certain times. With so many pupils in each school not all classes could be accommodated, so it was only the older girls who were able to benefit. Owing to the fact that the pool was an unheated, rather small, open affair and also to the vagaries of the English climate, we did not profit from many lessons. In fact I think I only managed four or five lessons in my time at school and never learnt to swim.

It was while I was attending Grammar School, that an outbreak of polio, or infantile paralysis occurred in Barnet. This was probably in 1936 or 37. A number of children were affected and parents were extremely worried, but I do not remember the schools being closed. I do remember seeing a boy from my brother's school who was previously very active in a normal boyish way, being taken about in a wheelchair. There were outbreaks in other parts of the country, causing quite a scare at the time, for many of the sufferers were confined to 'iron lungs' the only treatment available for serious cases of the disease. The 'iron lung' was a long metal case that enclosed the entire body apart from the head. It incorporated an artificial lung enabling the patient to breathe, but restricting all other movement. Most of the patients suffered from complete paralysis of the limbs due to the disease, therefore it is not surprising that parents were deeply concerned. Although some adults were also stricken the disease seemed mostly to affect young people. The 'iron lung' was first used in October of 1928 in Boston in Massachusetts and they continued to be used for many years until better methods were discovered. A polio vaccine was not discovered until 1959.

At the age of twelve I was given a new, black, larger size bicycle and my small green one was put aside for my sister. Ladies bicycles sported a dress guard to prevent skirts becoming entangled in the wheels or chain of the cycle. Mens and boys bikes differed by having a cross bar and no guard. After some practice on the road I was allowed to ride to school with my friend Betty. The busiest and fastest traffic was on the Barnet By Pass which we had to cross, but traffic was not as busy or as fast as nowadays. All went well until one day as we were about to turn into Furzehill road by the Home and Rest for Horses, a car came up close behind me and worried me. Instead of turning I continued straight on while Betty turned. The next thing I knew was a clash of metal as the car hit my bike and sent me sprawling on the grass verge. The car swerved into the ditch. I lay there conscious but dazed and as both the driver, who was unhurt and Betty returned to see the extent of the damage, I managed to pick myself up and ruefully survey the result. Apart from some bruises and a shock to my system, physically I appeared to have escaped serious injury. However my bike was not so lucky. It had some very wonky wheels and my coat was ripped all down the back. I believe the driver offered to take me home, but I was worried about my bike and as my legs seemed to be working I decided to walk as far as Betty's house. From there a message was sent to my parents who came to collect me. I was very upset about my bicycle and afraid what Mother would say about my coat. I expected her to be angry. As it was, my parents were so thankful to find me without serious injury, that the coat was considered unimportant. I had to give up cycling for a while due to the state of my bike and also to the state of my nerves as I was extremely apprehensive of crossing a road for at least three months after that time. I heard later, that my accident was used as a warning by the police, who went around all schools giving a talk on road safety.

Once I was fully recovered in both body and nerves, I was allowed to cycle again. My friend Betty moved to another town and instead it was another friend, Joyce and I who rode to school together. This time we took another route along the Elstree Way to the Barn Restaurant. A large and popular eating and entertainment place, then across the By Pass and over Rowley Green, an area of common land around which stood a number of large houses and then through Arkley and on to Barnet. The old tram lines were still in place on Barnet Hill and we had to be very careful not to get our bicycle wheels caught in them. The trams had been replaced by trolly buses with the overhead wires. It was the conductor's duty to swing the overhead connection to the right position when making the return journey. I remember travelling on a tram, although I cannot remember where it was, but I recall it had a driving position at both ends and also the backs of the seats could be moved in their slots from back to front, enabling the passenger to always face forwards, in the way the tram was going. The driver's position was mostly open to the elements where he stood moving his simple controls to activate the vehicle.

But, to get back to the bicycles. Sometimes we found some boys from the boy's school awaiting us on the road that passed through the common. For some time we ignored their presence, but it did not stop them following us the rest of the way to school. This went on for a week or two before one of them plucked up enough courage to hand me a note suggesting we meet one weekend. We still continued to ignore them until they actually stopped us and spoke one day. This seemed to be the way in which teenage boys began to show interest in the opposite sex. Perhaps it was a little slow, but that was the general approach to boy and girl relationships. For we had no lessons on the 'facts of life' as they were called and remained innocent unless such things were explained by parents, who were usually too embarrassed themselves to mention the subject. When boys and girls went out together it was generally in groups, for a cycle ride or some similar harmless and innocent activity.

Empire Day, 24th May was a special day for all schoolchildren in the local school and village. Girls wore white dresses and boys wore white shirts with their short trousers. It took place close to May Day celebrations when a May Queen was elected by the school children and there was dancing around the May Pole and processions with the children carrying posies or baskets of flowers, the celebrations attended by proud parents and onlookers. On Empire Day there was a flag raising ceremony of the Union Flag and a prominent member of the community made a patriotic speech to the assembled crowd. Best of all as far as the children were concerned, it was a day out of school. My husband told me that at the church school he attended in his infant years, the boys were asked to wear a white shirt for Empire Day and wear belts rather than braces for their trousers. As he was a little on the tubby side, his mother felt that a belt alone might not be sufficiently supportive, and cut holes in his shirt so that he might still wear his braces by putting the ends through the holes to button on to his trousers. He still recalls feeling very self conscious and embarrassed about this.

Empire Day was the anniversary of Queen Victoria's birthday and was inaugurated as Empire Day in 1902 by the Earl of Meath with the idea of teaching boys and girls of the true value of their heritage as citizens of the Empire also the duties and responsibilities of their citizenship. He also wished them to remember those who emigrated to settle in distant lands and forge links with the Mother Country. In 1959 Empire Day was renamed Commonwealth Day as by that time much of the old Empire had gained their independence, but still wished to retain some of the friendly 'family' alliance with 'The Old Country' of Britain.

Nearly every Sunday our parents expected us to go to chapel three times during the day. To morning service with them at eleven o'clock, to Sunday school after lunch when Mother and Father had a quiet rest at home, and again for the evening service at six o'clock. Our family attended the Baptist Chapel standing on the corner of Furzehill Road. It was an ugly building with a corrugated iron roof protecting two large rooms, one of them being the chapel proper with large pulpit and the organ on the left hand side at one end and the seating accommodation taking up the rest of this room. Dividing and folding doors separated the chapel from the second room where there was a stage and a small room at each side of the stage. One of these small rooms served as a vestry. Below a trapdoor in the stage was the large tank or bath in which people were submerged at Baptism.

Our minister was a pleasant but shy man until he climbed into the pulpit. There inspired with the fire of religious zeal he preached sermons to the congregation full of hell fire and damnation in a resounding fashion and at great length causing more than one Sunday lunch to be spoiled. Luckily I was not obliged to sit through many of these sermons, as before they began many of the younger children were allowed to leave. As my young sister and Alan were in this category I was allowed to leave also in order to take them home. The minister had a harassed wife and large family of young children who all lived in the Manse. I can remember a time when he made one of his visits to our home, our cat paid him particular attention. In spite of all our efforts to distract her, she kept returning to the minister even following him to the front door as he was about to leave. It was then we discovered the attraction. Our minister had done a little shopping for his wife on his way to us and had bought some fish that he put in the pocket of his jacket. No wonder puss was so attracted. Although we had not been able to smell it, she most certainly did!

To take part in entertainments such as dancing, theatre and all forms of games on Sundays was frowned upon by most non-conformist churches and as I enjoyed all these things I was a naturally rebellious member of this flock. However, I continued to attend with the family and was married there in 1946 when I left for a home of my own as a young wife. This Baptist chapel no longer exists as it was pulled down some years after the Second World War and has been replaced by a new one in Drayton Road.

CHAPTER 7

Shops kept long hours in the years before the Second World War, opening about eight a.m. and not closing until around nine p.m., but shutting for an hour at lunchtime. In my father's case, as a newsagent he started even earlier at 6am. By then the great bundles of newspapers and magazines had been delivered to the shop door step. They were taken in and put on a long table ready to make up the paper rounds. As the boys came in between seven and seven thirty, they were given their rounds in large canvas bags to be slung across their shoulders before setting out on their deliveries, some on bicycles and some on foot. By seven thirty to eight a.m. customers were calling for their morning papers on their way to work and buying their day's supplies of cigarettes or tobacco as they did so. Business remained brisk for some time. Once the workers had gone to catch their buses or trains, or simply disappeared into nearby factories, offices or studios, the pace slowed for a while.

The next group of customers, were usually the ladies of the house, who once the children were in school, took a more leisurely pace for their shopping. Before going home the ladies called in for copies of their favourite magazines, ordered every week so as not to miss episodes of the running serial story. They also bought their cigarettes or sweets in the hope that they might get a quiet sit down and read, before the family came home once more. After school, was the time when children came in to spend their pennies at the sweet counter. Two ounces of Dolly Mixture for a penny, or a farthing Gob Stopper that made the cheek bulge and lasted a long time. A halfpenny bar of toffee or chocolate was also a favourite. Bigger bars of chocolate such as Fry's Crème Chocolate bars then cost two pennies each, as did a quarter pound of many sweets. Prices remained the same until up to the outbreak of the Second World War. Bulls Eyes, Humbugs, Sherbet Dabs, sticks of Liquorice, some sweets with a sherbet centre which when sucked fizzed upon the tongue, acid drops and many other others that appear to have gone out of fashion. Children spent a long time feasting their eyes on all these delights before making up their mind just how to spend their pennies.

During the day 'travellers', representatives of the various manufacturers of the goods sold in the shop came to take orders for stock. Most of them had been doing the same rounds for many years and were well known to my parents. By five o'clock the evening rush had started with the customers returning from their daily work coming in for the evening editions of the papers. The Evening News, Evening Standard and others, each newspaper costing just one penny. By seven thirty most of the returning regular customers had gone and there was a quiet period in which paper work, checking of stock and other essential tidying up jobs could be done before the closing of the shop and cashing up took place. On Saturdays the shop was always extra busy as it was then people paid their weekly bills, stocked up the weekend cigarette and tobacco supplies and children had pocket money to spend. It was often ten o'clock at night before my father was able to get home. Sometimes he managed a little earlier and then he had a chance to sit down and listen to the radio and have a cup of cocoa before going to bed to sleep until starting the whole routine again early next morning. As he had a number of assistants to help him, he was able to slip home at times for a cup of tea and a sit down in his easy chair, but it was still a long day's work. Even when the shop door was closed some people still knocked on the door for the cigarettes or newspaper they had forgotten to get earlier. This was avoided once we had moved. When he was able to employ a manager for the business, he was able to take more free time. There was always a half day closing during the week, when all the shops in the village closed on the same day, but because of Sunday newspapers, newsagents had to open on Sunday mornings when other shops remained closed. There were only two days in the year when the shop remained closed all day; they were on Good Friday and Christmas Day.

Few goods were sold ready packed in the 1930s. In the case of sweets they were weighed loose on the brass scales before being put into a paper bag or paper cone wrappings. A square of white paper was twisted around the hand of the assistant to form a cone shape into which the sweets were poured and then the top and bottom of the cone folded over to enclose the sweets.

The Grocer's goods were also sold loose. Dried fruit, rice, lentils, sugar and other such commodities. Butter was taken from a large mound and a pound or half a pound patted into shape with wooden pats on a marble or wooden slab, sometimes marked with a patterned mould before being wrapped neatly in greaseproof paper and handed to the customer. Anchor butter from New Zealand was one of the first brands of butter to be packaged in 1924. It was the one Mother usually bought. Brook Bond tea came in packets with a dividend stamp showing the picture of a beehive. Mother collected the stamps to stick on a card. A full card was worth five shillings, an amount worth having at that time. Cheese was cut with a wire; bacon was always cut from the joint on a slicing machine, as were other cold meats. It was possible to buy oddments from the cuttings to make a cheap bacon and egg pie if you were hard up. Without refrigerators people bought each day for the day's requirements to be sure that the food was fresh, although I can remember seeing maggots on the bacon being sliced at the grocer's in very hot weather.

The Grocer's Shop

As there was no ready-made pastry all housewives made their own and flour, lard, or margarine was bought loose when needed. Meat puddings, dumplings, suet puddings, treacle puddings roly-poly jam puddings, Spotted Dick (a steamed pudding with dried fruit) were great fillers for hungry families, especially when topped with a creamy custard. A tin of Bird's Custard Powder was to be found on the pantry shelf in most British homes. Rice puddings and bread puddings were also popular. Apart from the rice puddings, rice was not much in favour as a savoury dish, although rice would have been known as a base for curry dishes by those who had travelled to India and such places. But few ordinary people had the chance to go abroad and not many left their native areas. It was possible and quite usual to place an order with the shopkeeper for supplies to be delivered to one's home.

Bread sold in the Baker shops was mostly white, never packaged or wrapped and never sliced. People had a bread board and a bread knife and were expected to cut it for themselves. Bakers did sell wonderful doughnuts full of jam and covered in sugar, also large cream buns among other mouth watering cakes that were regarded as a special treat by most children. Our village had two bakeries run by brothers of the name of Freestone who were in competition with each other, one at each end of the village. Bob Freestone had his Bakery in Theobald Street, his brother's bakery named The Dutch Oven built in the later 1930s had a roof of shiny blue tiles and stood on the corner of Grosvenor Road opposite my father's shop. The smell of newly baked bread drifted across the road each day causing the mouths of customers and shop assistants alike to yearn for a taste and when their morning break came the assistants would nip across the road to bring back their 'elevenses'. The Baker at The Dutch Oven kept some handsome cart horses who pulled the delivery vans on the daily rounds to customers, so mixed with the smell of bread one sometimes had a whiff of a good old country aroma.

There were many more haberdashery shops when I was a child, selling material, buttons, pins, needles, laces and trimmings and all other requirements for dressmaking, for most women made the clothes for their growing families, their own dresses and possibly husband's shirts as well. Some very pretty cotton material called 'Miss Muffet' in a number of patterns could be bought for six pence a yard. Almost every home could boast a sewing machine even if only used for turning bed sheets sides to middle or making curtains for windows. Worn clothes were patched and socks darned, dresses altered and many other mending jobs done in those days of all natural fibres. All items required for such tasks were found in the draper's haberdashery department.

The Draper's Shop

One of the fascinations of such stores for children were the cash railways which whizzed about above our heads. There was even one in Tucker's, our village drapery store which stood on the other side of the main road from the Chapel. Money for the purchase made was given to the assistant behind the counter who wrote out the bill. Then both money and bill were enclosed in a form of moneybox metal container attached to wires running across the ceiling of the shop. This container was then sent whizzing along the wires to the cashier who sat in a high cabin or cash desk above the level of the counters. She would remove the inner container, count the contents to check off against the bill, then return any change required along the same tracks. The metal container arrived with a clinking sound as it stopped. There were often a number of them travelling from different counters. Watching these moving cash carriers certainly kept children's eyes busy allowing their mothers to give more attention to their purchases.

Shops, which are no longer to be found, are the dairies. The Dairy was the local shop where one bought milk, butter and eggs and there was at least one in every reasonably sized village and even more in town, often on a corner site. Max Miller used to sing a song 'I fell in love with Mary from the Dairy', but it might be a little difficult to find such a Mary now. There were the United Dairies, the Co-op Dairies, Express Dairies and many more whose names I cannot recall. Our particular dairy was called Elm Farm Dairy and was run by the family of a local farm. They were specialised shops as were most shops then. All kept to their own trades and did not encroach on one another's preserve. Greengrocers and fish shops seem to have managed to survive the supermarket era, but not the grocers and even the butchers are finding the competition from the supermarkets hard to combat. The old ironmonger shops have almost disappeared having been ousted by the hardware stores and DIY stores where everything comes packaged in amounts of five or ten even when you only require one screw of a particular size. In the ironmongers they knew their trade and exactly what would be needed for certain jobs and repairs and could give expert advice on many tools, blades, hammers, saws, nuts and bolts and other items required. They also sold paints, oil and paraffin, paintbrushes and stoves, in fact most equipment needed to maintain and repair the home. Frequently they also possessed a yard where timber could be bought so that everything needed for setting up new shelves, making a bookcase, or a repair to a fence could be found here.

With the advent of time and technology another service to disappear from the scene is that of the Post Office telegraph boy. Young lads leaving school were taken on by the Post Office to deliver telegrams. Most children left Council School at fourteen, but Grammar and other schools in the private sector at sixteen to eighteen. Dressed in neat navy blue uniform trimmed with red and with their little round hats with a peak brim, secured by a chin strap, the telegraph boys could be seen on the Post Office bicycles peddling furiously to deliver an urgent message. The message would be in its yellow envelope, carried at their waist in a belted leather pouch. Many people used the telegram service to send important or urgent messages, also greetings for birthdays, weddings and other occasions. When most people had no telephone it was a vital service to deliver messages and answers very quickly. Of course during war time, a visit from the telegraph boy was treated with dreaded apprehension, for the War Office used this service to notify people of the death or wounding of their sons or husbands. Sometimes the message said "Missing, believed killed". However, in peacetime the messages were usually more cheerful, a quick method of indicating an expected time of arrival of a guest for instance. The telegraph boy waited whilst the message was read and if an answer was needed he took a return message to be sent from the Post Office. Post cards were frequently used for less urgent messages for the postal delivery service was excellent in its regularity of delivery. During the reign of George V one could send a postcard for the cost of one old penny. The cost jumped to two old pennies, or tuppence as we called it, in the short reign of Edward VIII.

The Telegram Boy

Other young lads seen cycling through the streets were the delivery boys on their trade bikes from the various shops, butchers, grocers, greengrocers etc. who were kept busy all day delivering customers orders to houses in the neighbourhood. It was a very convenient service where the customer, if they so wished, had a small order book in which they wrote their daily or weekly requirements from a particular shop which was then handed in at the counter. The shop assistants made up the order and with the bill it was packed into a strong cardboard box. It was then passed to the delivery boy who fixed the box into the metal basket carrier on the front of his bicycle and set off to deliver to the customer's house. The trade bicycles frequently bore the name of the shop painted on a metal plate across the cycle where the cross bar and chain guard were positioned. The system worked well and shops were keen to keep their customers satisfied. Most people dealt with the same grocer, butcher or greengrocer for many years. Shopping was much less complicated then, when the goods came without the expensive packaging and without so many different brand names.

The Delivery Boy

Miss Byer and her sister who ran a sweet and toy shop near the beginning of Furzehill road, encouraged children to save silver paper and gave a toffee for pieces of silver paper handed into her. Beside their shop was a house known as the Doll's Hospital where one could take a doll to be repaired. Since most dolls then had heads made of china, the hospital did good business. Next to the Doll's Hospital was Hunt's the butcher, run by Mr Young and then there was a largish house standing on the corner of Drayton Road. Mr Cherry was our local cobbler or boot repairer. He lived in one of the cottages on Shenley Road, the main road, near the dentist. His name matched his trade as Cherry Blossom was a very well known trade name for shoe polish and there would have been a tin of it in most homes.

Close by the Keystone stocking factory, was Starkes or Hanson's as it became, the sweet shop. Beside it stood the local Central Garage. On the other side of Hanson's was Read's the Greengrocer. Outside the garage on the wide pavement Mr Carpenter took his stand. Mr Carpenter owned a dairy and made an ice cream concoction that he sold at first by means of a horse and cart that he drove around the roads of the village. Later he acquired a tricycle that was strategically parked on the children's route home from school, by the garage. On the front of the tricycle was a large, square, refrigerator box covered by a removable lid. Another container held wafer cones. For one penny it was possible to buy a cornet cone filled with Mr Carpenter's own blend of ice cream. It was yellowish in colour with a delicious, slightly custard taste, greatly appreciated by all the local children who flocked to spend their pennies when he appeared on his tricycle complete with straw boater hat. As the lid was taken off the box a mist-like steam arose from inside into which Mr Carpenter delved to draw out large scoops of his special blend.

We occasionally saw other ice cream men with similar tricycles in our village. Eldorado was one, Wall's was another. Both men dressed in the uniform of these large firms and wore peaked caps. The Wall's outfit was blue and white and on the box containing the, this time, glistening white ice cream, was the advertising slogan started in 1922 "STOP ME AND BUY ONE" which we were encouraged to do by the ringing of the bicycle bell proclaiming his presence in the vicinity. If I recall correctly, the colours favoured by Eldorado for their uniform were white and orange.

Hanson's Sweetshop and Central Garage, Shenley Road

Tom Wingate who ran a kiosk type shop beyond Tuckers and the Co-op shop, in which he boasted to supply everything, was an extrovert character who was responsible for organising a number of different activities in the village, including the May Day celebrations.

Among street characters to come down our road, I remember the Knife Grinder and the Rag and Bone Man. The Knife Grinder arrived on his tricycle, on which was fixed a circular grinding stone worked by foot pedals. He called at each house and for a small fee sharpened any knives in need of attention. Mother usually managed to find one requiring his skills. He then started the stone wheel spinning and we watched as he moved the knife's edge across the stone and set the sparks flying. When the honing was completed to his satisfaction the wheel was stopped and the clean edged knife returned to its owner, the grinder receiving his fee. The Knife Grinder applied his trade in the streets of the towns and villages, certainly up until the outbreak of war in 1939 and a little after that time, but I cannot recall seeing any after the 1950s. I assume that as a trade they gradually faded as the older men died.

The Knife Grinder

The Rag and Bone Men on the other had still continue to make their calls in some areas of the country, although the horses and carts I remember as a child have been changed to open truck lorries. Their drawn out cries of "Rag and bo-n-es, Rag and bo-n-es" or "Old ir-o-n, old ir-o-n" echoing along the street ahead of them, warning of their coming. Along with the brass bell they rang, giving people time to put out their bags of rags, old pieces of metal and any other pieces the Rag and Bone Man was likely to take. Among the items might also be bottles and jars, for frequently these were re-used and often there might be a return of a penny or halfpenny on each one.

Children often collected and returned such bottles and jars to the shops to supplement their pocket money, or to the Rag and Bone man to receive a colourful windmill or balloon, and sometimes the Boy Scouts made collections to help their funds. As a child I remember the patient horses and the painted decorations on the cart, although the Rag and Bone Man himself was always dressed in flat cap or battered Trilby hat and shabby clothes which seemed to hang loosely about him. Many of these men made an excellent living from other people's rubbish.

The Tinker man who repaired pots, pans, tin baths, kettles and other such items also came around with his handcart once a week. He also sold candles and paraffin to householders. Before the days when one could buy garden manure neatly packaged in plastic bags, but relied on natural sources for provision, the horses of the rag and bone man, the milkman and the coal man sometimes left a reminder of their presence. It was then children were given a bucket and shovel by their parents and told to collect the 'reminder' "for the roses".

Other street traders seen in the more built up areas were the men with barrel organs, the organ grinder. The instrument was a small barrel or box on a single wooden leg. By turning a handle the barrel produced music. He was popular with the children who enjoyed dancing to the music he played. Often he was accompanied by a small monkey dressed in a short jacket and fez cap attached by a chinstrap. The monkey was usually secured by a light chain or lead and held a cup or cap in which to collect pennies from passers by and those who dropped coins from their windows if they had enjoyed the music. The barrel organ men were fast disappearing by 1935 to be replaced by buskers and street musicians. A number of ex-service men from the First World War, many of them disabled formed small groups of musicians and singers who entertained the theatre queues or played at the kerb side by the busy shopping streets in order to earn a living. Others stood on the pavements alongside the walls of buildings with a tray of matches or shoelaces and other small objects, the tray suspended from their necks. Many of these ex-service men wore cards saying "BLIND" or some other form of disablement.

The Cenotaph in Whitehall, London, was unveiled on 11th November 1920 in memory of those who fell in the First World War, but there was little done to help those who came home. There were also the Sandwich men who walked with a large board in front and another behind them joined by straps across the shoulders. The boards bore advertisements for various goods, or notice of forthcoming attractions. Those I remember most were the religious ones which sometimes threatened "THE END OF THE WORLD IS NIGH" or the more cheerful "JESUS IS THE LIGHT OF THE WORLD" and other such phrases.

The Onion seller sometimes visited our village. A Frenchman in typical black beret, blouson and loose waistcoat, he cycled his way from door to door with strings of onions hanging from his handlebars and around his neck, selling his wares direct to the housewives. Most of our onions must have been imported from France or Spain as when war began onions disappeared from view and householders could only obtain them by growing their own.

Another visitor to our village on a few occasions was the China Stall man. His stall would be set up in a convenient space and filled with a great array of coloured plates, cups and saucers and other china dishes and bowls. Then he would proceed to gather a crowd about him with his ceaseless patter while juggling with handfuls of plates, tossing them in the air and catching them to offer to bystanders at "bargain prices". With him would be his assistant who wrapped the china and took the money before the customer had time to change their mind! He was a great show as far as we children were concerned.

Tizer, a red coloured fizzy drink was very popular. It was bought by the crate from the lorry that came round at regular intervals and delivered to one's door. Other forms of non-alcoholic drink were probably carried as well, but we knew it as, the 'Tizer Lorry'.

Chimney Sweeps were very much in evidence as nearly everyone had coal fires. Black with the soot from the chimneys he swept, a sweep could be seen wheeling his handcart containing rods, circular brush and sacks in which to catch the soot brought down from the chimney. As children we used to wait in the garden in order to see the sweep's brush appear from out of the top of the chimney. It was a job the housewives liked to have done before they started the spring cleaning. A sweep could sometimes be seen at a wedding for it was considered lucky for the bride to have a kiss from a chimney sweep, although I do not know the origin of the superstition.

My husband, who was brought up in London, remembers a man in a boater hat who carried on his head a tray containing mussels, cockles and other shellfish for sale. He appeared every Sunday afternoon; ringing a bell and calling out his wares to proclaim his presence to the population whom were probably enjoying a Sunday afternoon doze. Since such shellfish were a popular snack with many Londoners, a wakening was welcomed rather than resented and women went into the street with bowls in hand to buy a tasty addition to their Sunday evening meal.

Not so popular were the gypsies who knocked on doors with their baskets of pegs, posies of heather and other odds and ends. They were persistent in their efforts to sell, or failing that try to persuade housewives to have their fortune told for the price of a piece of silver. Usually they had a small child with them and would spin a story of hard luck, as did one I encountered one day at our front door. Both my parents were out. I was about eleven years of age at the time when I opened the door to a knock. Standing in the porch was a swarthy gypsy woman with a small child. She immediately launched into her well rehearsed and practised sales talk. When I told her my parents were not at home and I had no money, she obviously did not believe me and spun a tale of having nothing to eat all that day and trapesing the street trying to sell her wares. I, being young and innocent felt sorry for her, but still had to refuse her. Finally she gave up and left. After shutting the door, pity overcame me for the poor hungry child and I dashed into the kitchen and cut a doorstep of a sandwich, which I put in a paper bag and then ran down the street after her. I caught up with her outside the baker's shop and thrust the wrapped sandwich into the pram the woman was pushing. Only to notice as I did so that she had several bags of freshly baked buns inside the pram, which had obviously just been bought by her from the Baker's shop. As I turned to dash back home, I caught a glimpse of the gypsy woman's face, her mouth open in astonishment, so surprised that her speech had deserted her. The episode gave me cause to wonder too. I learnt not to believe everything I was told, but to take such stories with 'a pinch of salt'!

At certain seasons of the year in the countryside one could often see bands of gypsies in their horse drawn caravans moving from farm to farm, or camped along the roadside en route. Their horses would be tethered to stakes along the wide grass verges and the families gathered around a fire of sticks and wood where the cooking and eating was done. They supplied farmers with casual labour when planting or picking of crops was done in the days before so many mechanical aids became available. It was in between these seasons when householders were subjected to visits to their doors. Sometimes parents would threaten naughty children that "the gypsies would take them away" if they were not good. It was implied that this would not be a pleasurable experience! Naughty Children were also threatened with 'the Bogy Man' who was always supposed to come in the dark. There was a song that went

"Hush, hush, hush, here comes the Bogy Man,
Don't let him get too close to you
He'll catch you if he can.
Just pretend that you're a crocodile
And you will find that Bogy Man
Will run away a mile".

The term 'Bogy Man' is believed to stem from Napolionic times, referring to Bonaparte.

CHAPTER 8

During the 1930s Boreham Wood became the proud possessor of an Odeon Cinema. It was a wonderful addition toward the social pleasures of the community. Previously the village had relied upon a visiting cinema that occasionally called and set up a show in a barn-like building in Station Road behind the chemist's shop, its arrival causing great excitement. Otherwise, it was necessary to travel to Mill Hill or Edgeware in order to see a cinema show and should one miss the last bus back it could mean a five mile walk home. 'Going to the pictures' was a developing weekly treat for most people during the 1920s when cinema was in its hey day. Once through its large glass doors, guarded by a uniformed commissioner, the cinema offered a release from the daily hum-drum of life and took one into a world of fantasy and glamour. For the space of two hours (or more if one stayed to see the film round twice!) a person could forget their cares and worries and indulge in a dream of romance, adventure, or comedy. Since all films were sensibly censored, people were not subjected to horrific scenes of explicit violence or sex and most people could be sure of enjoying a few hours of good, clean entertainment.

The cinema building itself was spacious with a pleasantly decorated foyer and lounge area where one could wait for friends, a kiosk where chocolates and sweets could be bought and of course a box office where tickets were sold. In many cinemas there was also a refreshment area where tea and cake could be enjoyed before or after the show. All served by waitresses in neat uniforms and clean white aprons. Small tables, comfortable chairs and carpets provided a pleasant social setting to an evening out. This was a great asset to young men and women in the early stages of courtship. Tickets for the screen show varied in price from nine pence for the front rows of seats nearest to the screen to one shilling and sixpence for the back rows and circle upstairs.

Once through the doorway into the dark interior of the building the usher or usherette guided patrons with the beam from their torch down the sloping aisle to the plush covered tip up seats. Feeling around in the darkness and trying not to tread on other people's unseen feet took some concentration until one's eyes became accustomed to the change. Until they did there was no knowing whether the occupant of the adjoining seat was male or female and might easily turn out to be someone known to you. The only light came from the screen itself and the beam of the projector high above through the small window of the projectionist room. The back row of the downstairs seating was the favourite position of sweethearts who could steal a kiss or two in the darkness away from prying eyes. Some cinemas even provided double seats. An invitation to "go to the pictures" was one of the first indications that a boy was interested in a particular girl or was 'smitten' with her, as the older generation would say.

The programme came in a continuous performance from 2 p.m. until around 10 p.m. consisting of a main film, a news reel, (probably the Pathe Gazette which began in the 1930s) and a 'B' or secondary film. In between the performances was an interval when local advertising was shown and the usherettes sold ice cream and chocolate from a tray strapped to a halter around their neck. A wrapped ice cream sandwiched between wafers or in later years coated with chocolate cost three pence and the larger ones in tubs cost sixpence. In the larger cinemas the interval was also the time when organ and organist appeared from the depths below the auditorium to regale the audience with a selection of music. Picked out in bright spotlights, his often huge instrument glittering in the brightness, patrons were cheered, romantically lulled or even made pensively 'triste' by the melodies played. When it became time for the film to recommence both organ and organist disappeared into the depths once more.

Posters advertising forthcoming films were put around the town, many shopkeepers displaying them and in return were given complimentary tickets. Usually the films were changed halfway through the week unless it was a particular attraction, then it might continue all week not changing until the following Monday. There were no films shown on Sunday.

The film world was making great strides, mostly in the U.S.A. The very first 'drive in' movie theatre with accommodation for 500 cars was opened in New Jersey on 6th June 1933. This enabled the audience to watch the films without even alighting from their vehicles.

The great heart throb of the early days of films, the Italian born, dark eyed, romantic Rudolph Valentino, the idol of millions, died at the early age of thirty one in the August of 1926. The news of his death supposedly caused a number of suicides. Mary Pickford and Douglas Fairbanks Senior and Lional Barrymore were stars who started in silent films and successfully adapted to talking films. Lional Barrymore was also a talented musician and artist apart from his acting career. Douglas Fairbanks Senior was the hero of many swashbuckling roles in which he did all his own stunts. He died in December 1939.

Later came the stars such as Bebe Danials, born in January 1901, Clark Gable born a month later in the same year, Marlene Deitrich, Claudette Colbert, Joan Crawford and the shy Swedish star Greta Garbo remembered for her comment "I vant to be alone". The "Come up and see me sometime" Mae West gained notoriety in 1927 when she spent ten days in jail after a police raid on the Broadway show 'Sex' in which she starred. The French star Maurice Chevalier was singing his light and charming songs, wearing his bow tie and straw boater hat.

In England another debonair actor and songster was Jack Buchanhan who also danced his way through films and stage. Ruby Keeler was an American actress and dancer born on 25th August 1910 who starred in the film 'Gold Diggers of 1933' among others. She was married to Al Jolson who starred in the first talkie film 'The Jazz Singer'. This marriage ended in 1940. In 1941 Ruby married John Lowe a real estate broker and retired from the silver screen. She did not return to acting until after his death. In 1970 at sixty years of age she took a leading role in a revival of the 1925, musical show hit, 'No, No' Nanette.' She died in 1993. All these people played romantic leads in the films of the time.

Gracie Fields, the popular British singer and actress starred in the film 'Sing As We Go' which portrayed some of the problems of unemployment affecting the country at that time. Another well known, humorist, film actor Will Rogers was killed in an air crash on 16th August 1935. We must not forget such immortals as Charlie Chaplin of course who gave amusement to so many, mostly without any speech at all. Walt Disney was developing his cartoon form of film. Mickey Mouse made his screen debut in the animated cartoon film 'Steamboat Willie' in 1928 and on June 9th 1934 Donald Duck appeared for the first time in a cartoon, called 'The Wise Little Hen'. The first full length Technicolor, animated film by Walt Disney was 'Snow White', produced in 1936 intended for the younger generation who found the wicked queen a little too scary, but was greatly enjoyed by the grown-ups! In 1939 came another children's story, 'The Wizard of Oz, which delighted everyone and made a star of the young Judy Garland.

Film Stars played a great part in influencing ladies fashions in dress and style. The severe hair styles of the 1920s such as the Eton Crop and the short Bob were replaced by the immaculate waves and curls of a longer hairstyle favoured by most Hollywood stars of the 1930s. Jean Harlow, the 'Blonde Bombshell ' of the period caused many women to emulate her and change the colour of their hair, a process frowned upon by many 'respectable' members of society. Such women were referred to as 'peroxide blondes'. The term 'Blonde Bombshell' came about from the title of the film 'Bombshell' in which Jean Harlow starred in 1933. Sadly Jean Harlow had a very short career, dying of kidney disease at the early age of twenty six on 7th June 1937. About this time in the 1930s, it became possible to have one's hair 'permed' for longer lasting curls. A 'Moderne' permanent wave in 1936 cost twelve shillings and six pence, if one was willing to go through such torture involving rubber pads and metal rollers attached to electric wires under a large saucer shaped metal hood, restricting movement of the head for some time. Such perms frequently had the disadvantage of making the hair brittle.

When films changed from black and white to Technicolor, they were inclined to cause the actor's faces to take on a greenish hue. In 1935 Max Factor the make up specialist managed to rectify this by inventing a pancake form of make up that gave a more natural look.

All films were censored and given different ratings. 'A' films were intended for those over sixteen years of age only, unless accompanied by an adult. 'U' films were open to all. When an 'A' film was on children under the age of sixteen would hopefully wait around the doors of the cinema, with entrance money in hand for some kind hearted adult to take pity and buy their tickets for them. So that then they could be seen as being accompanied by an adult. On Saturday morning there was the children's cinema when serial cowboy films were shown. The entrance fee was three pence. The cinema was filled with excited young people of all ages clutching their bags of toffees, the older children usually being detailed off by their parents to look after the younger brothers and sisters for the morning. All were eager to see the next instalment of the adventures of Buck Jones, or the Lone Ranger who the previous week they had had to leave in some precarious situation, the films always being cut off at a heart stopping episode to encourage attendance the following week.

Children's cinema was a great institution keeping the children happily occupied every Saturday morning and giving parents a chance to do their shopping, or any other activity in peace without the worry of wondering what their off-spring were up to. The children's behaviour was controlled by the manager and usherettes and was good, at least in our local cinema, as no child wanted to run the risk of being banned from seeing the next instalment.

As young children, for special days like birthdays or Christmas time, Father brought out the magic lantern projector and slides and treated us to a show. The slides were coloured, some of views of famous places but others told a short story. In spite of the advantage of colour they could not compare with Buck Jones and the cowboys who gave real action, and once we were old enough to attend the Saturday morning cinema the lantern-slides were rejected.

Another entertainment we enjoyed was the fair which came twice a year to set up its stalls and other attractions in the open fields in Theobald Street, or Radlett Road as it was usually known, not far from Doctor Neil's house and surgery. This position was some way from the village, but people were used to walking and we knew of some short cuts across the fields from our end of Shenley Road. As small children we were taken by our parents and given money to spend on all the various side shows. Sometimes we were able to make an extra penny or two on 'Rolling the Pennies', but more often than not we lost them. The round-about or carousel with their painted prancing horses was our favourite, while the blaring rumbustious music of the steam organs added to the excitement of the ride.

The real dare-devils among the young people tested their nerves on the flying Chair-o-Planes, or the Big Dipper while others took their girl friends on the Ghost Train in the hope that a scary ride might bring closer contact and a use for an encircling arm. Testing one's strength with the mallet and the bell, a shot at the rifle range, pitching at the coconut shy was a chance for young men to show their skill to watching females. The Dodgem cars where two could share one car was another opportunity for fun. The idea was, as the name implies to dodge other drivers but many chose to do the opposite and frequently used their car as a battering ram, or maybe as a means to chase some attractive female driver. There were many ways of making contact with the opposite sex at the fairground. The Dodgem cars were an American invention of the early twenties. Billy Butlin of the Butlin Holiday Camps took up the British Franchise in 1928, investing in their popularity.

The younger children were not forgotten as there was usually a round-about with little cars, motorcycles, fire engines and other things they could ride upon. As we reached a more adventurous stage, the boat swings were a great joy where one could work up to quite a height by pulling on the tufted end of the ropes hanging from the high bar at each end of its boat shaped cradle. If the showman felt that you were overdoing it and in danger of being carried away he lifted a board that scraped against the bottom of the swing slowing the swing to a more gentle and safe pace.

All the fun of the fair

The distorting mirrors side-show gave everyone the chance of a good laugh. Toffee apples, sticks of sugar foam, ice cream and other sweetmeats were on sale for those with a sweet tooth.

The brightly painted stands, side-shows and mechanical amusements all with their garish decoration, coloured lights, raucous showmen and strident music, in sharp contrast to the normally quiet life in our village, stayed with us two or more days before packing up and moving on to a new pitch to disturb the quiet idyll of some other village community.

To the same pitch once each year, came the circus. A week or so before the arrival of the caravans, trailers and cages of animals, posters appeared on bill hoardings, trees, walls and any other convenient place telling of the treat to come. We children gathered in the field to watch the circus hands put up the big top. Then before the first performance there was a procession with artists riding elephants, ponies and floats, while clowns cut capers and passed out hand bills along the route, all accompanied by the circus band.

By the time the first performance was about to take place, children were almost delirious with excitement. Many parents were also infected with their joy, reminding them of the pleasures of their own much earlier visits to the Big Top. Inside the huge tent tiers of wooden plank seating surrounded the central sawdust ring. The smell of canvas, sawdust and animals came sharply to the nostrils and as the musicians, dressed in the uniform suits of blue and gold started up their overture, a hush of expectancy descended on the waiting audience. The first to appear from behind the curtains hanging at the entrance to the ring was the Ringmaster in his red frock coat, black boots, black top hat and long whip. As master of ceremonies he introduced each act while the band played a fanfare.

There were jugglers with their balls, hoops and clubs, acrobats who performed amazing feats from a spring board or each other's shoulders, the trapeze artists with their daredevil flights through the air high in the big top so that we had to strain our necks looking upwards. I held my breath as a performer flew from one swinging bar to be caught in the nick of time by a companion hanging by his legs from another swinging bar across the breadth of the tent top. I felt very relieved that the safety net was there to catch them should they miss one another. Some spun high above us holding onto a strap by their teeth which certainly made my jaws ache in sympathy. Other members of the aerial acts were the tightrope walkers who rode bicycles or carried a companion in a chair on his shoulders in more death defying feats. We children liked to imagine that we too could do some of these things. In a minor way at least and practised hanging upside down by our legs or feet on the monkey ladder in the recreation ground or any other convenient rail, but usually when our parents were not around.

We loved the elephants that knelt or stood up on hind legs or balanced against one another at their trainer's command. When they left the ring each elephant caught hold of the tail of the elephant in front with their flexible trunks. For such huge animals they moved so softly and gently, especially when with their trunks they lifted some pretty girl artist up onto their backs.

The lions were scary. They were always kept in secure cages and were brought into the large cage in the ring through a tunnel cage coming from behind the curtains. They came on soft padded paws with lowered heads and low snarls and when the trainer already in the cage cracked his whip, they mounted stools. Further commands and cracking of the whip and a lion or lioness as they usually were, would leap through a hoop, or climb a stair, at times the hoop was set on fire before the animal went through. All very exciting as sometimes the lions snarled loudly and hit out with their powerful paws at the chair held by the trainer between himself and the animal. Accidents did happen and some trainers were mauled, so it was a time of tension for all those watching.

In between the acts while the apparatus was being changed clowns kept the audience amused with their antics. Each clown has his own particular make up and some became very famous like Coco, Grock, or Francesco. It was almost impossible to recognise the person beneath the white face, red nose, large lips, or shock of red hair and outrageous costume, but mostly the clowns were loved by children, although small children at first were apt to be terrified of these strange beings. The tricks they played on one another and sometimes the audience brought gales of laughter. The fairground and the circus were welcome diversions to towns and villages in the days before television, when the only way to see such things was to visit them yourself, a first hand experience including sound, smell and touch.

Although we had no such thing as television, there were

children's programmes on the wireless, as it was then called. A wireless set in those times was usually a fairly large box-like affair containing a heavy battery requiring a visit to Allistone's Elstree Radio Service shop to be recharged periodically, glass valves which sometimes burned out and had to be replaced. Each wireless also required an aerial which was a line of wire covered with a red and black woven material. This was attached to the wireless set (that belied its name) and was slung across the room in which ever direction obtained the clearest reception, often being hung out of a convenient window. BBC Children's Hour at five every afternoon was the time when we three children gathered around the wireless to hear Uncle Mac and Uncle David read stories or tell us things of interest. I believe that there was an Aunt on the programme also, but I cannot recall a name for her. The episodes of Toy Town with Larry the lamb, Dennis the dachshund, Ernest the Policeman, the Mayor and the irritable Mr Growser were particular favourites of the whole family. Humour was unsophisticated and gentle leaving us with an enjoyable feeling of happiness and well being. Romany, the Reverand Bramwell Evans in private life, introduced many children to the delights of the countryside encouraging an awareness of the natural world on our doorstep.

Radio Luxumberg which first began broadcasting on 29th December 1930, provided sponsored programmes such as the Ovaltineys. "We are the Ovaltineys little girls and boys". Ovaltine being a popular evening or bedtime family drink. The Ovaltiney Club was launched in 1935 and the programme was broadcast every Sunday evening between 5.30 and 6pm. The children on the programme were named Winnie, Johnnie and Elsie. At the beginning of the programme was sung:

We are the Ovaltineys little girls and boys;
Make your requests, we'll not refuse you
We are here just to amuse you,
Would you like a song or story
Will you share our joys?
At games or sports we're more than keen;
No merrier children could be seen,
Because we all drink Ovaltine,
We're happy girls and boys!
The programme ended with this verse;
And now the happy Ovaltineys

Bid you all adieu
And don't forget your Ovaltine
It's very good for you.
We will be here again next Sunday
With stories, songs and games
And so until we meet next week again
The Ovaltineys say goodbye to you.

Competitions could be entered and badges or small prizes won through these programmes. The broadcasts continued up until the outbreak of World War Two, when the club numbered 5,000,000 members. They then commenced again after the war up until the 1950s.

On winter evenings as we grew older we combined listening to the radio and keeping warm by the fire with rug making. The wool used in making the rug all helped to keep our legs warm as we hooked the pieces through the mesh and knotted them. Before we left home we had all made ourselves a rug to our own design to place beside our bed and keep our feet warm on frosty mornings.

Alan had his own 'Cat's Whisker' crystal set wireless. A very small contraption of wooden base with a primitive form of wire and battery on which we managed to hear faint sounds of music or speech through the air if the set was adjusted to a correct position for the aerial. Our parents enjoyed the presenter Christopher Stone's programmes of more adult or classical records during the 1930s.

The inventor of all these wonders of radio and wireless telegraphy was Guglielmo Marconi the son of an Italian father and Irish mother. He was born in 1874 and lived until 1937. His efforts and experiments in transatlantic radio transmission were derided by other scientists who were unconvinced of such a possibility until the captain of the ship on which he was at sea recorded the message he received. Marconi's invention enabled the police to arrest Dr. Crippon who had murdered his wife and was attempting to flee to America aboard an Atlantic liner. It was the first occasion on which radio was used for police purposes.

The first regular broadcasting station went on the air on the 2nd of November 1920. It was the KDKA station in Pittsburgh in the United States of America. In 1921 Pittsburgh began to broadcast religious services and in 1922 the very first radio advertisement a ten minute property commercial was broadcast in New York.

The first British programme was given on 17th September 1922 at 6.30 in the evening, and the first regular broadcast in Britain began on 23rd February 1923. It came from Writtle, a village near Chelmsford, Essex. Singer Norah Scott featured in the programme but a slight difficulty occurred when it was discovered that the radio station had no piano! The problem was solved by borrowing the piano from the local pub!

Radio started to become organised when on 1st November 1922 radio receiving licences were introduced at a cost of ten shillings. The milestones continued with the first daily news broadcast service by the British Broadcasting Company which began on 14th November 1922. At the beginning of the year 1923 the BBC started their regular weather forecast service and on 31st December 1923 the chimes of Big Ben were heard over the air for the first time. On 5th April 1923, further progress was made when the first mobile car radio receiver was tested on the streets of London. In 1923 on 28th September the British periodical the Radio Times was first published. In 1925 on 14th March came the first Trans-Atlantic broadcast. At a slightly earlier date of 30th November 1924 radio photographs had been transmitted for the first time from Britain to the United States of America. Radio continued to make headway. The popular sport of football was broadcast over the radio for the first time on 22nd January 1927 when a commentary was given at the Football League game between Arsenal and Sheffield United.

The voice of King George V was heard by the general population for the first time, when the BBC relayed his opening speech from the Wembley Exhibition in 1924. The British Broadcasting Company became the British Broadcasting Corporation (BBC) in 1927. Sir John Reith who was appointed general manager on 14th December 1922 became the Director General. It was said he ruled autocratically from his office on Savoy Hill. He was knighted in 1927. In this same year, wireless was installed in the Pullman carriages of the five past seven, Victoria to Brighton train for the benefit of early passengers. In 1929 the BBC began regional broadcasting services.

In 1932 King George V made a live Christmas Day broadcast from Sandringham on the Empire Service with a speech written for him by Rudyard Kipling. This has now become a tradition kept up to the present time by the reigning monarch. In contrast, 1933 was the year when the BBC was first used by the police to help track down a man suspected of murder. Canada had also been going ahead with its own broadcasting service and in 1935 on 15th May started a new trend by broadcasting the very first 'Quiz' programme. In New York in 1932 the Radio City Music Hall was opened to the public. Also in 1932 CBS radio in the United States started the Marx Brother's first radio series, Flywheel, Shyster, and Flywheel, a crazy trio of comedians.

Towards the end of the 1930s a revived interest in farming and new farming methods prompted the BBC to start a weekly programme for farmers and others who were interested in the land. This began in 1937. Panic broke out in America when on the 30th October 1938, Orson Welles's production of H.G. Wells 'War of the Worlds' on radio convinced thousands of people in the U.S.A. that Martians had landed on earth. On the 1st September 1939, two days ahead of the outbreak of the Second World War, the BBC Home Service began.

The inventor of television, J.Logie Baird who was born 13th August 1888, gave his first public demonstration of this new invention in Britain on 27th January 1926 to members of the Royal Institution in London. A fifteen year old office boy at Logie Baird's London workshop was actually the first person to be seen on television in the previous October when Logie Baird was testing his equipment. The first experimental broadcast of television did not come until three years later in 1929 on the 30th September, although WRNY studio in New York produced and broadcast the first scheduled television programmes on 14th August 1928 in America. The first play to be shown on television was on 13th July 1930 and the first regular BBC television service began from Alexandra Palace on 22nd August 1932. In the December of 1939 the premiere of Margaret Mitchell's 'Gone With the Wind' was televised in New York. The first such event of its type to be televised.

George Eastman had invented the Kodak camera in the late 1880s. Another fairly new invention by the Kodak Company in 1900, were the Brownie Box cameras. Alan was a proud possessor of one. He was no great expert in its use, but managed to provide a few rather fuzzy photographs of the family. His camera did not have the added sophistication of a flash bulb, as the photo flash bulb was only patented in 1930 and was at the beginning of its potential usefulness.

However, in spite of all these things, books were still my most constant source of pleasure. I was an avid bookworm and the despair of my mother on more than one occasion when my mind was so involved with the story I was reading, that I never heard her call me. In 1926 A.A. Milne published his stories of 'Winnie the Pooh'. I seem to have missed out on these when young but caught up on a few in later life when my parents moved to an area close to Ashdown Forest, the setting for many of his stories.

A number of well known writers of what are now called 'the classics' survived into the 1920s and 30s. Polish born Joseph Conrad, whose full name was Teodor Jozef Konrad Korzeniowski and who came into this world in 1857, departed it in August 1924, having left behind him a wealth of good stories including 'Lord Jim', 'Typhoon' and 'Victory'. Full of adventure, many of his stories had a sea setting, a result of his own experiences as a seaman. The writer Agatha Christie who had a list of more than 70 detective novels to her name, many of which are still produced as stage plays or television series. Perhaps the most famous featuring her detective Hercule Poiret, or Miss Jane Marples the elderly spinster who always found the answer to the mystery. This writer caused a further and real mystery when she disappeared from her Surrey home for many weeks in December of 1926. Her followers were delighted to see her eventual safe return and the continuation of her famous stories until her death in 1976.

The famous novelist Thomas Hardy, born in 1840 whose stories set in mythical Wessex are still serialised on television today, died in 1928. The great writer of the popular Sherlock Holmes stories, Sir Arthur Conan Doyle died in 1930 but his stories continue to enthral us. It is not so well known that he also wrote works on spiritualism. He was born in 1859. Also born in 1859 was the novelist of humour Jerome K.(Klapka) Jerome. His novel 'Three Men in a Boat' gave many a happy chuckle. He died in 1927. Novelist Arnold Bennett, born in 1867 wrote of the 'Five Towns' and their potteries in his stories of life in the north of England, typified in the novels 'Old Wives' Tale' and 'Clayhanger'. His stories came to an end with his death in 1931. A controversial author who scandalised most of the population with his novels in which the forbidden subject of sex played a prominent part, was D.H. Lawrence who was born in Eastwood, Nottinghamshire and died in 1930 of tuberculosis. He was twice prosecuted for obscenity over his publications. His book 'Lady Chatterley's Lover' published in Florence in 1928 was banned in Britain until 1961.

The author of the 'Forsyte Saga' which held television viewers enthralled when it was shown as a serial for many weeks, John Galsworthy who also wrote a number of plays, died in 1933 at the age of sixty six. 1936 saw the death of two more famous writers. in January the poet and author of many tales of India, Rudyard Kipling departed this life. His stories and poems earned him the Nobel Prize for Literature in 1907, but he will be remembered by many children for his stories from the 'Jungle Book' even if animated pictures of the Walt Disney film studios come first to mind. My father read tales from the 'Jungle Book' to my brother and I when we were small and as we grew older we read them again for ourselves. Rudyard Kipling was born in India in 1865. He was elected Rector, University of St. Andrews by its members in 1923 in honour of his achievements.

G.K. Chesterton born in 1874, the witty novelist who wrote the 'Father Brown' detective stories, also died in 1936 just six months after Rudyard Kipling. The year 1939 saw the loss of one of our well known poets, W.B. Yeats who died in January. The author of those popular 'Dr. Findley' stories A.J.Cronin, had a great success in 1935 when his book 'The Stars Look Down' was published. Margaret Mitchell first published her great and popular novel 'Gone With the Wind' in 1936. It had taken her 10 years to write and sold over twenty five million copies. It was subsequently made into a film with Clark Gable and Vivian Leigh taking the leading parts of Rhett Butler and Scarlett O'Hara in 1939 and has appeared periodically over the years since that time. The popular fantasy tale 'The Hobbit' by J.R.R. Tolkien was first published in September of 1937 and still continues to enchant its readers.

CHAPTER 9

Father came home for breakfast each morning after his early start at the shop. Sometimes he made the porridge we ate most mornings for our breakfast. I don't know where he learned to make it but it must have been much like the gruel he was made to eat at boarding school when he was young, and time had not improved it! I hated it and never ate it after I left home. He was very strict about finishing our food and when I refused to eat it at breakfast I was given nothing else. At lunch time the horrible mess was dished up to me again and I was forced to eat it or go hungry. One morning I ate my porridge without protest and I was given a penny for being a good girl. The truth was that my mind was so taken up with a story I had been reading that I had not even noticed or tasted what I was eating! I was just as amazed as my parents!

At other times we had a cereal called Force. The packet cover had a picture of a long legged man in early 19th century attire and wearing a monocle single eyeglass and a queue or what might be called a pony tail hair style, striding out across the front. His name was Sunny Jim if I remember rightly, and a little rhyme accompanied him;

High over the fence goes Sunny Jim,
Force is the food which raises him.

We enjoyed the packets of cereal as they often contained surprise presents of a small toy such as a miniature car, a farm animal, or some similar delight. At other times it was something quite large like a cup, saucer or plate and if enough of these packets were bought it was possible in time to collect a tea set or at least part of one.

Father also made the nightly drink of cocoa. I am glad to say that he was more adept at this and there were no complaints. Coffee, even during the morning, was not the popular drink with most people as it is today. We seldom had real coffee, but sometimes had a coffee flavoured liquid drink called Camp Coffee. It came in a tall bottle of which a spoonful or two was added to hot milk or water.

For those at Grammar School Wednesday was a half-day school. We arrived home from Barnet in time for lunch. Mother usually made a liver and bacon lunch on this day as it was one of our favourite meals. On Sundays there was always a roast joint of some kind with roast potatoes and Yorkshire batter pudding if it was beef. My sister reminds me of the time my brother decided to play a practical joke on my mother. He balanced a cushion on top of the door to the dining room. Mother, all unsuspecting, walked in and the cushion fell right onto the dish of roast beef and Yorkshire pudding she was carrying! The joke backfired on Alan for Mother was extremely annoyed. Alan was about nine years old at the time and had probably gained the idea from a comic paper.

Rice puddings, steam puddings, roly-poly Spotted Dick, treacle or jam tarts, bread puddings, apple puddings and plum puddings in season, all good filling dishes for hungry families, were dished up for desserts. There was competition among we children to 'scrape the bowl' if puddings and cakes were being made! Mother often put cloves in the apple pudding which my father and I both detested and invariably they arrived in our portion of pudding. Vegetables and fruit came in season, for without refrigerators and freezers the only way to keep food was bottled or dried. Beans could be salted for use during the winter, cucumbers and onions pickled, apple rings could be dried, other fruits made into jam or bottled, vegetables made into chutney, but fresh fruit and vegetables were only obtainable during their growing season. Such things as peas came in their pod and required shelling; carrots came straight from the soil along with their tops and often a good amount of soil as well. By only having these things at certain times of the year there was always a different delight in a new season.

In 'Aunt Kate's Day by Day Book' published in 1937, price two shillings and sixpence or 'half a crown' as it was known were hints on how to buy economically;

'Buy soap and candles in bulk, they harden by keeping and do not melt so quickly. Cleaning materials are cheaper bought by the dozen and soda, matches, oil, wood and fuel are also cheaper bought in large quantities. Tea, bought in chest or half chest, flour, meal, sugar, rice and grains by the stone and potatoes by the bag. When eggs are cheap buy in large quantities for preserving.

Buy in small quantities suitable for immediate use only, coffee, cocoa, butter, lard, suet, eggs, spices, syrup, treacle, coconut, cheese, chocolate and bread. The flour bin should be kept fresh and sweet. It should stand clear of the floor so that air can circulate underneath. A good idea is to stand it on two bricks. Keep the lid on to protect it from insects. The flour bin should be kept clear of pungently flavoured foodstuffs. Occasionally turn flour out and scald the barrel, thoroughly drying before returning the flour. This is to prevent 'mites' getting in.'

The new ice safes or boxes are mentioned in the book of 1937 'They have quite a large capacity in the food compartments and the water from the ice can be drawn off through a tap, while the ice supply need not be renewed every day.'

Frost boxes were an alternative.

'Frost boxes function on the principal of evaporation. Many emergency devices may be adapted from this same principle. Water sprinkled on stone or brick floors will set up evaporation and any food put either on these floors or in the room will keep cool. A towel or cloth which has its ends dipped in water will also provide evaporation and if wrapped round a food safe will keep the contents in good condition.'

Milk coolers helped to stop the milk turning in hot weather, other suggestions were to wrap a piece of flannel around the bottle keeping the flannel end in a bowl of cold water. 'Wrapping in greaseproof paper and putting lettuce leaves on top will help to stop butter turning rancid.' Is another suggestion. I well remember the horrid taste of rancid butter from the hot summers of childhood.

'To keep fresh meat, cover with butter muslin dampened in vinegar. If touched by flies, cut off affected part and wipe remainder with cloth dipped in vinegar and warm water.'

'When boiling milk place a pie funnel in centre of saucepan so that boiling milk will rise up funnel and over into pan and not over the side of the saucepan onto the cooker.'

These hints so clearly recall the problems that confronted housewives before all the labour saving devices became easily obtainable.

At tea time on our arrival home from school Father also joined us for a bread and butter meal with jam or honey and cake to follow along with tea to drink. After a five mile cycle ride we were always thirsty and ready for this meal. This was the last meal of the day, but at bedtime came the cocoa and a biscuit. When prepared for bed, prayers were said before settling down for the night. The prayer I learnt myself as a small child I have taught to my own children and grandchildren. It goes like this.

Jesus Tender Shepherd hear me,
Bless Thy little lamb tonight.
Through the darkness be Thou near me,
Keep me safe 'til morning light. Amen.

Just before turning out the light Mother would say,

"Pleasant dreams, sweet repose,
Half the bed and half the clothes".

To my sister and I.

Alan had a room of his own, Cindy and I shared a room and double bed. Our parents had a much larger bedroom. Our house had no central heating. Few houses did in the 1920-30s. In summer it was no problem, but when the winds began to howl and temperatures dropped, our bedrooms became like ice boxes. It took a great effort to leave the warmth of the living room with its open coal fire to venture into the hall and upstairs to the bedroom. We undressed and made ourselves ready for bed in the shortest possible time, exposing no more of our bodies to the cold air than was absolutely necessary. Then diving beneath the bedclothes hoping that the hot water bottle put in our bed by Mother or Father an hour or so earlier had warmed the cold cotton sheets. Two or more blankets and a feather eiderdown helped to restore our bodies to a reasonable temperature and enable us to sleep. Most beds had long bolsters beneath the pillows, ours was frequently used to divide off each half of the bed and prevent us encroaching on the other's portion. It also helped to make the bed more cosy as the bolster, like the pillows and eiderdown, was filled with soft, warm feathers.

We frequently awoke in the morning to see wonderful frost patterns on our window panes. Lovely designs of snowflakes or ferns provided by nature itself and hanging from the window frame, window sill and roof guttering were long shining points of ice. On mornings like this our breath hung in the air and strong willpower was required to forsake the blankets and feather quilt and move us from our beds to the bathroom. We would tuck our underwear into the bed to try and warm it before dressing. Sometimes the sun broke through later in the day and made the frost and icicles sparkle before slowly melting them away. Then it was wise not to be too close to the house as the sharp icicles broke away from their anchor on the guttering and dropped with a tinkling and shattering into tiny pieces on the hard ground. In retrospect, the winters seem to have been much colder and the summers sunnier and warmer in childhood.

On these cold frosty mornings it was no fun doing the weekly wash. Without the aid of machines, sheets along with everything else had to be washed, rinsed and wrung out by hand. On dry cold days the washing froze where it hung on the line lifted high by the wooden clothes prop. Fingers were nipped by frost when one tried to bring in the various items solid with ice. Then the drying rack, lifted to ceiling height by a pulley and ropes came into use and it was a matter of being nimble to avoid the drips from the melting clothes.

In the days before the 'all in one 'soap powder, ('Rinso' is a name that comes to mind, as one I remember Mother using in the 1930s) steam irons and 'magic' remover, these are some of the hints offered in 'Aunt Kate's Day by Day Book'.

'After washing *white things* let them dry thoroughly if unable to iron them the same day. Never roll them up in a half-wet state and leave them, as this encourages mildew stains. Mildew stains can be removed by applying a stiff paste made of white starch mixed in lemon juice. Hang stained article in the air for twenty four hours then re-wash and boil with soda.'

Cotton dresses were sometimes called 'tub' dresses. They were easy to wash in the tub or large bowl.

'Satin and other material with a sheen should be pressed when damp, a small area at a time until thoroughly dry.'

'White silk and crepe de chine should be washed in tepid soapy water to which a little borax has been added and rinsed in tepid water with a little methylated spirits in the last rinsing water. Then squeezed gently, wrapped in a clean towel and ironed on the wrong side before dry. Silk can be ironed lightly.' Further instructions are given for the care of Georgette, velveteen and chiffon, all washed by hand, also flannel and flannelette.

'Soap jelly is best for washing silks and woollens. Save all scraps of soap and make a home made jelly. Half fill a stone jar with the scraps of soap. Add boiling water and keep stirring until the soap becomes clear.'

'To protect waterproof qualities in raincoats. Wash coat in three gallons of cold water in which one pound of alum has been dissolved, using no soap.'

'When ironing starched articles the iron often becomes sticky. Rub it quickly over a bar of soap and rub vigorously on brown paper to polish. It will then run smoothly. As irons generally work better after being used for some time, iron course articles before fine ones.'

'Raw potato will remove mud marks on blue serge'

When doing the weekly wash, many articles required starching. Shirts, collars, blouses and aprons for example. Washing also required two rinses, possibly a third rinse for whites in water in which a cube of Rickets Blue had been dipped so that they came out 'whiter than white', as the advertisers say. All in all the weekly wash was a full day's occupation.

Many homes still had the big brick copper in the corner of the kitchen or scullery, but by the late 1930s smaller electric coppers were beginning to be available to boil 'the whites'. Otherwise it was possible to boil the white washing in large tin tubs on the gas or electric stove to obtain a really clean wash for badly soiled articles. A number of these articles once rinsed in clean water would require putting through the blue rinse, obtained by putting the Rickets blue cube in the clean water until the colour of the water changed to a pale blue. After this came the starching. This meant that the packet of Robin starch, (with its bright little picture of a Robin Red breast on the front of the packet), would be brought forth and a teaspoonful or so of the powder mixed to a paste with a little water. Then it would be added to another bowl where boiling water was poured on while the mixture was stirred. More water was added to cool the mixture when it would be considered ready to take the articles required for starching.

Another use for starch was a cosmetic one. It was useful to dust a little of the powder on to ones hair before giving it a really good brushing. This was a method used to clean dirt and grease from the hair if there was no time to shampoo it.

To return to the weekly wash; when all the above processes had been concluded, the next action was to put all the rinsed wet clothes through the mangle or wringer as it came to be called. They were neatly folded and placed between the rollers on one side to drop into the basket placed below the wringer on the opposite side, ready to be hung on the line. By the end of the wash, when all the clean clothing and linen was hanging on the washing line alongside the garden path. Hopefully drying in the sun and the kitchen and scullery was full of steam and moisture, the housewife would have been feeling as wrung out as her washing!

Although all these processes were certainly time consuming few women caused them to last all week, as in the song 'T'was on a Monday morning when I beheld my darling. a-doing of her washing oh!'

CHAPTER 10

Among people in the village whom I remember was Bert, the one armed postman. I do not know Bert's surname, or how he came to lose his arm, it may have been in the 1914-18 World War, but I do remember him as a most happy man, always cheerful, whose pleasant smiling face was a pleasure to see each day. He carried his heavy bag across his shoulders and managed to sort and deliver his letters most ably.

Mr Gates, the coal man delivered the fuel for our boiler and open fires with the aid of his assistant. He wore his peaked cap back to front to protect his neck, over this he wore a sack which came to a point above his head and hung down his back, again its purpose was to protect him from the heavy bags he carried in the course of his work. His assistant wore the same. This did not prevent them being covered in coal dust and I do not remember ever seeing Mr Gates with a clean face. Perhaps I would not have recognised him? However, he was an obliging man with a family who lived in a pleasant detached house near the recreation ground in Shenley Road. Unfortunately, his pleasant house was later blown to pieces by a bomb during an air raid in the Second World War. Luckily the family survived.

Another person who came daily to our door was Joan Freestone the baker lady. She was a cheerful, red haired and freckled, buxom, young lady, who coped with two baskets, one holding bread of different kinds, white, brown and currant loaves of varying shapes, farmhouse, cottage, tin etc. and the other basket, many kinds of cakes, fancy or plain on her ample arms. I loved the smell of the bread, but used to feast my eyes on the fancy cakes hoping my mother would buy some. Sometimes for a special treat, such as friends coming to tea or for a Sunday she might be persuaded, but usually Mother made her own, Victoria sponges, Madeira cakes with seeds in them (which I did not like) or rock cakes being her specialities.

Our family had always had a pet cat. Over the years we had lost our pets as their span of life is so much shorter, but they were much loved by us all during their time with us. Tibby a tabby cat that was with us from the time I was about seven years of age was with us still when I was into my teens. A most affectionate and docile cat, she allowed us to dress her in dolls clothes and wheel her around in my doll's pram. She enjoyed being petted and cuddled. Each morning Tibby came to our bedroom and woke me by gently tapping my cheek with her paw, then purring happily she would snuggle into bed beside me and stay until it was time to get up for school. After Tibby we had Smokey, a pretty, grey cat, but she was more my sister's pet and by that time I was busy with teenager's business!

I do not think it could have been easy to have pets neutered during those years, as I have recollections of a number of litters of kittens arriving. It was impossible to keep them all, so unless we had a positive offer of a home, Father would take all but one of the kittens before their eyes had opened and drown them in a bucket of water in the garden. This was always done when we children were not around. One kitten was always kept for the mother cat and usually a home was found for it when it was weaned. We of course hated parting with the adorable kittens, but understood it was necessary.

When I was twelve, I asked for a puppy for my birthday present. One day, our parents took the three of us to London to visit the large department stores. A treat for us all, as Mother enjoyed the shopping and we all enjoyed the train ride and the excitement of the big city and seeing the River Thames with its busy boats, barges and ships. It also meant a meal out in a restaurant, a rare treat. The shops had many floors and moving staircases, a novelty at that time. Sometimes instead of escalators, there were lifts, again a novelty, for none of these things were available in our village.

In Kensington there was, and probably still is, a department store on the roof of which was a garden. Begun in 1938, it had trees, shrubs and flowers and also possessed a decorative pond complete with fish and fountain, high above the roofs of any surrounding buildings and way above the traffic in the High Street one hundred feet below. It provided a pleasant spot to rest and gaze across part of the city and put us on a level with church spires. Derry and Toms and Bakers were two of the large stores in Kensington my parents enjoyed visiting. I cannot remember whether it was in one of these or in one of the equally large department stores such as Gamages or Selfridges in Oxford Street where I at last obtained my birthday wish. But in one of these stores was a large pets department. Full of young animals of many kinds, cuddlesome kittens and romping puppies, scampering mice and other creatures of whose names we were unsure. Guinea pigs and rabbits, long and short haired, of black, white, brown or mixed colouring. Tanks of colourful, aimless looking fish with flowing fins and tails. Cages of brilliant birds of all sizes from large green and scarlet parrots and white and yellow cockatoos, to tiny twittering Java Sparrows and other exotics from warmer climates.

We children would happily have spent most of the day in this one department should time allow, but while we gazed and admired and stroked kittens and puppies, one friendly little puppy in particular caught my eye. He was a little blue roan Cocker Spaniel with floppy ears and appealing brown eyes and so small as to fit easily into my father's hand. As I cuddled him he snuggled up against me and won my heart. I looked hopefully at my parents.

"Would you like to have him?" they said.

"Oh, yes please" was my delighted answer.

An assistant came forward. Pedigrees were produced; the price paid and Prince became my birthday present.

Through all my Teenage years Prince was my companion and friend. He walked with us and played with us and was even accepted by Tibby and our subsequent cats. When I felt sad he seemed to know, snuggling up beside me to give an affectionate lick of his tongue as if to say

"Everything is all right, I'm here".

When in later years I left home to join the Women's Royal Naval Service during the war, Prince remained behind with the family and became my father's companion. They walked together each evening 'around the block' before bedtime. This became such a routine that in later years after the war was over and I was home from the WRNS and about to be married, it happened that my father was unwell and my fiancé volunteered to take Prince for a walk in his place. Harry and Prince set off from the house in the dark, Prince walking to heel, or so Harry thought, until they met each other on the other side of 'the block' going in opposite directions! Harry, not realising had turned away from the established practice by going in the wrong direction to start with. Prince did not approve of the change and continued on the normal route on his own. Even after meeting they both continued in the way they had started and met up once more at the front gate, both satisfied that duty had been done!

Prince remained with the family after I had married and went into retirement with my parents when they moved to Surrey. He lived to a good age and was sadly missed when he died.

I suppose that a love of animals is an ingrained instinct with most children, but Alan and I were also aware that some animals were not to be treated as pets, but as working partners and some were raised for other purposes such as providing food.

Mother came from a farming background and we spent a number of holidays on farms belonging to relatives in the West Country. So we were used to the fact that cows were kept to provide milk and that many of the calves they produced, appealing as they were, at a certain stage were destined for the market as were the little piglets and lambs.

One of Mother's cousins was a gamekeeper. We knew him as Uncle Frank. Uncle Frank and his family lived in a charming old cottage on the outskirts of a wood in Wraxall Park in Wiltshire. He and Aunt May had three children, one son and two daughters. All were several years older than I was. During the summer holidays Alan and I were taken by car to spend one or two weeks with the family. Apart from the family Uncle Frank had three gun dogs all named after different parts of a gun. Trigger was a large black Labrador; Guard was a Springer Spaniel as was the third dog whose name I have forgotten. All these were working dogs and lived outside in kennels, but at times we were allowed to take them on walks with our cousins through the woods. These were wonderful walks of discovery, wild flowers; little springs and streams; wild strawberries, raspberries or blackberries; and sometimes, ripe hazel nuts or sweet chestnuts. Catkins and Pussy willow among other plants and trees were recognised or newly discovered. No matter what time of year, there were always things of interest to see.

Being so far from any shops, about four or five miles, and without a car, getting supplies was not easy, therefore self sufficiency was the aim as far as possible. To this end, the family kept two goats, chickens and of course grew their own vegetables. Among the creatures around the house, were sometimes coops of pheasant chicks being reared by a broody hen. The tiny speckled chicks scurried around on pin sized legs requiring large footed humans to take care where they trod. Each morning we accompanied our cousins when they went to milk the goats and later to collect the eggs. Snaring, or shooting, the many rabbits in the area provided meat.

A river valley led to the cottage and along the bank of the small river was a track that was a way to the nearest village. Frequently as we walked the track our cousins would ask us to stop and wait while they went ahead to check snares. They often came back with a dead rabbit. If a rabbit was not dead but caught in a snare, it would be a matter of seconds to my cousins to put it out of its pain, but they always made sure that we would not be upset by seeing anything unpleasant.

In its isolated position the cottage had no main drainage or even water laid on. Each morning we washed at the natural spring behind the cottage, its clear cold water soon banishing any sleepiness. If we were thirsty we had only to cup our hands and drink the soft, sweet water as it sprang from the earth. There were many of these natural springs around us in the woods, so we never had need of bottles of lemonade.

I suppose it must have rained on some occasions while we were there, but in memory the days were full of sunshine and the wonder of nature.

Aunt May, Uncle Frank, Alma and Lena Denslow with dogs plus Cynthia, Alan and me

Aunt May, whom I always remember as wearing a cross-over apron, was short, plump, with dark hair. Easy going, she kept the home running smoothly and had very few 'don'ts' in her vocabulary. We loved the freedom, but I hope, never took advantage of her good nature. Our meals were simple, but full of good nourishment and the open air life we led made sure we did them justice. Often, Uncle Frank dressed in boots and gaiters, serviceable knee breech trousers, waistcoat, large-pocketed jacket and trilby type shaped hat took

137

me with him when he was checking his pheasants, one of the dogs at our heels. Sometimes, he stopped suddenly, put his gun to his shoulder and fired. The first time it happened the loud report made me jump. I had never been that close to a fired gun before. It was usually a magpie that caught his notice, or perhaps a jay. Both birds were a menace to young pheasants, so were considered a legitimate pest by gamekeepers.

In the cooler evenings when Uncle Frank's work for the day was over, all the family sat in the soft light of the oil lamp, in the living room, around the warm open fire eating thick slices of buttered toast to which was added a large chunk of cheese. Nothing tasted better. Uncle Frank was kept busy with the toasting fork. This with a mug of cocoa was our supper. When we had finished our supper, carrying our little wax night-lights we made our way to bed in the little rooms under the sloping eaves.

Later Uncle Frank and his family moved to Burgess Hill where he took up another position as gamekeeper. After they had settled in their new home, Alan and I continued to spend part of our school holidays with them. This cottage had the convenience of piped water and electricity that must have been a great bonus for the family. Although, still some distance from the main road, the cottage could be reached by car within yards of the door. In a dip in the land close by was a pond surrounded by trees and bushes, which was the home of moorhens and coots. I enjoyed playing here and spent hours, cutting steps in the rather steep slope that led to the water.

Uncle Frank kept ferrets in hutches a short distance from the cottage. These weasel-like animals, were kept for catching rabbits. We were warned never to poke our fingers through the netting of the hutch, for fear of the ferret's sharp teeth. When once a ferret takes hold it is extremely reluctant to let go. One of the ferrets was a white albino with red eyes, the first I had seen. The others were creamy-yellowish in colour. All were constantly on the move, energetic, supple bodied little creatures.

There were more open areas in the Burgess Hill estate, some of them pasture fields where masses of cowslips bloomed in Spring and buttercups, daisies and other flowers made the fields bright with their colour in the Summer. Again as with Wraxall Park in Wiltshire, there were always new things to see. In this small cottage, I shared a bed with my cousin Lena and probably drove her mad when I sang myself to sleep each night. Had she complained I would have stopped, but perhaps she was too polite. I have no idea why I did this, as it was not a habit I pursued while at home. Another recollection I have is of my uncle's chair in the living room, a tall armchair whose back was draped with a striped black and white skin. I was intrigued with this as it was unlike anything I had seen before. From questions put to my cousin I discovered it to be a badger skin whose thick strong hair gave a smooth shiny surface. I never discovered why it was there, or how the poor animal had met its end. So far I have never managed to see a badger in its natural state. This skin is the closest contact I have had with such a reclusive animal.

As young children, we had stayed on farms of relatives in the West Country where other animals were kept, including goats that had to be tethered in safe places away from gardens. Goats are inclined to eat everything within reach, even managing such unappetising items as holly leaves with all their prickles. One summer we were on a farm when the harvest took place. There were no such machines as combine harvesters then; most of the work was done by manual labour. First, two men would enter the field to scythe the wheat growing round the edge of the field, the first man to scythe and his companion to tie the cut corn into sheaves and lay them alongside the edge or banks of the field. Once the perimeter was cleared, the next step was to bring in the horse drawn cutter and binder guided by one man. This cut swathes from the edges of the remaining corn while other teams of men followed behind to tie the cut corn into sheaves and after them came those men who stooked the corn into wigwam shapes to enable them to dry out in the sun. Many farm workers tied string around the bottom of their trouser legs to prevent rats running up them. A wise precaution especially at harvest time.

Alan, Cindy and myself were all too young to take part in any of the harvesting procedure, but it was a time when friends and neighbours turned out to help one another. In breaks in helping with the work impromptu picnics took place around the sides of the cornfield. The work was hard and inexperienced helpers often suffered with sore hands and knees from the lurking thistles among the cut corn, but the general atmosphere was one of happy sociability and good-humoured joking.

As the binder closed in on the final square of standing corn, the men went to get their guns and our parents moved us some distance away, for when the last of the corn was cut, the rabbits who had been sheltering there sprinted for safety among the hedgerows. Not all of them made the journey. The loud reports from many guns made sure that there would be rabbit pie for supper that and the following few nights.

Sheaves of corn being 'stooked' into wigwams

If the weather was good and the corn dried well, the next process was the threshing. For this a large steam engine threshing machine, fuelled by coal, was brought to the field. The engine built up steam that drove the strong, long belts to work the machine. Carts drawn by huge Shire horses were filled with the dried sheaves. Men with sharp and dangerous looking two tined pitch-forks collected the sheaf of corn and tossed it to one of two other men standing in the cart who lay them neatly in approved fashion around the cart until it was fully loaded and could carry no more. Then with a "giddy up" by the driver the patient horse carried the load to the threshing machine. In some parts of the country, one stook or shock of corn called 'the policeman' was left in the field. Not until this last shock was removed, were people free to go and glean the dropped ears of corn from that field. Up until then the wild life had free reign there and partridges and pheasants and others could take their fill. When threshing commenced the dried sheaves were pitch forked into the top of the machine. The separated grains emerged to be pipe blown into sacks ready to go to the mill, whilst the straw was expelled to be used for bedding for the animals and any other use the farmer found for it. Some artistically inclined people made Corn Dollies and other designs with the twisted straw.

Loading the sheaves onto horse and cart
ready to build the straw stack

Harvesting was a dusty process requiring many labourers, which we watched from a safe distance. A busy, tiring, but happy time, shared by many people. Although tractors came into use during and after World War 1 in a government bid to increase food production, I am glad to have seen the beauty of the old Shire horses in action. A number of farmers still continued to use horses into the 1950s. When the harvesting was finally completed, the farmers showed their appreciation by providing a harvest supper for all those who took part, the farmer's wife and other ladies having been preparing for this in the big farmhouse kitchens for days beforehand. One of my memories connected with farmhouse kitchens is of the large hooks in the ceiling used for hanging the hams. There was usually a good supply of ham in any farmhouse.

Another enjoyable time on the farm, at least for we youngsters, was in June when haymaking took place. I loved the smell of new mown hay and luckily suffered no symptoms of hay fever. The hay fields, full of wild flowers among the many kinds of grass, were allowed to grow to a reasonable height before being cut down in the hopefully sunny and dry month of June. Having been left to dry and raked and turned a couple of times it was gathered into bales and built into stacks to store for animal fodder for use in winter months. The stacks would be neatly thatched to protect them from adverse weather, and left, looking from the distance like rectangular cottages.

Thatching was still an active art in the 1920s and 30s, as many cottages, houses and some churches still retained their thatched roofs which might require repair or a complete re-thatch every fifteen to twenty years or so. Many thatchers had their own particular trademark or design, or even a symbol of some kind which denoted their work. Sadly after the Second World War the craft declined and the few skilled craftsmen still left are in demand by those who still delight in a thatched roof for their homes. Another difficulty is that fewer farmers grow the long stemmed corn required by thatchers to do their job, the shorter stemmed varieties bearing heavier heads of corn being more profitable. Some homeowners however, prefer a thatch of Norfolk reeds which, although more expensive as they are especially grown for the purpose, last longer and do a better job of protection.

There was a time when my cousins and I visited an old barn, not too far distant from their cottage home. Inside the dark interior were piles of straw. There were also other dark nooks and crannies which made it eerie fun to explore, but the piles of straw were our chief interest as they made a lovely shiny, smooth, slide. By climbing to the top of the pile and sitting on the sloping edge we did our best to transfer the shine to our backsides as we gleefully allowed our weight to take us to the bottom of the pile. Not everyone approved of our frolics, as while I stood watching my brother and cousins making their descent, a very indignant inhabitant of the barn made his displeasure felt. From out of a dark recess in the roof flew a large, white faced and white breasted barn owl, giving me a whacking thump on my shoulder. Taken by surprise we all stood gaping as he flew on and out of the open doorway, no doubt in order to find another place to roost where his peace would remain undisturbed. Apart from a small bruise I was unhurt, but it was certainly my closest encounter with such a large wild bird and it certainly left its mark!

When I was about ten years of age, our parents took the three of us to London Zoo. This meant a ride in the train to St. Pancras Station and on the underground railway to Regents Park. An exciting prospect in itself. At Regents Park we passed through the metal turnstiles into the Zoo grounds. There seemed to be miles to walk and hundreds of fascinating animals to see, some in large cages, others in pit areas or on terraces, penguins and other aquatic creatures in pools and exotic birds in aviaries. There was also a reptile house full of somnolent snakes, submerging crocodiles and alligators and lazy lizards. The insect house with strange vividly coloured beetles and butterflies, peculiar stick insects that so blended with the twigs on which they rested that it was hard to distinguish them from their background. The buildings housing the larger animals were popular with us. I had no objection to the smell of camels, giraffes and elephants and it was fun to offer Jumbo a bun and feel him take it from one's hand with the delicate touch of his waving trunk. But I disliked the smell of the reptile house and was not much interested in the aquarium.

The favourite of us all was the 'Pets Corner' where we could actually touch and fondle some of the more docile animals. My parents probably enjoyed this area also for it gave them a chance to sit down and enjoy a cup of tea whilst we were happily occupied. I have a photographic record of this visit, as children were invited to have their picture taken with one of the chimpanzees. Both Alan and I took up the offer and the chimp who was as large as ourselves obligingly put his arm around us as we sat beside him, a very strange feeling to be sitting with an affectionate ape, I found! Many of these animals were quite tame and one of the afternoon delights was to see the 'Chimps Tea Party' conducted by their keepers. They probably found as much pleasure in the performance as the spectators for they are intelligent animals. Other treats for the children were the elephant and camel rides.

Pets Corner, Zoological Gardens, London

The Zoo provided people with a close encounter with animals outside the pages of picture books, a place where one could not only see, but hear, smell and sometimes feel these animals at a time when most people were unable to travel to see them in their natural habitat. The zoo visit was a delightful, exciting, but tiring day for all the family and there was little reluctance to climb the stairs when bedtime was due.

With the car we were also able to visit the newly opened Whipsnade Zoo. This Zoo was one of the first to provide a more natural environment for the animals where there was plenty of open space for them in which to live and move. The opening of Whipsnade Zoo took place on 22nd May 1931. It was a revelation to see the animals moving so freely and seemingly contented in their surroundings after some of the cramped condition of cages in the Regents Park Zoo.

Elstree Reservoir was a close rendezvous for family and friends on a sunny afternoon. One area of water was sectioned off as a lido for swimmers and a smaller area for children to play in a safe pool. As we became older Alan and I were allowed to go in the company of other children of our age. Sometimes we would make the long walk of three to four miles from Boreham Wood, taking short cuts across the fields whenever possible, carrying our sandwiches and bottles of fizzy lemonade in canvas or paper carrier bags. When we became the proud possessors of bicycles, the walking time was cut by half and gave us a longer period to enjoy the water. Mother always sent us off with the warning that if there was a thunder storm we were to cover the shiny handlebars of our bikes with a cloth or bag, so that lightening should not strike them and that we must never at this time seek shelter under a tree.

There was and I believe still is, a small airfield close to the reservoir which gave us the added pleasure of watching a number of light aircraft taking off and landing, still a novelty at that time. I wonder if the summers in the 1930s were really as warm and sunny as I seem to remember them. I can still feel the heat of the sun, the dryness of the grass upon which we sat and the perspiration and thirst that we did our best to quench with large bottles of lemonade mixed from fizzy powder and water. If I wet my finger, stuck it in the powder and then put my finger in my mouth, I experienced a fizzy tingle on my tongue. It was lucky I left enough to make a lemon drink!

If pocket money could afford it we treated ourselves to a special bottle of red Tizer or Cherryade. Pocket money was just a penny a week until we were about eight when it was increased to two pence, but our comics 'Chicks Own' and 'Tiny Tots' were provided by Father. Later we progressed to 'Rainbow', 'Beano,' 'Dandy', and a girls equivalent to 'The Eagle' whose name I have forgotten. First published in 1937 the 'Dandy' featured the character 'Desperate Dan' who was a great favourite with the boys, probably because of his villainous looks as well as his desperate deeds. Another series of boy's stories was the Nelson Lee Library. Nelson Lee was a fictional schoolmaster/detective character situated in a public school, who, with his young assistant Nipper, solved numerable cases. In 1933 this magazine was merged with the more familiar boy's paper 'The Gem'. When we reached the age of fourteen, our pocket money went up to the great sum of six pence, a shiny silver coin.

There were also the comic strips in some of the national papers such as Pip, Squeak and Wilfred in the Daily Mirror, three amusing animals, one being a penguin, or other cartoon characters in other papers like Felix the Cat (who kept on walking). A non animal cartoon character was Popeye, the spinach eating sailor of great strength, who first appeared in the newspaper in U.S.A. on 1st July 1929 and seemed to make his way to Britain at a later date. Another cartoon character to appear about this time was Tin Tin, but apart from the name I don't remember much about it, but I do remember the stories about Rin Tin Tin, the clever and brave Alsatian dog. He became a canine superstar in both silent and sound movie films. Many young people were sad when he died in 1932. Superman appeared in Action Comics in 1938, but I left his adventures to my brother and other boys. I preferred more realistic tales by then.

I grew out of comics and into 'real' books by the time I was ten. I then became an avid reader of anything to do with exploration, travel, and adventure. But I was not above taking a sneaking look at our maid Catherine's 'Peg's Paper', for love and romance was still an unknown quantity and a great mystery which 'grown ups' wouldn't or couldn't explain to me. I always had the feeling that love and romance in particular ended with the wedding day.

CHAPTER 11

At eleven years of age I joined the Girl Guides. We met one evening a week in the wooden Guide Hut near the railway station, opposite the Gate Film Studios. The Company was run by the bespectacled Guide Captain and her somewhat rotund, but jolly assistant "Tommy". The group was divided into patrols, each with its patrol leader who wore two white tape stripes on the left hand pocket of her dark blue uniform. All girl guides wore a brimmed dark blue hat and the patrol and assistant patrol leaders had a white cord toggle. We also wore a leather Guide belt. When enrolled each guide promised to be "pure in thought, word and deed" and among other things to "do my duty to God and the King". It was also suggested that we should try to do at least one 'good deed' for someone every day. Each patrol was named after a bird I believe, although I cannot remember which particular bird I was supposed to be, probably a sparrow, I don't seem to remember anything exotic.

Captain kept us very busy with various tasks, working for our badges, the round emblems of which were sewn on our sleeves with pride when won. Lighting a fire was one task. For this we were taken to a spot outside well away from the hut and told to collect suitable twigs and sticks that we built into a wigwam shape around one small piece of paper we were allowed to use. As I enjoyed helping my father with the garden bonfires we built to clear the autumn rubbish, all this was no problem to me at all and I easily passed the test. Making a pot of tea was another skill we were required to have, but to have a number of guides all making tea at one time for this test would have been a waste of tea. So we made the tea at home and only required a written note from mother to confirm that we had actually done this.

Learning to tie and tell the difference between various kinds of knots was more tricky. We must know a reef knot from a granny knot and many others. We also needed to know the purposes for which they were used. I can always remember the bowline. For this we made a loop with one end of the rope standing upwards, that was the tree. At the bottom of the tree the rope formed a smaller loop, this was the rabbit hole. The other end of the rope was the rabbit. The rabbit came up the hole, round the tree and down the hole again, then both ends were pulled tight. If I remember rightly, this knot was to be used to rescue someone off a cliff face or in a similar predicament, but so far I have never had the opportunity to put my knowledge into practice. I found the knot business quite fascinating and when my brother Alan joined the Boy Scouts we practised our skills together.

The memory test was also intriguing. A number of articles were put on a tray. These we memorised for half a minute and then the tray was removed and we were asked to recount what the articles were. This little test also made an interesting party game. It was surprising how the simplest items were often the ones most easily forgotten.

Tracking was fun. Following clues left by the leader such as chalked arrows on trees, walls or pavements, knotted grass or crossed twigs, we worked our way through part of the village and hoped that we would finally catch up with our quarry. We were also taught to recognise tracks of birds and animals. Games, both team games and others were enjoyed outside when the weather was fine and inside the hut when it was wet.

Girl Guides camp, Woodbridge, 1937
L-R: Margaret Benjiman; Gwen Acason; Marion Hazel; Joan Chessal; Renee ?

Cooking party with 'Tommy' in charge

Songs were learnt and sung with gusto in unison and also in rounds. In fact all were kept busy in a most happy and healthy fashion. The meetings always began and ended with a small ceremony and a guide salute. The uniforms and customs may have changed in present times, but I hope the present day Girl Scouts, as I believe they are now called, have as much fun as we did then.

The biggest adventure in my time in the Girl Guides was going to camp. My very first time under canvas and away without my parents was in 1937 when I was twelve. What a time we had preparing for the great day of departure. Bell tents; rubber ground sheets; palliasses (large bags made of strong cotton); suitable clothing; wellington boots; swim suits; buckets; pots and pans; cutlery; unbreakable mugs and plates all marked with our name; sheet sleeping bag; blankets; toilet bags and loo paper; torches; writing paper and fountain pens; and anything else we felt we could not do without. But as far as I remember, no soft toys or anything that was not strictly practical. My father lent me his old army kit bag to carry my belongings. It had been with him to Mesopotamia and back during the First World War.

Departure day dawned and everything was piled onto the coach that was to take us to our destination, a field on a farm near

Woodbridge, Suffolk. Our first task on arrival was to put up the bell tents. Those who had previous experience took charge. The tent was spread out flat on the ground and then one brave soul was required to crawl inside the enveloping folds with the centre pole that she was to fix in the top of the tent and gradually lift whilst the rest of the team pulled on the guy ropes to be secured by pegs hammered at an angle into the ground by the girl in charge of the mallet. When one side was fixed the rest of the team then moved to the other side of the tent to do the same there. Only when the tent was secured safely all round could the girl inside come out and fill her lungs with fresh air once more.

Mealtime around the campfire

It all sounds simple, but when trying it for the first time things did not always work out as planned. Helpers tripped over guy ropes and pegs in their eagerness to comply and plaintive sounds would come from within the folds with requests to "get a move on" whilst she struggled valiantly to hold the rocking pole in place. The 'she' in the case of our group, being me! Once the tent was up and guy ropes and pegs had been checked by Captain, we were directed to the farmer's barn to fill our palliasses with straw. These were to be our mattresses on which we were to sleep for the coming week and it was up to us to see how comfortable we could make them. If they were packed too loosely we should soon be noticing the hard earth. It is amazing how much straw it takes to fill a six foot long palliasse and as we stuffed the prickly stems down as deep and as firmly as possible, we coughed and sneezed in the particles of dust flying around us. When filled to our satisfaction we then had to lug our unwieldy mattress on our backs, across the field to our tent where they were placed on the ground sheets. There were five girls to a tent and the ground sheets and palliasses were placed so that we slept with our heads toward the outer perimeter of the circle while our feet pointed towards the centre pole. It did not leave much room for manoeuvre and we learnt to pick our way carefully or displeasure would be expressed in a number of flying objects!

Our bell tent
Gwen, Hazel, Joan, Margaret and Renee

With the tent now ready for night-time occupation, our attention was given to various tasks for the communal welfare of the camp. One section was sent to a suitable area by a nearby wood to dig a trench for the latrines over which a form of commode was placed and a screen erected around the whole. A shovel and a pile of soil was handy to the area. Other sections were detailed to help Tommy, who was chief cook, set up the fire and bars on which to hang the cooking pot, also to collect fuel from the woods, others to collect buckets of water from the water tap. I don't think we were required to pump it although pumps were certainly still in use in many places in 1937.

The occupants from each tent were responsible for setting up their own wash areas by making stands for the washing bowl with suitable receptacles for holding soap, towels and face cloths, all this had to be done with sticks and string. The resulting furniture may not have been entirely stable at first, but when accidents such as the collapse of the bowls supports caused a soaked uniform or sandals, we learnt to remedy our mistakes pretty quickly and our final stick wash stand was considered a work of art! Any other form of furniture required had to be made in the same way and I for one found it a challenging and enjoyable exercise imagining how early pioneers or castaways on an island would have coped in similar circumstances.

Each day the tasks for each group were changed around, so that all had a fair share of jobs, pleasant or otherwise. Each evening the day finished with a sing-song around the camp fire until darkness descended and we took our torches to go and clean our teeth before finding our beds. Captain or Tommy came round to check all was well each night and after her visit it was 'lights out'. Any flickering glow from torches could be seen through tent walls and our tent leaders were very strict about obeying camp rules.

Songs such as the 'Kookaburra Sits in the Old Gum Tree' sung as a round was a favourite, another round sung was 'London's Burning' and three years later it really did. 'Oh, Jemima' and 'John Brown's Baby's Got a Cold Upon Its Chest' were also popular. In the last song names were gradually replaced by actions. One song, in which we could really let rip with war cries, was something to do with Red Indians. I wonder if these same songs are sung around camp fires after more than fifty years? I am sure with sleeping bags and modern tents camping is more comfortable, but I doubt if it can be more fun!

During a part of each day we went to the river to swim. There was a reasonably shallow area for us to disport ourselves and a friend tried to give me swimming lessons, supporting me with her hands while I tried a breaststroke, but as soon as she started to remove her hands I panicked and sank. I still have visions of bubbles arising as I went down.

All our meals were cooked on the camp fire and we learnt to make a few delicacies such as Indian Toast when meat paste was spread on a slice of bread which was then fried in fat until it was crisp. We also made Cheese Dreams, cheese sandwiches that again were fried in fat and tasted wonderful. Over the years I have forgotten some of the other tasty dishes, but I do remember that we all ate ravenously, the fresh air giving everyone a very healthy appetite. We had a little trouble with a plague of wasps and at one time needed to shield one's slice of bread and jam with one hand, while taking it towards the mouth with the other, wiping off the wasps as we did so. Luckily there were not too many casualties among the girls, but quite a number among the wasp population!

On the very first night of camp there was a thunderstorm. Our tent leader with one other guide put on mackintoshes over pyjamas and with torch in hand went around the tent loosening the Guy Ropes which otherwise would have tautened with the rain and pulled out the pegs, thereby causing the tent to collapse. I knew nothing of this activity until the following morning as I slept through it all! Something else we had to remember was not to touch the fabric of the tent while it was wet or the water would drip right through. It was also necessary to dig a shallow trench around the tent to guide the water away from the tent floor in case of heavy rain. We all learned many useful lessons in that first camp, some of which came in handy in later life.

At the end of the week, a fine and sunny time apart from that first thunderstorm, we reluctantly packed up our pieces of equipment and took down our tent, again with a volunteer inside holding the pole. A further lesson was learned when trying to fold it e.g. everything must be done in a correct way if it is to be successful. Latrine ditches were filled in and wash stands, which had been our pride and joy, dismantled. Pots and pans had to be scoured out with sand and newspaper and the camp fire area cleaned up. There was to be no litter left anywhere. The straw from our palliasses was emptied back into the farmer's barn. In fact the only evidence left of our camp were the circles of flattened grass where our tents had been and the bare patch left from the camp fire.

The Boy Scouts general programme was very similar to that of the Guides as Alan and I found when we compared notes. One of the things that all Guides and Scouts had to learn was the Morse Code, so Alan and I could test one another to improve our skill. I fear that with the passing of time the only letters I now remember are S.O.S. and V from the V for Victory sign used in wartime. Sometimes Guides were asked to assist the Boy Scouts with their concert and vice versa. In one Scout Concert they were performing a skit on Henry VIII and his wives and the Captain received a request for six volunteers to play the part of the wives. It seems that such parts were not fancied by the lads. Along with five others I went along to help out and enjoyed the fun.

Lord Robert Stephenson Smyth Baden-Powell founded both the Boy Scouts and the Girl Guides. The Scouts in 1908 and the Guides, two years later with the help of his sister Agnes. Lord Baden-Powell was a distinguished soldier and the defender of Mafeking during the Boar War, when with one thousand and two hundred men in a time of sickness and famine he held the town for two hundred and fifteen days until its relief on 18th May 1900. The first Scout Troop was formed 24th January 1908 and Scouts in USA were incorporated into the movement in 1910. By 1937 over two million boys and girls were members of these organisations, with their various branches, the Rovers and Rangers, Sea Scouts, Wolf Cubs and Brownies. Lady Baden-Powell became Chief Guide. She and her husband shared not only the same interests, but the same birthday, February 22nd, apart from the year. Lord Baden-Powell was born in 1857 and died on the 8th January 1941 in Kenya during the Second World War.

CHAPTER 12

Like many before World War II we possessed an upright piano. It stood against one wall of our sitting room, not far from the large French windows leading into the back garden. These windows provided ample light for reading the music. As we had the piano and I was keen on singing, my parents decided that it would be a good thing for me to have music lessons. So once a week after school, Mrs Garnsey, the piano teacher arrived to give me my lesson. Mrs Garnsey was a widowed lady of about fifty years of age, comfortably built, with wiry, wavy hair turning grey, almost disciplined by being tied in a bun and fixed with long hair pins at the back of her neck. She always seemed to wear a long coat whatever the weather and a felt hat with small brim, all in neutral colours. She also wore an extremely strong and pervading scent that wafted before her and remained with us after her visit, that, combined with a hint of talcum powder confirmed her presence. I soon became accustomed to the aroma and never let it worry me, but my young brother was not quite as polite in his description, referring to 'the pong'. When I had asked to wear scent, Mother remarked "some people used it to cover up other smells", but I noticed she sometimes used it too on special occasions, 4711 Eau de Cologne being her usual choice.

I must have been about nine years old when the lessons started and at first I was quite keen to learn. Practice was required of half an hour each day of scales, exercises and small pieces of music, on all of which I was tested when the next lesson came around. I used to like to hear Mrs Garnsey play a piece first before I tried it, as I found it easier once I knew how it was supposed to sound. Sound was easier to remember than all those little black notes.

As I progressed I was expected to take the various grade exams. To do this meant a trip to London to play before the examiners. I did not do too badly at first managing to pass the first three without trouble, having been warned by my teacher that sometimes the examiners attempted to distract the pupils by dropping pencils on the floor or tapping on the table in order to test the pupil's concentration. Once the exam was through, then came the treat. Mrs Garnsey always took her pupils to a London restaurant for tea with bread and butter and jam and then a choice of delicious cream cakes. This was indeed a day out of the ordinary and an exciting experience to be in a busy restaurant being treated in such an adult fashion among the teeming population of the big city. One of the most popular teashops of the time was J.Lyons who had a number of teashops on corners of many main London streets. They were referred to as Lyons Corner House and consisted of a number of different restaurants on several floors of the same building. One was therefore able to make a choice of restaurant depending on what sort of meal was required. All meals were served by waitresses at the beautifully laid and discreet tables. There was no overcrowding, but a clean and efficient atmosphere served by the neatly uniformed waitresses in dark dresses covered with a short, frilled edged, white apron, and an attractive white headband threaded with navy ribbon keeping her hair away from face and food. Lyons Corner House caused a great sensation when it first opened on the 23rd October 1933.

A Joey Lyons tea shop in the 1930s

The management employed as many as one thousand staff to cater for an expected two thousand customers. After tea we would look in a few big department stores and travel up and down on the recently installed moving stairs escalator before finally making our way back to the railway station and home.

Mrs Garnsey had no car and must have spent much of her time travelling on buses and trains in the course of tutoring her pupils for she lived at Mill Hill, some distance of four miles or more by bus from Boreham Wood. Once a year, in the summer she gave a party at her home for all her pupils. There were games to play in the garden, one being clock golf I remember, with prizes for the winners of small competitions and a wonderful tea with all the things children liked to eat on the long table in the dining room. Each child was expected to do a party piece of some kind. I usually sang a song. One, I remember was one sung by the child film star Shirley Temple called 'Animal Crackers in my Soup'. Shirley Temple won an Oscar in 1934 when she was only five years of age. Her films were very popular as most people fell for the charm of this five-year-old child with her curly ringlets and winning ways. She left films early in life and went into politics. I don't think that we as children realised how hard our teacher worked for us all, we can only now, as adults appreciate the thought that went into her efforts for us.

My lessons continued until I was around fourteen years of age, by then I had progressed to playing reasonably difficult pieces. One of my favourites was the waltz from Coppelia by Delibes. It is a lovely piece of ballet music. By that time increasing homework from school and an interest in other pastimes made me lax in my piano practice and my parents stopped the lessons. Some years later as a young Wren in training at the WRNS establishment in Mill Hill, I went to the house I recalled to see Mrs Garnsey, only to discover that I was one week too late. She had died the week before. I was very sorry, I believe she would have liked to know that she was remembered with affection by at least one of her pupils.

Apart from the piano, our sitting room boasted a wind up gramophone. This reposed inside a wooden cabinet standing on four legs at a convenient height for manipulation. The top opened by a hinged wooden lid disclosing the turntable and arm holding the needle at the appropriate distance for the records. Some of the

78rpm variety small size, as well as the larger records of classical music appreciated by my father, (if not the younger members of the family), were housed in the lower part of the cabinet. Long-playing records were first demonstrated in New York by RCA Victor in September 1931. All records were then made of shellac. They broke quite easily and sometimes if they were left in the sun, went out of shape, leaving the record resembling an ocean swell. In the corners beside the turntable were the receptacles for the needles, one for the new and one for the used, for needles were supposed to be changed for every one, or two at the most, records played. On the front of the cabinet were two hinged doors hiding the loudspeaker. These were to be kept open while the records were played.

Besides the classical records were selections from 'Chu Chin Chow' described as 'A Musical Tale of the East told by Oscar Asche. Music by Frederick Norton'. Some of the most popular songs from the show were 'Any Time's Kissing Time', 'The Robber's Chorus' and a favourite of my father's 'The Cobbler's Song' sung by Peter Dawson, an Australian singer with a very deep and rich bass voice. 'Chu Chin Chow' held the record for the longest running musical- and very spectacular-show from its opening at the then His Majesty's Theatre, London on 31st August 1916, until well into the 1950s. The New York cast had film star Tyrone Power's father in the lead role, played in London by Oscar Asche who also wrote the piece.

There were other popular musical shows such as 'Maid of the Mountains'; from whence comes the song 'Under the Deodar'. (The Deodar being an East Indian Cedar tree, prized for its light coloured wood, so I am informed) and 'The Arcadians' from whence came the song 'Arcady', whose popular tunes were heard on the wireless. Songs sung at the time came from a number of different shows. 'Show Boat' by Jerome Kern and Oscar Hammerstein which was played at His Majesty's Theatre in 1916 during the First World War and has had many revivals since, brought us 'Old Man River', 'After the Ball', 'Bill', and 'Only Make Believe'. The Show's initial Broadway premier was in 1927 and the first London performance at Dury Lane Theatre in May 1928. Cedric Hardwick (later Sir Cedric) played the part of Captain Andy, and Paul Robeson, that great bass singer, the part of the Negro servant Joe. The show was adapted from a novel by Edna Ferber and the lyric to the song 'Bill' written by P.G.Wodehouse.

'I Dreamt I Dwelt in Marble Halls' coming from 'The Bohemian Girl' composed by the Irish composer Michael William Balfe who lived from 1808-1870 was still sung and heard on the wireless programmes. The plot concerned the kidnapping of a nobleman's daughter when a baby, by gypsies who brought her up as one of their own children, but she has these dreams of marble halls, a memory of a past life. Two films were made of the story. The first, a British silent film in 1922 with Ivor Novello and Gladys Cooper and the second in 1936 with Laurel and Hardy of all people! The song 'I Dreamt I Dwelt in Marble Halls,' was included by a lady, who after playing the part promptly died. In her case it is most likely that the vocals were dubbed onto the sound track as the lady was not known as a singer. The song 'I Dreamt I Dwelt in Marble Halls has since been revived on compact discs by Eyna, a popular modern singer and by Aled Jones. Sigmund Romberg, a Mid-European who emigrated to the United States of America where he died in 1951, wrote 'The Desert Song'. It was performed in London in the late 1920s. The star of the show being Harry Welchman. It was so popular that he went on playing the part in various revivals and tours, on and off for the rest of his career. Three films were made of this musical, an early sound one with John Boles in 1929, the second film with Dennis Morgan in 1943 and the last one in 1953 with Gordon Macrea. John Hanson took the lead in later stage productions. 'Won't You Now Come to the Ball', a song my Mother liked to sing, came from 'The Quaker Girl' by Lional Monkton, produced about 1910, starring Gertie Miller and Joseph Coyne. A year later it went to New York and was revived in Britain again in 1934 and again in 1944.

'Rose Marie' was a very popular musical in both Britain and America and probably had some effect in making the Canadian Mounted Police Force (known as 'The Mounties') very popular among young boys in both countries. Their motto being 'The Mounties always get their man'. 'Rose Marie' had some very stirring tunes as well as haunting melodies, 'The Indian Love Call' being one of them. It was still popular in the 1940s when it was made into a film with Jeanette McDonald and Nelson Eddy in the leading roles. The musical show 'Rose Marie' was written by Rudolf Friml.

Edward German, the composer of 'Merrie England' Henry VIII Dances and other delightful light music, popular with many people, sadly died in the November of 1936. Although German by name, he was an English, or maybe Welsh composer as his correct name was Edward German Jones.

Amongst the records in our cabinet, there was one called 'In a Country Churchyard' full of bird song, church bells and other country sounds. 'In a Monastery Garden' which I believe was on the other side of the same record, was a rather haunting piece of music which was used as a background for a very sad film Mother and I went to see, which had us weeping buckets of tears!

Records bought specifically for we children included 'Teddy Bears Picnic' first produced in 1932, 'Let's All Sing Like the Birdies Sing', ' Oh, The Chirruping of the Birdies on the Sycamore Tree', 'Wedding of the Painted Doll' and 'The Laughing Policeman'. The last of which sadly came to grief when one of Alan's friends sat on it! Records made during the 1920s and 30s were easily cracked or broken, they were also liable to melt with heat, so many had a rather short life. If damaged the needle frequently became stuck in a particular groove causing the same phrase to be repeated over and over again until the arm was lifted, to be replaced at a point further on in the record. Another problem with the wind up gramophone, was that someone always had to be handy to rewind it when the spring reached its end, or the speed of the song became slower and slower and the voice of the singer deeper and deeper, until sopranos ended up sounding like basses and the basses became a groan! However, it gave us all a great deal of pleasure in its time. The first automatic gramophone was introduced to the public in 1924 by His Master's Voice who produced many of the records, always recognisable by the picture of the terrier dog sitting beside the large horn from whence came 'his master's voice'.

Aunt Kate's Day By Day Book even gives a hint for putting new life into old records. 'Place them one at a time in warm soapy water. Move them about gently and rinse in clean water. Pat them dry with a clean towel and leave standing on edge for a few hours. This treatment cleans them and usually improves the tone very considerably'.

The piano was also a pianola. By opening up the front, large rolls of paper marked with patterns of little holes could be affixed and by pressing a lever the keys of the piano started to move up and down without the help of human hands and the sound of music poured forth. Only father was allowed to work this piece of mechanism and he did not do that very often, so I doubt if we ever heard the full repertoire.

Music played a great part in our lives one way or another, although none of our family were great musicians we all enjoyed listening to music of various kinds on the piano, gramophone or wireless. My father to his classical chamber music, Mother preferring the light classics and musical shows which I also enjoyed, as well as the ballads and dance music played by orchestras such as Henry Hall's, Ambrose, Harry Roy, Billy Cotton, Caroll Gibbons, Paul Whiteman and Jack Hylton. Henry Hall started his musical career with the Salvation Army. His signature tune 'Here's to the Next Time' was a main theme of a tune he composed while in the Salvation Army. One of the songs sung by singer Sam Brown with Jack Hylton's band was 'There Ain't No Sense Sitting on a Fence, All By Yourself in the Moonlight' brought out in 1928. I think Alan and I enjoyed singing this song because we were able to say 'ain't, normally a forbidden word in our home! Writers of popular music whose melodies never seem to tire were the Gershwin brothers, Ira and George. Some of their earlier songs, 'I Got Rhythm', 'Nice Work if You Can Get It' and others were all the rage in the 1920s and 30s. They also wrote many melodies for the films of the time. When George Gershwin died in 1937, his sorrowing family provided him with two funerals, one in the film world of Hollywood and the other in the city of New York. George Gershwin's opera 'Porgy and Bess', 'Rhapsody in Blue,' premiered in New York in 1924 and countless popular songs, had people singing, humming and playing his tunes around the world.

Cole Porter whose melodies are perpetually popular wrote a number of musicals and his show 'Anything Goes' opened in New York on 21st November 1934. It has had many revivals. Cole Porter studied at Harvard intending to become a lawyer but then changed direction to study music instead at the Schola Cantorum in Paris. He went on to compose other musicals as well as many songs until his death in 1964.

Turner Layton and Clarence Tandy Johnstone joined forces to become a singing duo with piano. Known as Layton and Johnstone, they made many records and were frequently heard on the radio. They also performed on stage. Some of their well known songs at the time were 'Bye Bye Blackbird', 'Me and My Shadow', 'My Blue Heaven' and 'Love Letters in the Sand', the last of these recorded long before it was discovered by Pat Boone who also recorded it in the 1950s. I loved to dance and sing to these and knew most of the popular songs of the day. The very first pop music chart was published in 1936 by the Billboard Magazine in New York.

Popular dances of the 1920s were of course 'The Charleston and the One step and Two step, very catchy dances, but I was not yet of an age to be able to learn them. Mother took me to my first dance held at the film studios where I had my first job, at the age of fifteen. By that time the Charleston, One Step and Two Step were out of fashion being replaced by the Foxtrot, Quickstep, and Waltz, with a selection of a few South American dances such as the Tango, and Rumba taking their place. Alan and Cindy enjoyed the records and songs produced for children such as those already mentioned. As children we knew all the nursery rhymes and songs played on 'Children's Hour' which now seem to be replaced by jingles from television. Having been brought up in Ireland as a child, my father also enjoyed Irish music and songs. I inherited his love of these and learnt them by heart. A favourite singer was Count John McCormack, a great tenor singer of Irish songs often heard on the wireless, who was born in1884. He died in 1945.

A man who had a particular interest in folk music was Cecil Sharp. He had died in 1924, but during his life had been aware that many of the old folk songs were being forgotten and lost. He made it his personal crusade to travel around Britain to save as many as possible by getting those of an older generation who still remembered, to sing them and as they sang he wrote them down, so saving them for future generations.

Mother and Father had been keen singers in their time belonging to various choirs. Mother as a member of her choir had had the privilege of singing in the Crystal Palace, a marvellous glass building which Father had always promised we should visit, but before we ever managed to get there, it burned down on 30th November 1936. So we only ever saw it from a distance, a silhouette on a hill against the skyline.

Some days, when our parents had time, we gathered around the piano for a singsong with mother and later, myself playing the air of the song.

At school I had joined the dancing class taken by the games teacher Miss Sharp, an extra subject to the regular curricular. Wearing a short form of Grecian tunic, we formed a circle doing flowing movements to the music, dancing barefoot in the Isadora Duncan style. Isadora Duncan pioneered a completely new style of dancing in the 1920s, but sadly her dancing days came to an end in September of 1927 when her long flowing scarf became entangled in the wheel of the car in which she was riding and strangled her.

What I really fancied myself as doing was ballet or tap dancing, but this was the best I could get at the time. I had of course been to see one or two films featuring that great dancer Fred Astaire and tap dancing had become quite a vogue, many youngsters dreaming of themselves as future Fred Astaire's or a female counterpart. Many little girls also dreamed of being a ballerina and wearing a tutu dress. The great ballet master Serge Diaghilev had only died in fairly recent years in 1929. In 1909 he had founded the Ballets Russes Company and toured Europe and the American continent bringing Russian Ballet to the notice of the West. The ballets he produced gave male dancers strong dancing parts of their own in contrast to the mainly supporting role for the ballerina, usual until then. We had also heard and seen pictures of the great ballerina ethereal in her pose and net tutu who almost every young girl would love to emulate no matter how chubby she might be! Anna Pavlova, who died in 1931 at the age of 49, was most famous for her role 'The Dying Swan' created for her by Fokine.

More losses in the musical world came with the death of two well-known classical composers in 1934. The English composer who was of Swedish descent, Gustav Holst who died in May and was renowned for his suite 'The Planets'. But who also wrote choral works and operas. Almost a month later on 10th June, another English composer Frederich Delius died. His works included operas, choral works, orchestral, romantic, impressionist pieces and church music.

At the end of the 1930s a new sound in music was to be heard. American bandleader, Glen Miller, was composing and orchestrating dance music in a new way of which we were to hear much in the following decade in this country. His theme tune 'In the Mood' was recorded on 1st August 1939.

As we became old enough to spend a full day in London with our parents, a few weeks before Christmas we would be taken to the Houndsditch warehouse where my parents bought stocks of toys for the shop's Christmas season. This huge warehouse was like an Aladdin's cave to our wondering eyes, full of a multitude of toys to delight any child's heart. There were beautiful dolls, as well as cots and prams to put them in, plus all the other accoutrements for would be 'little mothers.' There were model cars, aeroplanes, trucks (or lorries as we called them then). Numerous other kinds of toys, games and meccano sets with all their complicated pieces of metal bars pierced with holes, in which to fit the accompanying screws, nut and bolts, enabling one to build the various illustrated models. Our parents must have watched us closely as often a particular toy we had admired was by our bed when we woke up on Christmas morning

The wrapping department of the warehouse was a fascinating place to us. Any item bought was sent to this area to be neatly parcelled up for customers to collect and take away. At wide, wooden counters, staff took goods as they arrived, placed them on wide sheets of brown paper, folded here, folded there, a turn with the lengths of strong string protruding from metal containers, a twist or two and there was a neatly shaped parcel, no matter how awkward the shape of the purchase to start with. They worked with such speed and deftness that no one was kept waiting for long.

Having saved up some of our pocket money, we chose to spend it in one of the smaller, and more familiar towns around our village. Usually we chose one large enough to contain a Woolworth Store. The trip under the watchful eyes of our parents might be to Watford, Barnet or possibly Edgeware, which also had the nearest tube station to the London Underground train service. Woolworth was known as the sixpenny store where nothing cost over six pence in price. Woolworth catered for items for the household such as pokers, screwdrivers, pots and pans and other utensils, to cosmetics and toys, all displayed on open counters grouped in rectangles behind which assistants watched to serve customers and take the money. Almost anything within reason could be bought from Woolworth for six pence or under. It was a wonderful place to shop in, as one's pocket money seemed to stretch such a long way.

Christmas decorations, displays, cards or goods did not generally appear until a week, or possibly two weeks before the actual event and so it was a delightful period of anticipation which had no chance to fade or become mundane before the great day. This also applied to Easter. Easter Eggs, bunnies, cards, again, did not appear until about a week before the holiday. These few preceding days were a time of frantic preparations, secrets and joy when we stuck our coloured strips of paper together with flour paste to make paper chains. These we strung from one corner of the room to another with the aid of drawing pins, fixing them to the ceiling near the pendent light rose and to the wooden picture rail bordering most walls, along with a decorated frieze in the 1930s.

Making Paper Chains

On these same picture rails were hooks of burnished metal supporting pictures such as 'When Did You Last See Your Father?' 'Mother and Son' (a mare and foal) or 'Raleigh's Boyhood'. Around these pictures a piece of Holly or tinsel would be added as decoration. On Christmas Eve the tree was decorated, complete with clip-on candles and fairy doll, but of course the candles were not lit until Christmas Day, with due ceremony by my father.

The Christmas Pudding, or sometimes several puddings were made some weeks before Christmas Day. The ingredients including plenty of dried fruit and candied peel were bought, along with the mincemeat for the mince tarts in preparation for a busy cooking session. When the initial stages such as the weighing out had been done, all ingredients were tipped into a very large yellow pottery mixing bowl and a spoonful or two of brandy added for flavour. This was the only time my parents touched any alcohol, for they were both teetotal, the brandy in the Christmas Pudding was the exception to the rule. With a large wooden spoon to stir the currants, sultanas, raisins, into the basic mix of butter, sugar and flour, along with candied peel, beaten eggs and brandy, until a rich brown mixture was produced. It was then that the family members were called to take their turn at the stirring and at the same time make a silent wish. The wish not to be divulged to anyone, or it would fail to come true.

The stirring completed, the mixture was spooned into pottery pudding basins, the top covered with greaseproof paper and then a cloth secured to the rim with string tied in a slip knot and carried over the top of the basin to form a handle. The four corners of the cloth also taken over the top and tied two at a time to form a top knot by which the puddings could be lifted. Before putting on the cover it was the custom to drop a new and shiny, silver threepenny bit coin into the mixture of each pudding, to be discovered by some lucky member on Christmas Day. With so many rules and regulations regarding food in the present day, this custom would no doubt be frowned upon as a health hazard, but at least our family came through unscathed.

The copper was often used to boil a number of puddings that required to be cooked for at least four hours. A single pudding might be boiled in a large saucepan, but it was necessary to continue to top up the water to ensure that the pan did not boil dry and so burn the pudding.

On the day of eating, the puddings required re-heating for one and a half to two hours before serving. When thoroughly heated they were lifted from the pan by a fork placed under the top knot, the covers removed and the pudding turned upside down onto a large plate. Brandy was poured over the top and sides and set alight. A piece of Holly stuck in the top and the whole flaming edifice carried into the darkened room for all the Christmas Cracker pulling, paper hatted folks to enjoy, along with hot mince pies, custard and cream and brandy butter.

Looking back, apart from the Christmas decorations, the predominant colours considered suitable for furnishing in the 1930s seem to have been mostly shades of fawn, brown, rust, or green. Primary colours appear not to have been in 'good taste'.

Something that happened early one Christmas morning was definitely NOT in good taste. New Neighbours had moved in next door, a couple with a four year old child. We did not see much of the wife who seemed a reasonably quiet person, but the husband was burly in build, although of medium height. I must have been twelve at the time, for Prince was still a young puppy. I had risen early on this Christmas morning to go downstairs to see him, the rest of the family were still enjoying a lie in bed. All at once I heard a great commotion from next door; shouting and crying and then the sound of doors opening and running feet. Looking from our front window, I was amazed to see the wife running out into the street, dressed only in her petticoat, with her long hair streaming down her back, being chased by her husband wielding a hair brush, with which he proceeded to beat her, while she cried and begged him to stop.

Such behaviour shocked me. It was quite beyond any I had ever witnessed before. A disagreement or tiff was understandable, but for such uncontrolled behaviour as for a man to hit his wife and particularly in such a public fashion, was well beyond the code of moral standards we were brought up to expect. While I stood watching too horrified to move, some sense must have returned to the man's head, for he stopped the beating, turned and went back into the house, leaving his wife sobbing in the road. I rushed upstairs to tell my parents, wondering if there was something we should do. They were as shocked as myself, but when we looked again from the window, the wife had picked herself up and was walking down the road away from us. She returned later with a policeman, who seemed to manage to calm the situation and we heard no more from next door. This experience on the morning when all should have been peace and goodwill to all men AND women, left an indelible mark on my memory and made me realise that not everyone followed the standards of behaviour which we were taught. Soon after this the couple involved moved to another area and a quiet middle aged couple from the north of the country took their place as our new neighbours.

Victorian childhood had been full of proverbs, and Mother had one for every circumstance. If we were about to try out something new and daring, it was a case of "Look before you leap". Should we decide to spend all the money we had been given for a birthday rather than putting some aside into savings, we were told "Look after the pennies and the pounds will look after themselves". If I was reluctant to repair a garment in need of mending, I was reminded that "A stitch in time saves nine". When we lost patience and were frustrated by some small thing we wished to do, but which refused to go right, or when sewing, the thread knotted, we lost the needle, or lost a nut we were trying to fix on our bicycle and became exasperated, it was "Little things are sent to try us", or this rhyme:

'Patience is a virtue,
Possess it if you can.
It's seldom in a woman
And never in a man.'

Getting in one another's way when trying to do some job, we heard "Too many cooks spoil the broth". On the other hand when help was required, it was "Many hands make light work". If it was a job needing to be done, but we were loath to do, Mother came up with "Never put off until tomorrow what you can do today" or " Hard work never hurt anyone". If it was essential that the job should be done immediately, we heard "Strike while the iron is hot" or "Time waits for no man". When a job we were doing went badly and we said "That pen is no good" complaining about the implement we were using, "A bad workman always blames his tools" was all the sympathy we received, or Mother quoted this rhyme:

'If at first you don't succeed,
Try, try, try again.
'Tis a lesson all should heed,
Try, try, try again.
If those other folk can do
Why with patience should not you.
Only keep this rule in view,
Try, try, try again.'

The rhyme goes with a little tune and Mother often sang it.

A broken toy or expected treat which failed to happen and caused us to dissolve into tears brought "It's no use crying over spilt milk", or possibly "Every cloud has its silver lining".

If noisy or chattering too much, there was another rhyme we heard:

'A wise old owl sat in an oak

The more he saw, the less he spoke.
The less he spoke, the more he heard.
Now wasn't he a wise old bird?'

When Mother was harassed and was late with her household chores through interruptions, her favourite expression was 'I'm all behind like the cow's tail'.

If we were caught out in a little fib, she had another little rhyme.
'Oh what a tangled web we weave
When first we practice to deceive.'

I believe there is more to this poem, but here memory fails me. If over ambitious in some scheme we had in mind, it was 'You must cut your coat according to your cloth'. Complaining of each other's or someone else's behaviour or faults, we were reminded that it was a case of 'The pot calling the kettle black' (as most pot and kettles were in Victorian times), and 'People in glass houses shouldn't throw stones'. A quarrel between brother and sister, or friends when blame was cast and unkind words spoken produced 'Least said soonest mended'. We were encouraged to clear our plates at mealtimes with 'Waste not, want not'. If after a series of mishaps everything came out all right, it was 'All's well that ends well'. There were of course dozens more sayings that Mother had up her sleeve for the right occasion, but they would fill too many pages here.

Mother was inclined to be slightly superstitious. She avoided walking under ladders, for to do so was considered to be unlucky. It was also unlucky to bring May Blossom into the house. To break a mirror would bring seven years bad luck. On the other hand if one saw a pin on the floor it was lucky to pick it up. As the saying went 'See a pin and pick it up, all the day you'll have good luck'. To spill salt would bring bad luck, unless one took the precaution of throwing a pinch of the spilt salt over one's left shoulder. For the same reason when seeing a new moon it was advisable to turn over the money in your pocket. 'Touching wood', I still do automatically when something is going well, and also 'cross fingers'. I suppose most people still retain something of the old superstitions at times.

Mother had two superstitions concerning knives or scissors. The first was 'Stir with a knife and stir up strife'. The other concerned the giving of knives or scissors as a present. Should one receive such a present, then in return one gave a small coin to keep the friendship. It was considered lucky to touch a sailor's wide collar.

During the Second World War, many a sailor on leave would feel a light touch on his back as people remembered the old superstition. It is good luck for a bride to kiss a chimney sweep on her wedding day. Fine for the sweep, earning a useful tip from the bridegroom! It was even considered lucky to accidentally put on underclothes inside out, but unlucky to correct them.

As children we arranged the stones from our plate of prunes and custard neatly around the edge of our dish, at the end of the meal counting out the rhyme 'Tinker, tailor, soldier, sailor, rich man, poor man, beggerman, thief' to the number of stones accumulated. The resulting answer being your future husband or career. The rhyme then continued, 'Silk, satin, cotton, rags', giving the form of apparel in which you would be married. It was all good fun for the children and ensured that the prunes were eaten! My brother became a sailor, but I doubt that was due to the prune stones!

Another clue to the identity of a young girl's future husband, was to peel an apple in one long unbroken piece, then to fling the piece over the shoulder to see what initial it formed when it landed. This was supposed to give the first letter of the true love's name. Before the age of tea bags, fortunes were told from the left over tea-leaves in the bottom of the cup. The dregs in the cup being swirled around three times, before the cup was tipped upside down on the saucer. The resulting pattern left indicated one's near future.

Another superstition connected with weddings involves what the bride should wear. 'Something old, something new, something borrowed and something blue'. The bride's white dress was intended to indicate that she was a virgin. It appears in today's social and (im)moral climate, that many young brides' dresses should be heavily spotted, or at least a little off white! The Wedding cake also plays a part in these old beliefs. If the young unmarried girls slept with a piece of wedding cake under their pillow, they would dream of their future husband.

A rather different subject, is the phrase 'Spending a penny'. This phrase came into being when the new public toilets were first built. The gentlemen had free entrance to the men's toilets, but the ladies were charged one penny, one 'old' penny. It was necessary to insert the penny into the slot of a metal container on the door of the lavatory. The dropping of the coin released the lock and so allowed the door to open. Hence the spending of the penny!

CHAPTER 13

After the end of World War 1, the younger generation of the 1920 era seemed to go a little wild. 'Flappers' wore short skirts and short hair casting aside most of the pre-war restrictions of dress and decorum. In 1923 Paris fashion houses decreed that women's clothing should become more comfortable. Materials for dress should be lighter with less of them. Hailed with delight by the young 'Flappers', the new ideas were considered immodest by others. Wealthy young people had mad parties going on into the late, late hours of the night or early morning, dancing to the latest craze 'The Turkey Trot' or 'the Charleston' that became the rage in 1925, listening to the Jazz bands and drinking champagne and the newly invented cocktails. Jazz originating with the black population in the city of St.Louis in Missouri, USA, became the new sound in 1920. One exponent of jazz was JellyRoll Morton. Among others, the popular trumpeter Louis Armstrong and his groups 'The Hot Five' and 'The Hot Seven'. A form of singing called 'The Blues' became very popular and of the exponents of the art, black singer Bessie Smith became known as 'The Queen or Empress of the Blues'. She made many recordings, some with Louis Armstrong and in 1929 starred in the film 'St. Louis Blues'. In 1937 she was hurt in a car crash and bled to death while, it was said, waiting for an ambulance in Mississipi. Segregation of the races was still very strong in southern USA at this time. Bessie Smith was not white, and could not use a 'for whites-only' vehicle, no matter how serious her injury. In February of 1928 people were outraged when dancer Josephine Baker performed in Vienna, Austria dressed only in a bunch of bananas. In 1923 the International Congress of Dancing Masters had condemned the Foxtrot and Tango dances.

Other parts of the United States chose to ignore new ideas, such as in Tennessee where in 1925 a law was passed prohibiting the teaching of the theory of evolution as it was believed to challenge the text of the Bible. A biology teacher John Scopes was convicted in 1925 for teaching the theory of evolution in a Tennessee State School.

In other areas fresh ideas were emerging, old rules relaxed and new rules made, but class barriers remained and in contrast to the wealthy 'Flappers' and their friends, people of the working class in Britain were suffering great hardships of unemployment and poverty. Some benefits had been introduced in 1912; a sickness benefit of ten shillings a week, unemployment benefit of seven shillings a week and a maternity benefit of thirty shillings, but it was hardly enough to keep a family. More than this, working men wanted a change in the poor working conditions. Those who had been away fighting for their country found that working conditions had not improved on their return. On 14th January 1923, 100,000 people made a mass demonstration in London's Trafalgar Square against unemployment. It was dubbed 'Unemployment Sunday', but their voices were ignored by the Government Ministers of the time who snubbed the event. Prime Minister Mr Bonar Law resigned due to poor health and on 21st May 1923 Stanley Baldwin took his place. In December, only a few months after taking office he called a snap election. It ended in defeat with the intention by the Labour and Liberal Parties to throw the Tories from power. On 23rd January 1924 Ramsey McDonald formed the first Labour Government. It proved to be a short-term government lasting only until the November of the same year. He did not regain power until 1929.

In an effort to escape from slum dwellings and depression of this period, over the two decades of the twenties and thirties, some of the inhabitants of those poorer areas of London bought plots of land. Advertised at £5 a plot, in parts of the Essex countryside, twenty-five miles outside the city. On these small plots they hoped to make a better life for their families, away from the dirt, smog, smoke and disease of the town in the clean fresh air of the open country. Salesmen advertised these plots as 'a little bit of paradise' but this hardly matched up to the reality as there was no mains water, sewage, gas or electricity and no nearby shops for provisions. Many of the families lived in tents until they were able to build some sort of shack. Life was hard. By making a vegetable garden on the virgin land they hoped to provide much of the food needed to sustain themselves and their children. Some settled and thrived, forming their own distinct communities. Many of their shack like

Gales Garden, London, 1923

bungalow homes were still in use in the area of Billericay and Basildon in the 1960s and 1970s although most had been bought by building developers by the 1980s.

Union leaders trying to negotiate better terms for workers came up against stubborn refusal on the part of the bosses. When the Samuel Commission recommended that the miners should have a reduction of pay, The secretary of the Miners Union, Arthur Cook replied, "Not a cent off the pay, not a minute on the day". This rallying call was taken up by all the miners. The Trades Union Congress put a ballot to all the members, who voted to strike. This resulted in a call for a general strike starting on the 30th April 1926. More and more workers joined until the country's industry and transport was almost brought to a halt. The Government (once again headed by Baldwin who was back in power from 1924 and remained until 1929) and bosses refused to give way, instead the government called for volunteers to man the transport system. These came forward and with police protection, drove the capital's buses. Less than a month later on 12th May, the workers were forced to give in. If anything, their conditions were worse than before. Baldwin was instrumental in ending the strike. In the November of 1926, further trouble occurred when the miners of

Frickly in Yorkshire, unable to make any headway in the improvement of conditions in their mine, came out on strike. The situation became ugly and riots ensued. Other miners joined in the strike that quickly spread.

On the 24th October 1927 came the Wall Street Crash in the United States of America. The collapse continued with more panic selling in October of 1929 on the New York Stock Exchange. The repercussion was felt through out the world and in spite of changes in government, the depression continued through the 1930s when there were further protest marches by the unemployed of Merseyside and a mass hunger strike in 1932. A harsh Family Means Test had been imposed by the government in 1931. This made the conditions of the unemployed even more difficult. The government was so concerned about the effect that the film 'Love on the Dole' might have on the population that they banned it from the cinema screen. It was only the outbreak of war in 1939 and the need for ships, planes and guns that caused the heavy industries of Britain to get moving again.

In 1918 women in the United Kingdom over thirty years of age became entitled to vote. This right was gradually widened to include further groups until in 1928, after a long and hard fight, all women over the age of twenty-one in Britain were given the opportunity to vote. New Zealand had been the first country to give full women's suffrage and this they did in 1893, obviously valuing their females. Australia had followed suit in 1902; Norway in 1906 and Britain and the United States of America were the late starters with U.S.A. women's suffrage coming into force in 1920.

Women had proved themselves perfectly capable of doing men's work throughout the period of the First World War when most of the male population was fighting in the armed services. They also felt themselves equally capable of deciding whom they would choose to represent them in parliament. They had relaxed their campaign for the right to vote for the duration of the war, but after the armistice felt that they were due for consideration and granting of the right to franchise as equals. With the granting of suffrage to those over thirty, their demands were only partially met. Their fight continued for another ten years, before men's attitudes changed sufficiently to allow the vote to all those women over the age of twenty-one to put them on an equal footing with men in local and national elections.

Women also gained recognition when in 1920 Oxford University passed a statute admitting women to study for degrees. On 25th May 1921 the first woman barrister gained her qualification. Sex barriers took a little longer in other areas of life and it was not until 1930 on 16th June that mixed bathing in the Serpentine in Hyde Park was first allowed. The Lido had been built by George Lansbury, the first Commissioner of Works in the Labour Government of Ramsey MacDonald, who felt that ordinary Londoners should have the opportunity to enjoy the pleasures of the Park. In these changing times, in 1925 on 7th August the Summer Time Act was made permanent in Britain when clocks were moved on, or back an hour according to the time of year. Spring Forward, Fall Back, was a helpful reminder. The change was first made in 1916 to boost production during the First World War.

CHAPTER 14

Investments were made in improvements to public transport. The first almost entirely enclosed, red double-decker buses were seen in London in 1925. On 10th December 1928 a new underground station in Piccadilly Circus was opened. Four years later on 9th May 1932 Piccadilly Circus itself was first lit by electricity. Further north, the Liverpool Mersey Tunnel, begun on 16th December 1925, was formally opened on 18th July 1934. Communication with our far distant dominion was improved, when a telephone link was established from Britain to Australia at the end of April 1930. The dial 999 emergency service came into use in the United Kingdom on 1st July 1937. The World's first telephone emergency service. It is surprising to discover that the first car phone was actually exhibited in Germany in June 1925! The inventor of the telephone, Alexander Graham Bell had died in August of 1922. Also in Germany, in Kiel Harbour the first practical tests of radar were carried out on 20th March 1934. We were to hear much more about this invention in the next decade. On 26th February 1935, Robert Watson-Watt demonstrated Radar, radio detection and ranging, in England at Daventry.

Into the 1930s across the Atlantic, The Empire State Building was opened in New York on 1st May 1931 by President Herbert Hoover. It was then the tallest building in the world having 102 storeys. On America's Pacific coast, we heard of the opening of the famous Golden Gate Bridge in San Francisco on 27th May 1937. Also in America, a new trend was being set with the opening of the first Laundrette, opened in Texas on 18th April 1934. With the increasing popularity of the motor car the world's very first motel was opened in California in 1925 on 12th December and a few years later on 6th June 1933, the first drive-in movie was opened in Camden, New Jersey. Henry Ford's Model T Ford motor car number 15,007,003 was rolled off the factory production line in 1927, the last of its kind. Henry Ford had built his first petrol driven motor car in 1893.

Another famous bridge, that of Sydney Harbour in New South Wales, Australia had its two halves joined together on 19th August 1930 and was finally opened in 1932. Holland's engineers were also busy and on 28th May 1932, the closing of the twenty-mile dyke connecting North Holland with Friesland reduced the Zuider Zee to an inland lake. In Russia, or the Soviet Union as it was now named, the Moscow Metro underground railway was begun in 1935 and completed in 1938. A very fine piece of engineering and architecture, its marble decoration differed at every station and all was unspoiled by commercial advertisements. A small but very practical aid to modern life was the sale of the world's first box of matches by its inventor John Waller on 7th April 1927. A boon to busy housewives and also to smokers who no longer had to use the old 'lucifer to light their fag'. Another invention that may have pleased the male population was that of the first electric razor, patented by Jacob Schick in the November of 1928. The supermarket trolley appeared for the first time in a store in Oklahoma, USA.

Since coming to Britain after the French Revolution, Madame Tussaud's Wax Works had become a great attraction to visitors to the City of London. In 1928 on the 26th April, the descendants of the original Madame Tussaud opened a brand new building in which to house and exhibit the amazing lifelike wax figures to the public. The Wax Works continue to be a main attraction for visitors to the Capital. Also in 1928, the now famous Harry Ramsden opened his first fish and chip restaurant in a hut near Bradford. Up until then, it was customary for fish and chips to be bought at the counter of the local shop where the frying was done, and the hot contents, salted and sprinkled with vinegar were then wrapped in greaseproof paper and yesterday's newspaper to be taken away and consumed elsewhere. Harry Ramsden went one better and provided a place to eat them. Canned beer was introduced in 1935 to Americans by the Kruger Brewery of Richmond, Virginia, but it did not go on general sale in Britain until some years later. Prohibition of alcohol had been in the force in the United States, banning the manufacture, sale and involvement with alcohol from 1920 and was not repealed until 1933. About the same time as the introduction of canned beer, William Wilson founded the self-help group of Alcoholics Anonymous in Ohio.

The Burmese Pavilion, The British Empire Exhibition, 1924

In 1924 there had been a great exhibition held at Wembley. The British Empire Exhibition included pavilions of crafts, culture and design from every part of the British Empire. Thousands of people attended the exhibition and learnt a little more about our far flung outposts of empire, on which it was then said' the sun never sets'. The year 1927 saw even the British Army begin to modernize its procedures when the use of the lance, a long metal, spear-like weapon, was abandoned except for ceremonial use. A designer engineer of other notable edifice, whose name is given to this most famous of his structures, was Gustave Eiffel. He lived to the grand age of ninety-one and died at the end of 1923, but his tower in Paris remains to his memory.

In 1924 0n the 3rd of January, the English explorer and archaeologist, Howard Carter discovered the sarcophagus of Tutankhamun in Egypt's Valley of Kings. He had discovered the tomb earlier in 1922, in his expedition with Lord Carnarvon, but had not expected to discover the wonders he found on reaching the sarcophagus, for most tombs had already been stripped of all of their treasures by grave robbers. The discovery of this tomb which had been sealed in 1337BC caused a great sensation at the time, the wonder at the artifacts found there remains to this day, continuing to bring interested visitors to the exhibits up to the present time. Howard Carter died in March 1939 after a long period of ill health. Lord Carnarvon had died earlier on 7th April 1923 due to a mosquito bite. A rumour had started that there was a curse on those who entered the tomb. A few years after Howard Carter's discovery, in 1927 another archaeologist in China found the tomb of the Mongol conqueror Genghis Khan, but this discovery did not have the world wide and lasting excitement of the Tutankhamun tomb.

The Palace of Engineering, The British Empire Exhibition, 1924

A discovery made by astronomers on 13th March 1930 was that of the planet Pluto. Planet Earth suffered a 'close shave' astronomically when the 500,000 ton asteroid Hermes shot past the earth in October of 1937. It missed earth by 485,000 miles, but in astronomical terms it was close. From the heavens to the deep sea, a fish, which was thought to be extinct for sixty five million years, the coelacanth, was caught by a fisherman off the coast of South Africa on the 2nd of December 1938. A discovery that was to have devastating effects in the following decade, was that of American scientist A.C.Urey who on the 29th December 1931 publicly announced his discovery of Heavy Water, and in the following year Heavy Hydrogen. Something we were to hear a great deal about in later years, Radar, was patented in 1935 by a group of scientists led by Robert Watson-Wattt. In October of 1939 scientists in America informed President Roosevelt that it would be possible to develop an atomic bomb. That same year Nobel Prize winner Otto Hahn, a German Chemist revealed he had discovered how to split the atom. In the January of 1934 a 500 caret diamond, believed to be the stolen half of the Cullinan diamond found in 1905, was found near Pretoria, South Africa.

More down to earth discoveries had been going on in the new twentieth century. The days of David Livingstone may have been past, but we, as children were brought up on the stories of the great and courageous explorers of previous years, such as Scott of the Antarctic and Sir Ernest Shackleton who had died comparatively recently on 1st May 1922. The Nowegian explorer of these cold regions; Roald Amundson who reached the South Pole in December 1912, one month ahead of Captain Scott was killed in an air crash on 18th June 1928. A few years later we heard of the death of Fridtjof Nanson, another Norwegian explorer of arctic regions and a Nobel Prize winner for his Russian relief work with postwar refugees. He died on 13th May 1930. Fridtjof Nanson, born in 1861, attempted to reach the North Pole by drifting in the ship 'Fram'. His group travelled further north than anyone before. Nanson was a man with many interests, a scientist; he also worked with the League of Nations.

Indian Pavilion, The British Empire Exhibition, 1924

Sir Ernest Shackleton had been born in 1874. An adventurous British explorer, he led an Antarctic expedition in 1907-9 which located the southern magnetic pole. He returned again to the icy wastes in 1914-16 when his ship the 'Endurance' was lost on the Antarctic crossing. A further expedition in 1921-22 to Enderby Land was his final venture, for he died on this expedition. An early advertisement of 1909 used Shackleton's name and likeness to advertise Bovril, a popular meat extract. Adding a teaspoonful of the extract to hot water made a nourishing and warming drink. It was a popular drink with our family during cold weather.

The Malaya Pavilion, The British Empire Exhibition, 1924

The American explorer Robert Peary, who was the first man to reach the North Pole in 1909, died at the beginning of the 1920s on 20th February. Another man fascinated by these vast areas of ice, I have already mentioned, was the American Navy Commander Richard E. Byrd. He led five Antarctic expeditions including the expedition of the discovery of Marie Byrd Land in 1929. He died in 1957. The Icy wastes held a fascination for another adventurer, Sir George Hubert Wilkins. His ambition was not to walk on them, but to travel under them in a submarine. His dream was to take his craft under the North Pole. An Australian by birth, he spent a number of years in the Antarctic and Arctic and was knighted for the flight he made over polar ice from Alaska to Spitsbergen in 1928. It was in 1931 that he attempted to sail a secondhand submarine he named Nautilus (as in the book by Jules Verne), under the ice to the North Pole. He was unsuccessful due to problems with both craft and crew, but he was the first to take photographs under the ice. He wrote several books about his adventures. When he died his ashes were taken to the North Pole and scattered to the wind.

All these men were held up to us as model heroes and we were encouraged to read of their exploits of bravery and perseverance in the face of great difficulties.

One of our very early explorers, Captain James Cook was remembered and honoured in 1933 by the Australian State of Victoria which paid £800 for the cottage, built in 1755 in which the great explorer spent his childhood.

Not an explorer as such, but a man of great courage, Lawrence of Arabia, Colonel T.E. Lawrence, soldier and writer, leader of many brave deeds with his Arab friends against the Turks during World War One, died six days after a motor cycle accident in a Dorset Lane. He had left the army after the end of the war and joined the new Air Force as Aircraftman John Hame Ross and during this time wrote a book about life in the ranks that he called 'The Mint'. He later adopted the name T.E.Shaw, borrowing the name of his friends Bernard Shaw and his wife. He kept a low profile about his previous career. He had a home in Hertfordshire. The sad news of his death on 19th May 1935 stunned the population and revived interest in his activities of the war years. He had only finished his book 'The Seven Pillars of Wisdom' in 1935 shortly before his death.

Another man of great dedication was Albert Schweitzer who spent much of his life caring for the sick of Gabon in French Equitorial Africa. He set up a hospital at Lamburene where he catered for the medical needs of the local population. Few white people would have traveled in this area in a jungle subjected to many kinds of unpleasant insects, wildlife and tropical diseases, but Albert Schweitzer made it his life's work to help the people living there. He was a cultured man. A well known organist in Europe, he gave many concerts that helped to fund his hospital. Known as 'Le Grand Docteur' Albert Schweitzer was also a writer, philosopher and missionary being awarded a Nobel Peace Prize in

1952. He lived until 1965.

There were other men who explored the high places of the world. George Mallory was one of these. His ambition was to be the first to climb Mount Everest. When asked "Why?" He answered "Because it is there!" He made his attempt, but disappeared from view when 1,000ft from the summit. No one succeeded in any attempt until 1953 when Sir Edmund Hillary and Sherpa Tenzing succeeded in the year of the coronation of Queen Elizabeth II.

It was no great hardship for me to read of these great people. I admired their daring and initiative, for my ambition was also to travel to these exciting places, although I must admit the frozen ice lands held no great appeal for me. However, visions of myself machete in hand, hacking my way through virgin forest, or being shipwrecked on some small Pacific island filled my dreams in my early teens, but in 1939 such thoughts were put aside whilst all our energies were spent on surviving the traumas of World War II.

CHAPTER 15

There were other heroes for children and adults in the world of sport, but I do not remember any great fanatical behaviour from fans who, I believe were more restrained in their behaviour than in the present day. Perhaps it was that generally, sport was played for pleasure, not money. We saw no tantrums on the tennis courts, no tears from the loser, a good game was more important than winning and one was expected if losing, to do so with good grace and good fellowship. Spectators clapped, not booed, threw bottles or other items when teams lost. It was the spirit of the game that counted not the outcome. Managers were not sacked if their teams failed to win. Neither did players receive fantastic wages. When big business stepped in, sportsmanship died.

Fans could be intense in their support for individual teams, though generally well behaved. However, one Football Association cup final was almost cancelled on 28th August 1923 due to 75,000 spectators who scaled the walls of Wembley Stadium and invaded the pitch. One policeman, P.C.Storey, riding his white horse saved the day by clearing the pitch. No call then for riot shields. The final score when the game finished was Bolton 2 goals and West Ham 1. In the 1930s Stanley Matthews, who played for Stoke, Blackpool and England during his time, was a hero to many small boys. Sir Stanley Matthews was the only footballer to be knighted whilst still a player. He started as an apprentice at Stoke City Football Club and was a professional at eighteen. He played for England still at the age of forty-two, and continued playing until he was fifty in league football. Tom Finny, a player for Preston North East and England was another well known footballer of the time. There were eighty football teams in the 1920s. All played with leather boots and balls which became very heavy in wet weather. Matches were reported on the wireless. A British attendance record was set up when 149,547 people watched Scotland play England at Hampden Park, Glasgow on 17th April

Sir Stanley Matthews

1937. Football Pools also commenced around the 1920s. The first World Football Match took place in 1930 and was won by Uruguay.

Cricket was a popular game taught at most schools and after school played on many a village green or town park. Most villages and towns supported their own cricket teams who made a brave sight when they appeared on the pitch all dressed in white flannels, shirts and pullovers if the weather was a little chilly. Wives, sisters, and girl friends supported their men by providing food for the after match tea. Cricket heroes of the time included Wally Hammond of Gloucester and England, Jack Hobbs and Herbert Sutcliffe of Yorkshire who also played for England. D.R. Jardine was another great name and two gifted amateurs who played for England were Percy G.H. Fender who played for Surrey and R.E.S. Wyatt a player for Warwickshire. Harold Larwood and Bill Voce who played for Nottingham, caused great controversy with their bodyline bowling during a test match in Australia in 1932, in which a number of players were injured and which almost developed into a political situation and threatened trade between the two countries. Don Bradman of New South Wales was the Australian captain at the time. Don Bradman set a record scoring 334 runs in one game in 1930. In 1938 England cricketer Len Hutton beat this record by scoring 364 runs in a final test against Australia. Professional cricketers named 'The Players' were a class apart from the amateur 'Gentlemen' cricketers and were still a minority in the 1930s.

Hobbs and Sutcliffe

After being abandoned for over one thousand years Olympic Games commenced once again in 1836. However the first Winter Olympics did not begin until the January of 1924, when they were held in Chamonix, France. Consternation was caused in the British athletics team at the Paris Olympics of 1924 when Scottish Sprinter and missionary Eric Liddell refused to run in the 100 metres race on religious grounds because it was held on a Sunday. He did however run in other races winning a bronze and a gold medal.

Sir Malcolm Campbell and 'Bluebird'

186

Politics intruded into other sporting events during the 1930s, Particularly with regard to Germany where Hitler was trying to build up his 'Master Race'. Boxing had become popular as a sport during the 1920s to the outbreak of war in 1939, and many a young lad learned to use his fists, but usually to the Marquis of Queensbury's rules. Jack Dempsey who came from a tough background in New York to become the World Heavyweight Champion fought and beat the Frenchman Carpentier in 1921, was finally beaten by Geny Tunny in 1926 and again in 1927. In 1936 there was a match between Max Schmeling of Germany and the black boxer Joe Louis of U.S.A. To Hitler's great satisfaction, Schmeling won the fight and returned to Germany in an airship to be congratulated. In 1938 there was a return fight that was won by Joe Louis, which certainly did not please Hitler. In August of 1936 the Olympics were held in Berlin. Hitler turned the occasion into a great show of Nazi strength. When the black runner Jesse Owens who in 1935 set six world records in just 45 minutes, won four gold medals, Hitler noticeably failed to congratulate him, leaving the stadium in disgust. The 1936 Games were the last Olympic Games for twelve years.

Motor car racing became popular in the 1920s. The first, a 24hour race at Le Mans in 1923, and Motor car racing began at Brooklands near Weybridge in Surrey, where earlier in the century a race course had been built by wealthy landowner Hugh Locke King on his private estate. The first British Grand Prix was run here on 7th August 1926. Admission to the events held there in 1937 cost three shillings and sixpence for adults and two shillings for children. Malcolm Campbell the racing driver used Brooklands as his base. Malcolm Campbell, later Sir Malcolm Campbell, in his famous speed car 'Bluebird' was frequently in newspaper headlines and on newsreels in his attempts to break the speed records, at first on land, which he did in 1935 and then on water in his speedboat, also named 'Bluebird', in 1939. His last attempt to increase the record cost him his life. We saw the actual explosion and disintegration of his craft on the newsreels at the cinema. This took place in later years in 1949. After the sinking of the 'Bluebird', Sir Donald's Teddy Bear mascot 'Mr. Whoppit' was found floating on the surface of Coniston Water. It was retrieved and given to his daughter Gina.

Greyhound racing as a sport began in White City, London on

Belle Vue in the 1930s

20th June 1927. It was first introduced in 1926 and gave a modest alternative to horse racing for the working classes, but is believed to have originated earlier in Swaffham, Norfolk by the Earl of Orford. Manchester had its own popular Belle Vue Dog track. Of course for the rich and fashionable, Royal Ascot was the big day in the Horse Racing world even in the early 1920s.

A small matter of note in 1930, was that for the first time the King's Prize at Bisley for rifle shooting was won by a woman on 19th July. A great champion in women's tennis was the American Helen Wills-Moody. She won the singles title eight times at Wimbledon in 1927-30, 1932-33,in 1935 and finally in 1938 at the age of 32. This was a record that no other player had equaled. The first woman to swim the English Channel was Gertrude Ederle in August of 1926. Her time was just over 14 hours. The first British woman to swim the English Channel from France to England was Mercedes Gleitz. Born in 1900 she made the swim in 15 hours 15 minutes on 7th October 1927. Johnny Weissmuller who later played the leading part in the Tarzan films we watched so avidly as children, in July of 1922 became the first man to swim 100 metres in under a minute, taking 58.6 seconds. I remember him as a big man with broad chest and shoulders who uttered very few words in his films. Youngsters like myself would dream of swinging from tree to tree as effortlessly as did he.

The University Boat Race, first started in 1829, caused quite a lot of excitement among the population in the 1930s, whether or not individuals had any connection with the universities, or even the towns of Oxford and Cambridge. For some days before the race, shops were selling buttonhole favours of light blue and dark blue representing the two teams of rowers. These came as ribbon bows and sometimes a small, dangling, fluffy doll in light blue for Cambridge and dark blue for Oxford. Everybody seemed to sport a favour, adult and child alike and the merits of both teams were a constant source of discussion, small boys even coming to blows in guarding the honour of their favoured team. The members of our family supported Cambridge except for my mother who preferred Oxford.

On the afternoon of the race, all gathered around the wireless to hear the BBC broadcast with John Snagg giving the commentary from the River Thames. It was and is a unique race of four and a half miles from Putney Hard to Mortlake, passing under two bridges, Barnes Railway Bridge and Hammersmith Bridge. As a small boy my husband lived in Hammersmith and used to stand on Hammersmith suspension bridge to cheer the straining and

A day at the races. Royal Ascot, 1921

perspiring rowers as they passed underneath. We who could not be present at the race followed the wireless broadcast with tense interest and later would probably see it on the Pathe newsreel when we paid our weekly visit to 'the pictures'.

Since the event took place in March or April, it was usually cool Spring weather, but there was an occasion in around 1948 or 1949 when it actually took place in a snowstorm! For twenty years or more, up until 1935, B.H.Streeter, a great scholar, philosopher and Provost of Queen's College, Oxford, stood at the starting point of the race and in the minute or two before the gun, recited a limerick to the Oxford crew. This was probably to relieve the nervous tension the rowers would be under. At the sound of the starter's gun, the teams in their long boats, guided by a light-weight Cox sitting in the stern, the only member of the crew able to see where they headed, set off from Putney rowing the course up the Thames to the final post at Mortlake over four miles on, their long oars dipping lightly into the ruffled water.

Wimbledon 1930 Champion Hellen Wills-Moody
who won the title a record eight times

Crowds lined the banks and bridge under which the boats sped, each boat's Cox trying to take advantage of the varying current and banks. Cheering boys raced along the tow path and river banks, following as far as they could, while small craft gathered behind the official's boats followed the course on water. Among the crowds, the ice cream men and vendors did a roaring trade and excitement ran high as the crews neared the finishing post.

As the winning boat passed the post the umpire waved a flag; the supporters cheered and threw their caps in the air. The winning crew celebrated by throwing their Cox into the river. At this time it was an all male crew. No women took part. I wonder if the women Coxes of today undergo the same treatment? The fervour lasted while celebrations went on, Policemen turning a tolerant eye to student activities on that evening even if one or two of them lost their helmets in student pranks. It is difficult to realize the excitement that the boat race generated in these days of television and excessive amounts of football coverage. It seems that the boat race has almost been obliterated.

The Boat Race

Basket Ball was becoming a popular game for men in the U.S.A. and 1927 saw the founding of the famous Harlem Globetrotters team. The nearest game to compare with this in Britain was Netball. Normally played by schoolgirls.

A quieter form of recreation, hiking, became very popular in the late 1920s and early 1930s and in 1931 saw the founding of the Youth Hostels, basic accommodation for those hikers. For those of the population who preferred mental stimulation indulged in from an armchair, rather than that of physical exertion, The Times Newspaper published its first crossword puzzle on 1st February 1930. They were a little slow off the mark, as the very first crossword puzzle, compiled by Liverpool born Arthur Wynne had appeared in the American publication of the New York World in December of 1913.

CHAPTER 16

Apart from Sportsmen and Explorers, other portraits to grace the cigarette cards were those of the film world and theatre. The famous stage actress of earlier days, Ellen Terry, died in July 1928. She was born in 1882 on 24th October. Not a long life, but a full one in which her name became world famous. Another great name in earlier theatre was that of the French tragedy actress Sarah Bernhardt. Known as 'Divine Sarah' she died in Paris at the beginning of the decade in March 1923. The world mourned its loss of its 'greatest actress'. Dame Sybil Thorndike was enchanting audiences in the theatre thoughout the 1920s and 30s, while George Bernard Shaw, a dominant personality, continued to write his controversial stories and plays. Born in Dublin, Ireland in 1856 he could be a scathing dramatist critic, just as his plays showed recurring themes of social satire. He wrote 'Candida', 'Mrs Warren's Profession', 'Major Barbara', 'Pygmalian' and 'Saint Joan' among others that won him the Nobel Prize for Literature in 1925. He was a prominent member of the Fabian Society and an ardent socialist. He died in 1950 at the age of ninety-four, a prickly individual to the last. He and his wife had a home at Ayot St. Lawrence, a small hamlet in Hertfordshire, between St. Albans and Hitchin that he gave to the National Trust in 1944 on the death of his wife. I was too young to appreciate his work until the 1940s when some of his plays were made into films. The plays and stories of Bernard Shaw and other authors became more easily available to the general public when in 1935 the first Penguin paperback books were published, at a cost most people could afford.

Two people responsible for bringing many good plays to public notice during the 1920s and 30s were Sir Gerald Du Maurier, the actor manager who died in April 1934 and the well respected, theatre manager Lilian Baylis who died in November 1937. Lilian Baylis was adept with the mandolin and once played it on stage in Don Giovani. A kind, but not particularly physically attractive lady, she always wore gold pince-nez and her hair tied in a form of bun. She was never the less an excellent theatre manager and under her direction 'The Old Vic' thrived, becoming the home of Shakespeare plays and of opera. Some of the actors and actresses who drew the crowds in the years preceding the Second World War were Lawrence Olivier who in 1938 was playing the unmentionable Scottish King, MacBeth. Sir Lawrence was born in 1907. Also born in that year was Peggy Ashcroft who in 1936 was playing Juliet to John Gielgood's Romeo.

Lillian Baylis also ran Sadlers Wells that became the home of Sadlers Wells Ballet, later the Royal Ballet. When Lillian Baylis took over The Old Vic, it had previously been a low Music Hall, but within a short space of time she ran seasons of Shakespeare plays with many famous actors.

In 1920 Noel Coward was a young actor learning his craft. By 1921 he had started to write short plays and articles for American New York magazines 'Vanity Fair' and 'Metropolitan'. Throughout the 1920s he continued to write plays and musical pieces for his shows which included 'Hay Fever', 'Dance, Dance, Dance Little Lady', 'Poor Little Rich Girl' and 'Bitter Sweet' from which came the songs 'I'll See You Again' and 'Zigeuner'. His productions in the 1930s included 'Journey's End', 'Private Lives', 'Cavalcade', 'Conversation Piece', 'Red Peppers' and many others. Many of his plays featured the popular comedienne actress Gertrude Lawrence, as the leading lady. He composed many songs, subtly satirical as 'Mad Dogs and Englishmen', or 'Stately Homes of England', as well as the more romantic kind such as 'Some Day I'll Find You' and 'I'll Follow My Secret Heart'. As an actor, playwright and composer his work was witty and sophisticated and very popular. He was knighted by the Queen in his later years and died in 1973 at the age of 74.

Born on 15th January 1898, Ivor Novello was an up and coming name in the 1920s, a composer of romantic musical plays. Many of his musical plays were staged in Dury Lane Theatre between 1935 to outbreak of war in 1939 and then again during the war when the government allowed theatres to open once more. He wrote the song 'Keep the Home Fires Burning' for his mother during World War I. Though not a particularly brilliant actor, he took part in a number of his own plays. He had a particularly poor singing voice and never actually sang in his musicals although all the rest of the cast did. His musicals included 'Glamorous Night', 'Crest of the Wave' in Coronation year of 1936 and in 1939 'The Dancing Years' and King's Rhapsody'. Others were staged after the war.

Those who remember the American musical 'Annie Get Your Gun' shown in London after the Second World War, may be interested to know that the actual heroine of the piece, the sharpshooter of the west, Annie Oakley died in1926. Her real name being Phoebe Anne Oakley Moses.

1932 saw the opening of the Shakespeare Memorial Theatre at Stratford-on-Avon on the 23rd April, St. George's Day. This provided an alternative venue for actors and lovers of Shakespeare to the Old Vic Theatre in London.

Richard D'Oyley Carte ran the Savoy Theatre putting on the ever popular operettas of W.S.Gilbert and Arthur Sullivan. 'The Mikado', 'The Gondoliers', 'Trial By Jury' and H.M.S. Pinifore' being just a few of them. Many of W.S.Gilbert's witty librettos contained jibes at the political figures of the day. These are often now amended to fit modern day events. The composer George Gershwin tried something new when he put his operetta 'Porgy and Bess' on Broadway in New York for the first time on 10th October 1935.

Looking back, the 1930s was a period of coy 'Drawing Room Comedies' with French windows up centre back stage and young men entering and asking "Anyone for tennis?" except for the plays of G.B Shaw, J.B.Priestley and a few others in that category. Words were beautifully articulated so that speech could travel to the audience without the aid of microphones and amplifiers as yet not invented, thank goodness! No performances were allowed on a Sunday by law and the British censor wielded a firm rod. Reading a play was allowed as long as one wore ordinary clothes, but no hint of costumes or make up were allowed to be worn. With the coming of films, many old theatres and music halls had been converted into cinemas.

An influx of actors, singers and directors from Europe in the troubled times of the 30s brought fresh impetus to the British Theatre. There many stories told by theatrical folk of well known characters in that world, amusing and otherwise, of which I was far too young and sheltered to be aware of at the time, but some have come to my ears in later years, such as the following. Sir Donald Wolfit, an actor who loved the limelight, constantly toured with his company in his productions of Shakespeare when he and his wife took the major parts. They had just played 'Hamlet' at the Theatre Royal in one of the provinces where the house had been a somewhat 'lively' one. When Sir Donald stepped on to the empty stage and raised his hand for silence. He ended his usual speech with" and next week, we shall be performing the Master's 'MacBeth'. I shall of course be playing the Thane, and my wife Miss Rosalind . . . (when from the 'God's' came the call "Your wife's an old hag, mate!") Sir Donald paused, hand to mouth for several seconds, then glancing from whence had come the call, he continued "Never the less, she will play Lady MacBeth!"

The world lost some famous singers and composers during the two decades between 1920-1940. In December 1921, Camille Saint Saens, the French composer of 'Carnival of the Animals' died at the good age of eighty-six. In November 1924 Giacomo Puccini, the Italian composer of operas including 'La Bohime', 'La Tosca' and Madame Butterfly' died at the comparatively early age of fifty-six. Enrico Caruso, the famous Italian operatic tenor died in February 1921. He had been one of the first singers to record his voice on gramophone records for his public admirers. The German Wagnerean Lilli Lehmann made her final farewell in the May of 1929. Another famous singer from Australia, Dame Nellie Melba, said her last goodbye in February 1931.

She had announced her retirement in 1925. This great soprano's name lives on in the form of a Peach Melba dessert named after her. Dame Clara Butt, the British Contralto followed a few years later in January of 1936. The first performance of the Glyndebourne Festival of Opera opened on 21st May 1927 with Mozart's 'Figaro'.

Between 1932 and 1937 several famous composers left this world. The American John Philip Sousa, famous for his marching tunes, died in March 1932. Sir Edward Elgar, the British composer of' 'Dream of Gerontius' and 'Enigma Variations' in which he gave musical pictures of his friends, died in February 1934. He had composed music for Queen Victoria's Diamond Jubilee. A second British composer, Sir Edward German died two years later on Armistice Day 11th November. The following year on 28th December 1937, the French composer of the 'Bolero' and other popular pieces, Maurice Ravel departed this earth.

Within a year of one another in 1925 and 1926 the art world lost two of its talented painters. The American portrait painter John

Singer Sargent in April of 1925 and the French artist of many water lily pictures, one of the leading impressionist painters, Claude Monet in December 1926. Monet was born in Paris in November of 1840, but the house, his home for the final years of his life at Giverny with its beautiful garden and water lily pond, is still a place of pilgrimage for the many admirers of his art.

Notoriety was obtained by others who made the headlines of the news. Not for their good deeds, bravery or abilities in art or sport, but instead for their criminal activities. The United States and Chicago in particular acquired a reputation for gangsters. One Mobster was Al 'Scarface' Capone, who in 1931 was charged with 5000 offences under the prohibition laws. He received a ten-year sentence of imprisonment and a heavy fine of $80,000 for tax evasion. Some of these criminals profited hugely from American prohibition laws begun in 1920, through dealing in the sale of illegal alcohol.

Prohibition continued for fourteen years. Alka Seltzer the tablet to help dispel headaches and hangovers came on the market in 1931 in time for the end of prohibition! John Dillinger known as America's most wanted bank robber met his end when, after thirteen months on the run, he was shot dead by FBI men outside a Chicago cinema in July 1934. A couple who also came to a well deserved end when they were shot dead in a road block ambush by Texas Rangers near Gibland, Louisiana on 23rd May 1934 were Clyde Barrow and Bonnie Parker. Better known as Bonnie and Clyde, they with their gang, which included Clyde's brother and his wife, had been robbing and murdering together over a period of two years. Bonnie Parker had been working as a waitress when the two first met. When Barrow was jailed for robbery, she smuggled a gun to him to aid his escape. Together, they continued a life of crime robbing banks, not hesitating to kill in the process, until their fateful meeting with the Texas Rangers. Bonnie Parker had written a poem called 'the Story of Bonnie and Clyde' or 'The Story of Suicide Sal' in which she predicted their death.

CHAPTER 17

Although I was much too young to be interested, a number of events were happening on the political scene in the two decades of the 1920s and 30s which were to affect all our lives at a later stage. Looking back one can see that situations of unrest and signs of aggression from certain parts of the globe were gradually building to a peak culminating in the Second World War.

The 1920s had started in hope, with the founding of the League of Nations on the10th January 1920. The intention was to resolve the world's political problems and "to prevent future wars by establishing relations on the basis of justice and honour, to promote co-operation between the nations of the world." It was also planned to do social and economic work in an effort to improve the lives of those who suffered deprivation. In the U.S.A. the senate voted against joining. But other nations went ahead. A ceremony for the funeral and burial of the unknown warrior was carried out at Westminster Abbey on Armistice Day 11th November 1920 and on the same day one year later the first Poppy Day was held to raise funds for the wounded of World War 1.

Germany was admitted to the League of Nations in 1926 by a unanimous vote. Unfortunately, all these good intentions came to grief in the mid-thirties with the advent of Hitler and Mussolini. In October 1933 the Nazi government withdrew Germany from the League of Nations, and by September 1939 the world was at war once more.

Although Britain was not directly involved in actual conflict until 1939, certain political moves abroad had a bearing on home politics and Britain's overseas dependencies and colonies. British Civil Administration began in Palestine on 1st July 1920 and in 1922 on 11th September a British Mandate imposed by the League of Nations was proclaimed there. Arab States rejected it. On 25th May 1923 Jordan achieved independence. Independence was also granted to 26 counties in Ireland that became known as the Irish

Free State, or Eire, as was printed on the stamps of the time. It was hoped that this would calm the disorder in this troubled land. Six counties in Ulster Northern Ireland chose to remain in the United Kingdom. This change took place on 6th December 1921. The Irish Home Rule Bill had been given Royal Assent in 1914. On 21st January 1919 Sinn Fein MPs proclaimed an Irish Republic with Eamon de Valera as President, as the IRA (Irish Republican Army) attacked British Authorities in Ireland. Michael Collins, a leader of the Sinn Fein, became Prime Minister of the Irish Free State in 1922. He played a large part in the negotiations with Britain. Later that same year, dissidents killed Michael Collins in an ambush between Bandon and Macroom. The Irish Free State held their first elections in September of 1923. In June 1938 the Gaelic scholar Douglas Hyde became the first President of the Irish Republic.

In Europe, Mussolini seized power in Italy on 20th October 1922, after marching on Rome and forming a fascist government there. In the 1929 elections of March, Benito Mussolini claimed to have won 90per cent of the Italian vote. The King of Italy remained on the throne, but he was without political power. In Germany where there was rampant inflation and the cost of a loaf of bread was 200 million Marks and the price of butter made it too expensive to be served in restaurants, Black Friday of 1927 was the day that signalled Germany's total economic collapse. Looking in my old stamp album I see German stamps to the value of hundreds of thousands of Marks whose worth was actually very little. Some stamps of originally 200 Marks were over printed to 2 Millionen, others of a 1000 Marks over printed to 125 Tausend. The rate of exchange in 1923 became 4.2 trillion Marks to the dollar! This inflation continued until the Mark was eventually revalued.

Adolf Hitler attempted a 'putch ' in Munich on 8th November 1923. It was unsuccessful and led to his imprisonment, during which time he wrote 'Mein Kampf' his book of his ideology, published in July 1925. In the following year (1924) he resumed leadership of the National Socialist (German Workers) Party. This had been founded by Anton Drexler in Munich on 5th January 1919 and was better known later as the Nazi Party.

In Russia, Lenin, the communist leader died on 21st January 1924 aged fifty-three. Vladimir Ilyich Lenin was exiled twice for his anti-government activities, but returned to Russia to overthrow the government Council of Peoples Commissars. He became chairman of the Communist Party and virtually dictator of the Union of Soviet Socialist Republics formed in 1922 and in which Joseph Stalin, the son of a shoemaker was the General Secretary. Stalin took over power on the death of Lenin and from 1927 was undisputed ruler of the Soviet Union. Stalin became a ruthless dictator. And from 1930 carried out constant purges against sections of the population. He referred to these as merely 'purifying' the Soviet Union.

The beginning of communism was taking place in China where in 1921 the Communist Party was formed. I remember my father once pointing out a man of our village and telling me that he was a communist. I was very young at the time and had little idea of what a communist was. Ten years later, in London, opposing groups of communists, (the Red Shirts) and (Brown Shirts) fascists, founded and led by Sir Oswald Moseley clashed in fights in the streets of the city. These mostly took place on Saturday nights it seemed, with the city's police force doing their best to keep the conflicting groups apart. Fascist groups made attacks on the Jews as in the Cable Street Battle when the police were hardpressed to keep the peace. Sir Oswald Moseley's fascists marched in military style uniforms through the streets of London. It was not until 1945 that such uniform marches were outlawed. Sir Oswald Moseley and thousands of other fascist sympathisers were interned by the British Government on 31st May 1939. Other riots with a so-called religious basis, i.e. Catholics v. Protestants, took place in Ireland, Liverpool and Glasgow, where the football matches between Celtic and Rangers frequently took the form of a battle. It seems that men can always find an excuse to fight.

Country boundaries, names and ruling governments were changing. After the First World War of 1914-18, Tanganika (now Tanzania) was taken from German control and became a British Mandate in 1920, which gave Britain control of almost the whole of East and South Africa. France created the State of Lebanon on September 1st of the same year. In 1922 the last Sultan of Turkey was deprived of his authority, being deposed by Mustafa Kemal Ataturk who carried out many reforms to modernise Turkey. On the 25th March 1924, the country of Greece was proclaimed a Republic, its Monarchy rejected. 1924 saw a change of name for the capital city of Norway when Christiania reverted to its original name of Oslo, the name used before 1625. 1928 saw the kingdom of Albania formed, with King Zog as its first monarch. In 1929 the various states of Serbs, Croats and Slovenes in a section of middle Europe were named Yugoslavia for the first time. In 1930 Ras Tafari, Haile Selassie was crowned Emperor of Ethiopia, an African country still involved in slave trade. He abolished slavery there in 1932. In 1931 New Delhi became the new capital city of India. On the other side of the Atlantic Ocean, in 1932 Franklin Delano Roosevelt, although stricken with polio in 1921, fought against physical disabilities to become the 32nd President of the United States of America. In July of 1934 he became the first U.S. President to sail through the 41 mile long Panama Canal.

In Britain, the royal family was held in high regard and any royal happenings were treated with respect. When the widowed Queen Alexandra, wife of the late King Edward VII died on 20th November 1925, the country mourned. Happier royal occasions which gave cause for celebration, were the wedding of Princess Mary, the Princess Royal, in 1922 and the wedding of the Duke of York to Lady Elizabeth Bowes-Lyon 26th April 1923 at Westminster Abbey. Three years later came the birth of their first child; Princess Elizabeth on 21st April 1926 (our present Queen) and in 1930 on 21st August their second daughter Princess Margaret Rose was born.

A few years later we heard of the death of the young and popular Queen Astrid of Belgium who was killed in a motor accident. I well remember the black edged stamps among my stamp collection. From the age of nine I had been following my father's example collecting stamps, both British and foreign, in a not too serious fashion, but in the course of this hobby I picked up a reasonable amount of general knowledge about the various countries. King George V was also a keen collector of stamps and was reputed to have 325 albums.

I must have been nearly ten years old, when the country and of course our village, celebrated the Silver Jubilee of King George V and Queen Mary, on May 8th 1935, when the cost of posting a letter was still a penny in old currency and a newspaper cost two pennies. A Grand Fete was held in a second recreation ground in Shenley Road where the tennis courts were situated. Coloured bunting was brought out to decorate the recreation ground and main street. Stalls, side-shows, and competitions were held including baby shows, beauty and knobbly knee competitions, but what I remember most clearly was every child being presented with a pottery mug on which were the likeness of the King and Queen. In his Silver Jubilee broadcast in 1935, the King sent a special message to the children saying, " The King is speaking to you". Speeches were made in honour of their Majesties and three cheers given by all present. The tea tent and the beer tent did a roaring trade, celebrations were enjoyed by everyone in the village and Union flags flew in profusion. In the evening beacons were lit throughout the land.

Receiving a Silver Jubilee Mug

Sadly King George V, 'The Sailor King', died in January the following year and once again the country was in mourning. His eldest son Edward (more often called David among his friends) came to the throne as Edward VIII. Unfortunately, he was involved with a twice divorced American lady, Wallis Simpson (who was still married to Mr Simpson at the time) whom he wished to marry and make Queen of England. The situation was discussed whenever adults gathered together and although the British newspapers at that time were far more restricted in the news they printed, particularly with regard to the Royal Family, foreign news was full of the scandal and so news percolated through to the British population. The news was finally broken in the British Press on 3rd December 1936.

Divorce was very much frowned upon generally and the majority of the people in the United Kingdom felt that Mrs Simpson would not be a suitable Queen for the country. Therefore, the then Prime Minister, Stanley Baldwin had to make the situation clear to the King. Edward decided he could not live without Wallis Simpson by his side, and gave up the Crown to retain the lady. He abdicated in favour of his younger brother the Duke of York. For a short time after renouncing the Throne and all his titles, he became plain Mr Windsor. Edward married Wallis Simpson in Paris on 3rd.June 1937, leaving Britain to live in France. The new King, George VI, gave them the titles of Duke and Duchess of Windsor. All this made headline news for the media whose front pages were entirely taken up with the affair. Edward VIII's reign lasted just three hundred and twenty five days. The Duke and Duchess of York became King George VI and Queen Elizabeth, a popular decision with the general public and the British Government, who had been more than a little concerned of Edward's admiration of the rising German leader Adolf Hitler.

The coronation of George VI and Queen Elizabeth on the 12th May 1937 was a time of great rejoicing for the country, for they were a couple well loved by the people. The ceremony took place in Westminster Abbey. Celebrations were held in every town and village, with children gaining another commemoration mug of this occasion. The widow of King George V, Queen Mary, became the Dowager Queen and her stately upright figure was with us for many more years. She was born on 26th May 1867 and married George V in 1893 when she was Princess Mary (or May) of Teck. The World's largest (at that time) passenger liner 'The Queen Mary' launched on 26th September 1934 was named after her.

Launch of the Queen Mary, 1936

Other European royal families were having their problems also. In an effort to overcome strife among Serbs, Croats and Slovenes, King Alexander of Yugoslavia had established a dictatorship there in 1929. He was assassinated at Marseilles, France on 9th October 1934. His son Peter, who was a teenager at the time, fled to Britain for sanctuary. King Carol returned to the throne of Rumania in 1930, replacing his own son Michael. He remained King until 1940 when Michael replaced him. The communist take over in 1947 ended Michael's reign. Queen Marie of Rumania had died in 1938. In 1938 on 20th November, Queen Maud of Norway had also died. Happier news came with the wedding of Princess Juliana of the Netherlands to German aristocrat Prince Bernhard zur Lippe-Biesterfeld on 7th January 1937.

Political unrest in Europe was increasing. The Rhineland, an area of west Germany flanking the River Rhine, having been de-militarised in 1925 after World War One was evacuated by the Allies in 1930. In 1936 the Rhineland was reoccupied by Germany. Paul Von Hindenburg, the German Military and Political leader and President of Germany died on 2nd August 1934. He had appointed Hitler as Chancellor in 1933 and thereafter served only as a figurehead in German politics. In 1933 the Social Democratic Party in Germany was suppressed and the German Catholic Party was dissolved. The Nazi Party under Adolf Hitler banned all opposition parties. Dr. Englebert Dollfuss, the Austrian Statesman and Christian Socialist Chancellor from 1932 was forced into an alliance with the Austrian Nazi Party and assassinated by them during an attempted coup by the Nazi's on 25th July 1934. His murderers were executed a few days later.

In the March of 1933 Hitler proclaimed Germany's Third Reich. Many Jews took this as an ominous sign and a large number left the country. They were well advised so to do for the next move of the Nazi Party was to set up concentration camps. To them were sent opponents of the Party, along with Jews and gypsies. The Nazi's went to all lengths to quell any possible opposition. On the night of 30th June 1934, 'The Night of the Long Knives' over the course of this one weekend, hundreds of possible opponents to Hitler's dictatorship, including many old comrades who had helped him to power, were brutally murdered.

Hitler had been helped in his rise to power by Franz Von Papen, the German Chancellor in 1932 who organised a coup d'etat in Prussia. On the 12th September 1932 'The Reichstag', the parliamentary assembly of the German Weimer Republic formed in 1919 was dissolved. An indication of Hitler's aggressive ambitions was seen when he ordered conscription of Germany's young men for the army on 10th March 1935. In 1936 Joachim Von Ribbentrop, a Nazi leader was appointed ambassador to London. In 1938 he became the German Foreign Minister.

On the other side of the world, in 1926 on 25th December, the Emperor Hirohito acceded to the throne of Japan and was formally enthroned as Emperor of Japan in November 1928. Japan had launched the first purpose built aircraft carrier the Japanese Hosho, in 1922 and from the early 1930s Japan had been showing signs of aggression in the Far East. She had occupied Manchuria, setting up the Republic of Manchukus in 1932. Japanese troops captured Shanghai in China on 28th January 1932. Also in 1932 the Japanese Prime Minister Tsuyoshi Inukai was assassinated in Tokyo. Japan continued her hostile policy invading China whose National Government had been established in 1926. In 1934 China was at war within itself. The army of Communists led by Mao Tse-tung fighting against the National Army led by General Chiang Kai-Shek. By 1937 there was a full-scale war going on between China and Japan. It was not until 1938 that the League of Nations denounced Japanese aggression. In November of 1924 the last Manchu emperor 18 year old Pu-Yi, was forced from his palace in Peking and in the March of 1925 the Chinese Revolutionary leader Sun Yat-sen, known as the father of modern China, died.

There were also problems on the continent of India where in 1933 Mohammed Nadir Shar, the King of Afganistan was assassinated. In India, when in 1920 the Indian National Congress voted to adopt Mahatma Gandhi's campaign of non-co-operation with the British Colonial Government, further trouble flared. In 1930 Mahatma Gandhi had started a three hundred mile march to the sea in protest against the British salt monopoly. He continued to make peaceful protests against the British Raj at every opportunity with his vast following of supporters. It was not until 1947 that India was to get the self-rule she was seeking,

Britain had in 1931 recognised the independence of its dominions within the Commonwealth and in 1936 had signed an alliance with Egypt. Farouk had become King of Egypt on 28th April 1936.

Meanwhile Mussolini seeking power beyond Italy invaded Ethiopia in 1935 using gas warfare against warriors armed only with spears, capturing Addis Adaba and annexing Ethiopia for Italy in 1936. When Haile Sellassie appealed to the League of Nations, which had been founded in 1920 to try and prevent war, they were unable to offer him any help. Mussolini also attacked and annexed Albania in Europe. In 1939 the King of Italy was proclaimed Emperor of Abyssinia and also accepted the Crown of Albania. King Zog of Albania became another royal refugee.

The country of Spain was declared a Republic in April of 1931 after King Alfonso XIII abdicated and fled the land. In July of 1936 a civil war began in Spain then governed by the Republican Party. In October of that same year General Francisco Franco became the Supreme Ruler of Spain. By now I was old enough to realise that the world around us was, to say the least, insecure, although up until this time our family and friends had not been affected by its 'disagreements' and life appeared to go on as normal in our own surroundings. However, the news of the unrest in Spain between the Republicans and General Franco's Party was brought closer to us when young men from Britain volunteered to join the combating forces. Hitler gave his Luftwaffe some practice when he sent them, at Franco's request to bomb the Republican town of Guernica in Northern Spain on 26th April 1937. The famous painting by Picasso commemorates the event. When refugee children from Spain were brought to England, a group of them were accommodated in a large house on Rowley Green, near Arkley, Barnet. Parties of girls from our school went to make contact with them, but we could do little other than smile and make signs as they spoke little or no English and we spoke no Spanish. I seem to remember that we made up parcels of goods for the cause, but whether we sent them to the people of the Republic cause or the other side I do not know.

Later one or two Spanish girls attended Queen Elizabeth's School as pupils. A year or so earlier a girl from Germany joined our class, but it was only years later that I realised that she too was a refugee from Hitler's persecution of the Jewish population there.

On the 25th January 1938 people as far south as London's West End in Britain and throughout Western Europe were amazed to see dazzling lights playing across the sky. It was the Aurora Borealis or the Northern Lights as they are often called. The Vikings believed that the lights were caused by the flashing armour and spears of Odin's handmaidens, the Valkyries, riding out to collect warriors slain in battle to take them to Odin's palace of Valhalla. Scientists tell us that the lights are due to intense sunspot activity, but could they have been an omen or portent of the conflict in the forthcoming years and the Vikings had the right idea?

Neville Chamberlain had replaced Mr Baldwin as Prime Minister on 28th May 1937 at a time of heightening tension in Europe as the Nazi Party became ever more aggressive. Ignoring the terms of the Treaty of Versailles, Hitler had now formed a large army and was building up an extensive Air Force and Navy, which Britain and France failed to take any steps to stop. By 1938 the threat of war in which both Britain and France would be involved against the governing forces of Germany, looked imminent. Chamberlain met with Hitler at Berchesgaden on 15th September 1938 to try to resolve the situation.

Just as people had gathered to discuss the issue of Edward's abdication, now they gathered to discuss the possibility of war. There were many worried people in Britain's high streets, pubs and homes. Most people of my parents' generation had sharp memories, still fresh of the horrors of World War One and women were concerned that their husbands and sons would be called to fight. Therefore, when after Chamberlain returned from a second meeting with Hitler, this time in Munich on the 30th of the same month, waving a piece of white paper which declared "the desire of our two peoples never to go to war with one another again", there was understandably a great sense of relief. Smiles returned to faces, people feeling as though a great burden had been lifted from them. Life could go on, as before, there was no need to worry.

Most people did not realise that this agreement had been obtained at great cost to the country of Czechoslovakia. Hitler had demanded that Czechoslovakia cede him the Sudetenland, the western corner of the country in which a number of German speaking people lived. Chamberlain won Hitler's agreement not to go to war, but to annex the Sudetenland 'peacefully'. Hitler lost no time. He had already taken over command of the military forces at the beginning of February that year and was now the complete dictator in both political and military matters. Chamberlain had barely returned home when we heard that German troops had, on 1st October entered Sudetenland. On the 5th October President Beres of Czechoslovakia resigned. Very soon the Nazis had taken over the whole country.

On the 18th day of March, German Troops entered Austria and the following day forced a union (anschluss) of the two countries of Germany and Austria. Hitler's preparations for increasing his own and Germany's power continued in the build up of its air force, army and navy. Many planes, submarines (U-boats) were built and on 14th February 1939 the battleship 'Bismark' was launched. Continuing his thirst for power, Hitler had invaded Bohemia and Moravia on 15th March 1939 and on 23rd annexed Memel, a city in Lithuania. Many people must have been distressed when on 2nd January 1939 the American Time Magazine named Adolf Hitler as its 'Man of the Year'. The Mathematical physicist Albert Einstein wrote to President Roosevelt of America in 1939 warning him that German scientists were using uranium, probably to make an atomic bomb. He urged the President to start an atomic project.

There was mourning throughout the world, when at the age of eighty-one Pope Pius XI died on 10th February 1939. His successor Pope Pius XII was formally crowned on 12th March in the Vatican. Round about the same time, actually on 29th March, although the official end was not until April 2nd, the Spanish Civil War ended when General Franco's troops took Madrid after three years of fighting and the loss of many thousands of lives. Franco took over the country and remained firmly in control as Dictator until his death in 1975.

Each time Hitler invaded another country, he declared it was his 'last territorial claim'. Since no-one could trust his promises, everyone was very sceptical with regard to any of the German propaganda, but it was not until the end of 1945 that the world knew the great evils he had instigated in Germany and the countries his armies had occupied.

As the Nazis consolidated their occupation and power in Europe, the British Government, having followed the policy of disarmament for so long, began to try and make up for lost time by rearming. Preparations were also made towards the protection of civilians in time of war and on 1st February 1939 a white paper on Civil Defence in Britain was published. Consideration was given to gas attack, as it had been used by the German forces in the previous war of 1914-18 and in July 1938 gas masks had been issued to the civilian population of Britain for the first time.

On 29th May of the same year, the two Dictators of Germany and Italy signed an alliance in Berlin. The year continued in high tension for all in Britain and France. Veterans of the First World War recalled their experiences of the dreadful slaughter in Flanders and other areas, the terrible conditions of trench warfare and the loss of many comrades. Women remembered the young men they had loved, who never returned; the bombing raids by the Zeppelin air ships and the unfamiliar roles they had had to play whilst the men were away. My father spoke of his lucky appendicitis, which caused him to be transferred to a hospital in Alexandria, Egypt, while his battalion was posted to the horrors of Gallipoli. All those who had experienced World War One had their fears reawakened.

As a girl of thirteen, I sensed the tension and fears, but could not fully understand them, lacking the adults' experience. I believe most youngsters of my age indulged in a kind of excited curiosity to discover what all the concern was about. Young people continued to attend school as usual and meet with their friends, but underlying everything we did was the feeling that something momentous was about to happen. By March 1939 it had become obvious that appeasement was not the way to deal with such a man as Hitler and that only a greater force would prevent his armies over-running Europe. The British Government had begun conscription of its young men in the April. Housewives were buying extra tinned food and other supplies to keep in store 'in case' the worst happened, just as they had done in the crisis of 1938.

On the 1st day of June, newspaper headlines shouted a new tragedy when the British submarine 'Thetis' sank in Liverpool Bay. More than seventy people died. Some of those aboard at the time were invited VIP (Very Important People) guests. The reason for the sinking appeared a mystery as the day was calm and sunny. The sinking held the headlines and radio news for some time over three days of rescue attempts, to no avail. Some time later the submarine was refloated, renamed 'Thunderbolt' and played an active part in World War Two, by sinking two U-boats and bombarding enemy positions. In March 1943 it had the great misfortune to be sunk again with the loss of sixty-three officers and men.

By August it was clear that Hitler had designs on Poland as next in line for occupation by his armies. Chamberlain, speaking for Britain was joined by the French Government in guaranteeing Poland that they would not condone Hitler's aggression against that country and Hitler was warned that should he attack Poland, then both Britain and France would declare war on Germany. Hitler did not believe that the treaty with Poland would be backed by action from Britain and France, and on 1st September 1939 his armies marched over the border and started to attack the Poles who fought back valiantly. Britain gave him an ultimatum saying that if he did not withdraw his forces, we should declare war on Germany.

He did not withdraw. And so it was that on Sunday 3rd. September 1939 at 11o'clock in the morning we heard our Prime Minister speak on the radio. He sadly and quietly told us that we were now at war with Germany.

Almost immediately after the Prime Minister had finished speaking, the tall air raid siren recently constructed next to the blue and white Police Box on the Shenley Road near the recreation ground only three hundred yards or so from our house began to wail. Its eerie sound rose and fell, penetrating the deafest of ears around the area. It took us by surprise coming so soon after the Prime Minister's broadcast.

Along with my parents, Alan, Cindy and myself was my school friend Joyce. Joyce and I had arrived home from a bicycle ride, enjoying the last few days of our school holidays, just in time to hear the PM's announcement. With the wail of the siren we expected to hear the sound of approaching enemy planes and probably the scream of descending bombs, for we had just been bombarding our worried parents with questions "What will happen now?" "Do we still have to go to school? The sound of the air raid siren was our answer.

Mother was the first to take action, having memories of Zeppelin raids during World War One. "Quick, she said "gather all the cushions and put them on top of the table and then get underneath!" Then she drew the curtains across the window. Doing as she commanded, we youngsters crouched there under the table, waiting for the excitement to commence, while my parents sat nearby in armchairs with apprehensive frowns upon their faces. We waited, listening for unfamiliar noises for several very long minutes. Nothing happened. No planes, no guns, only silence apart from our breathing, until at last the sustained note of the 'All Clear' siren burst forth and we crawled out from our improvised shelter, feeling rather foolish.

This first alert we decided, was a bit of an anti-climax, especially when we discovered that there had been no enemy aircraft, but that it was only a practice alert. Never-the-less, it was for we school children the first of what was to expect when a raid was signalled and we were to have plenty of experience of the real thing complete with bombs, guns and a great many other unpleasant ingredients in the days to come.

Over the next few months there was much activity on the civilian front as well as the armed forces as we prepared ourselves for the expected onslaught. One of the first changes was the issue of gas masks for all the population. Notices were posted up throughout the village specifying on which day and time to report to the local church hall to collect and take instruction on the wearing of this hideous and uncomfortable object. Such lists were arranged in alphabetical order and as our name came at the beginning of the alphabet, our family were among the first to gain experience of these rubber and webbing contraptions which gave one the appearance of being from outer space, or an elephant minus half a trunk. The rubber clung around the face whilst the tight webbing straps, adjustable by a buckle, fitted closely over and around the head. The early form of plastic window gave a restricted view and the respirator drum through which air was filtered required the wearer to breathe with a steady rhythm. Not an easy thing to do in a crisis when feeling frightened. As the window frequently misted up, vision was limited while breathing was constricted and awkward and the awful smell of rubber assailed the nostrils.

There were special gas masks for young children called 'Mickey Mouse' masks. These had a small red, rubber balloon on the outside of the mask in the nose area, which supposedly inflated when children breathed out and which hopefully would keep them amused. Young babies were provided with another form of protection. This necessitated putting the baby inside a form of mask resembling a diving suit, or perhaps more akin to the modern spaceman type of helmet. Once the baby was inside, the mask was fastened under the body between the legs. It was then necessary for the mother to activate a concertina shape air pump by pushing it in and out. I pity any poor mother who had to carry such a contraption, as they were extremely heavy.

We practised under the instruction of air raid wardens and were then sent on our way with our respirators, or gas masks as they were more commonly known packed in their brown cardboard boxes attached to a cord enabling them to be carried as a shoulder bag or school satchel. Wardens advised that we should practice wearing the masks for ten minutes each day in order to familiarise ourselves with them. In the event of any raid using gas bombs, wardens would patrol the streets sounding wooden rattles of a kind heard at football matches. In the event of mustard gas being dropped, burns were to be treated with a 'Number 2' ointment kept in small tins at First Aid Posts.

The 'Black Out ' started on the first day of war. Ever since the 1938 crisis, plans had been going ahead with regard to actions to be taken by the civilian population in the event of war. The time had now come to put them into effect. The 'Black Out' when no lights were to be shown after dark was the first big change for everyone. All streetlights were extinguished including all advertising lights. Car lights and cycle lights were restricted to mere slights of light, as lamps were blacked out with dark paper, as were all torches. This caused a number of accidents in the early years of the war. Houses and other buildings, of course, must show no light and housewives were required to make curtains of black out material, used in addition to normal curtains, so that no slither of light shone through.

Apart from the blackout curtains, windows were pasted with

crosses of sticky brown paper to reduce the possibility of shattering glass in the blast of bombs. Many shop owners boarded up their windows apart from small areas, to protect the plate glass and prevent further damage, or injury from broken glass.

The evacuation of many children from cities considered to be in danger of attack from the air, had been carried out on the day war was declared. It was a traumatic exercise for many families, with young children being parted from their families for the first time, to go to live with strangers in an unfamiliar part of the land and a different way of life. Many of these children, used to city streets, but totally strange to the country, saw a cow or sheep for the first time of their lives. In the lull that followed the declaration of war, many parents took their children back home and a second evacuation had to take place when the bombing of cities became really serious in the August of 1940. On 30th September, identity cards were issued in which one's name address, date of birth and National Registration Number were noted. All adults were required to carry these with them at all times and they became an extra accoutrement to one's normal dress along with the gas mask in its brown cardboard box.

Warden Posts appeared in town and villages where volunteers issued with arm bands and tin helmets marked with 'W' to denote 'Warden' took turns at duty and practised first aid and emergency drill in preparation for times to come. Policemen also carried tin helmets, in their case marked with the word 'POLICE'.

It was a time of uncertainty and apprehension. Catherine decided to go back north to her family. We all missed her, but understood her feelings. Young men disappeared from the village to return some weeks later in smart uniforms of khaki, navy or air force blue. The autumn continued with little enemy air activity over Britain during the next few months, although the U-boats were already active at sea. Their first victim was the liner ''Athenia', torpedoed and sunk on the first or second day of the war, September the 3rd or 4th. The war at sea continued with 'Ark Royal' sinking a U-boat and then another U-boat sinking our aircraft carrier' HMS Courageous' with the loss of 518 men and the Commander. Merchant shipping suffered heavy losses in the early years of the war; unable to protect themselves from the ravaging U-boat packs lying in wait for them in the Atlantic. Britain was truly shaken when on 17th October 1939 a U-boat sneaked past all defences to the British naval base in Scapa Flow in the Orkney Islands and sank one of our biggest battleships 'The Royal Oak' at anchor in the harbour. It was an audacious act by a clever young U-boat commander. For Britain it was the loss of a fine ship and 24 officers and 809 valuable men. It was also a lesson to all to look to their defences and be more alert, even when in port. The war was no longer at a distance, but right on our doorstep and husbands, sons and brothers were being killed.

In December war was carried to the American continent when the 'Battle of the River Plate' in Uruguay took place. British battleships 'Exeter', 'Ajax' and 'Achilles' trapped the German battleship 'The Graf Spee' cutting off any escape and causing her commander to scuttle her on 17th December.

The Territorial Army had been armed with what equipment was available and under the title of the British Expeditionary Force, had been sent to France, where the French were relying on their Maginot line of defence to hold the German armies back. A faith soon shattered.

It was believed later that it was due to General Franco's great personal dislike of Hitler, that Spain did not also join the Axis Forces against Britain and her Allies, but decided to remain neutral in the struggle. A small mercy to be thankful for in a time of increasing troubles.

And so we come to the end of another two decades. A short period of just over twenty years of peace for Britain between two World Wars. The first of which had been fought with the same opponent in the hope that it was a war to end all wars. Now once again the world had to face man's senseless destruction of man for the gratification of a fanatical dictator obsessed by power. Does mankind never heed the lesson?

CHAPTER 18

Housework demanded time and effort in the days before World War two and for some years after the end of hostilities. There were few of the easy clean remedies that now fill the shelves of the supermarkets. Coal fires also caused more dust and dirt generally throughout the house when most women were without such items as vacuum cleaners, washing machines and tumble-dryers, instead, relying on broom, dustpan and brush and 'elbow grease'. Aunt Kate's Day by Day Book gives plenty of helpful hints for the busy housewife.

'Coal fires are often responsible for the dingy look of picture and photograph frames. Give them a weekly rub with a sponge moistened with oil of turpentine. Do not wipe dry. An occasional rub over with a paraffin rag will keep mantlepiece ornaments polished and cared for.'

On fires. 'For a fire for a short time only in a room, plunge a brick into paraffin oil and leave to soak for a few minutes. Then place in the empty grate and set light to it. It will burn for half an hour giving a splendid heat, leaving neither dirt nor dust.' And 'Place chalk instead of bricks at back and sides of the grate. Chalk throws out more heat. Cinders soaked in paraffin make good fire-lighters.'

'To break up large lumps of coal, cover lump with a piece of newspaper and hammer over it. The paper will prevent the pieces flying into the eyes. Bank up a fire with a mixture of slack, coal dust and potato peelings. Mix a little salt with the peelings to take away the smell.'

Paraffin seems to have been the housewife's standby for many purposes. E.g. 'Kitchen salt moistened with paraffin keeps baths clean and white.'

'Paraffin added to water when washing steps, helps prevent hands being chaffed.'

White hearthstone would be used for whitening door steps and a useful hint to stop them freezing in frosty weather was to add a crushed Asprin dissolved in a cup of warm water along with a tablespoon of methylated spirits to the washing water. Another use for Asprin apart from curing headaches was to sprinkle crushed Asprin on the soles of stockings, for the ease of sufferers of chilblains.

Scrubbing the front step

Further help was on the way to keep women's hands from being chaffed during the 1930s when a small Gloustershire company realised that rubber gloves would be an excellent way to protect women's hands. During the 1930s many middle class women were forced to do much of their own housework as domestic servants became scarce. For working class women now had the opportunity to take jobs in the fast emerging factories in light industry.

Unfortunately, although the idea was there, production of Marigold rubber gloves did not become established until 1950, after the end of the Second World War as the rubber latex was produced in Malaya, a country occupied by the enemy.

Other hints from 'Aunt Kate' explained how to improve the look of tiles by washing over them with milk, "Just enough milk to dampen the cloth."

Another;

'A coffee stain should be rubbed with glycerine and left for an hour, then rinsed in warm water.'

'To clean white piano keys, moisten a soft cotton cloth with methylated spirits and dip in a little whiting. Rub soiled parts and polish with a soft duster. A little milk on a cloth will improve black keys.'

'Marks on mirrors can be removed with fine whiting, washing blue, or powdered French chalk.'

Here is a hint on cleaning white straw hats.

'Dissolve a few crystals of oxalic acid in hot water. Dip a nail brush into the solution and scrub well, then rinse in cold water.'

And for velour hats,

'Sprinkle with ground rice and rub well, using a soft cotton cloth for the purpose. Finish by brushing well with a clean hat brush. The same treatment may be applied to felt hats.'

Even ostrich feathers were remembered, no doubt for the benefit of the maids of debutantes of the time.

'Draw the feather to be cleaned very gently through the loosely closed hand from base to tip in strong, luke-warm soap suds. Rinse in clear luke-warm water. For white feathers, add a little blue. Then tie a piece of string to the end of the quill and hang up to dry. Shake the feather while drying. For loose curling, shake the feather over a warm stove; for tighter curling, curl each tiny feather with a silver fruit knife, running it along the frond.'

One was even told how to make one's own blue from;

'Two penny worth of oxalic acid and Prussian blue mixed together. Put the mix in a quart bottle (two pints or 1.13646 litres) and fill up with water. Only a very little at a time is needed when rinsing clothes.'

'When washing glass, add a little vinegar to the rinsing water.'

'Stains can be removed by soaking in warm water containing vinegar and salt.'

'Heat marks on a polished table may be removed by rubbing with camphorated oil.'

Once read, newspapers came in handy for many other uses before being used to light the fire.

'Placed under an ironing sheet that 'wriggles', sheets of newspapers will keep it flat and firm.' They can also be used for rubbing spilt grease off the warm stove when cooking is finished.

'To save dishes from being cracked by necessary heating in the oven, place folded newspapers beneath them. The paper breaks the heat and the plates are comfortably warmed.'

Remembering that non-stainless steel cutlery was widely used; these are some suggestions for keeping such utensils clean.

'Non-stainless steel knives can be cleaned of stains by rubbing with raw potato. Rusty knives can be made bright by covering with garden earth and rubbing with a pad of paper. An efficient knife cleaner can be made from a piece of linoleum tacked to a board, used with a little powered brick poured on it.'

Care for the housewife's cleaning tools was also suggested.

'To remove fluff from brushes and brooms. Nail a piece of open mesh wire netting to a wall or fence just outside the kitchen door. Rub the brush up and down the wire and fluff will fly off easily. Before using a new broom, place it in a bucket of water for some hours. This will swell the wood and hold the bristles firmly in place.'

Since the housewife may be the gardener of the household as well, this piece of advice might also prove helpful.

'Night lights besides lighting dark corners of a house, can be useful for bringing on young plants for the heat they give out. To keep away frost, put several night-lights in the frame. The heat may be conserved by suspending a sheet of tin above the lights. A night light placed in the bottom of one flowerpot with another pot of the same size inverted, placed over the first, will give out a fair amount of heat.'

Wooden bead necklaces were very fashionable and so came hints to clean them.

'Put a mixture of bran and magnesia in a bag and shake the beads in this.'

'Glass and porcelain beads should be put in a bag with salt and immersed in warm water.'

Craftwork was also remembered;

'Bent celluloid knitting pins can be straightened by pouring hot water over them. Straighten with fingers and then harden by placing them in cold water.'

There are many more hints for cleaning wire mattresses, Venitian blinds, wicker-work furniture, linoleum, bedroom tiles, cork mats, iron pans, kettles, wringers and how to enamel a bath. Finally one is told how to make use of old gloves and stockings.

'Old gloves and stockings can be used for interlining iron and kettle holders (irons and kettles were heated on the stove until electric forms of these utensils were invented). Old woollen stocking feet slipped on hands with a pad for the palms are excellent for polishing floors etc.'

In 1937 'Aunt Kate' was recommending the January sales to buy cretonne for new cushions and curtains adding 'Remember too that the dress department may have just what you are looking for in the way of furnishing fabrics. Tweed is now very popular for upholstering suites and ideal for cushions and curtains.' By the 1940s the trend was completely reversed and women were raiding their scrap bags to find furnishing material to use for clothing!

Perhaps there is still a use for some of 'Aunt Kate's' hints in present day homes?

CHAPTER 19

Boreham Wood as I knew it no longer exists. Soon after the end of World War II in 1945, much of the land surrounding the village was sold by Hertfordshire County Council to London authorities, for new housing to re-house people from badly bombed areas of London. The vastly extended village became known as a 'New Town' and eventually even changed the format of its name to blend the two words into one Borehamwood. When the fields and woodlands began to disappear, my husband and I with our two young children moved to the west of England. Fifty years later on a return visit, there were less than a dozen buildings at most in the centre of the village which I recognised, The old post office, the church, the Crown Public House, the parade of shops, (among them my father's) and a few buildings down Theobald Street, including the Wellington Public House were the only familiar landmarks left of the old village.

The old post office no longer carries out its original function; the church was still recognisable though the trees, shrubs and gates that adorned its front had gone replaced by an attractively paved area; the Crown pub was woefully neglected, shabby and dirty. It had in the 1920s and 30s been the main hotel and busy meeting place from its prime position close to the railway station. Naturally the shops had changed owners and trades over the years and my father's shop had become a Chinese restaurant. The Wellington pub alone continued to conduct business as usual with the addition of a few modern accessories but managed to retain its old ambience and atmosphere. We had no time to visit the church, but assumed it carries out it parochial services to the community as churches have done for centuries past. I wondered if the tennis courts were still there? My friend writes of how the vicar, the Reverend C.F.G. Curgenven allowed the young people of the village to play there and how his housekeeper would provide lemonade to be enjoyed by them all. When the Reverend Curgenven retired in 1932 and the Reverend Maddock took over, he continued the custom allowing the young people to use the court. A second visit by me at a later date proved that the tennis courts have now been replaced by a quiet community garden with seating for tired shoppers, tucked between the new shop buildings. The cottages originally there, all gone long ago.

Mrs Pritchard, whose memories go back to the early 20s, remembers starting Sunday School at the age of seven in 1923 at the Old Parish Room in Theobald Street. It was also the venue for meetings of the Girls Friendly Society and the Band of Hope. The 'New Church Hall beside the actual church was not built until the late 1920s, or early 30s. Apart from the Parish Room, there was a Working Men's Club, a blacksmith, a short road with a few cottages where the district nurse lived and then the coal merchant W.H. Gates and also Nelson Staples the undertaker. I also remember Braithwaite the upholsterer had his business here. On the opposite side of the road were some shops. Bond's the fishmonger, who Mrs Pritchard says, "made very tasty fish and chips"; Bob Freestone's bakery and shop; Rastall Hardware and Ironmonger and Tompkins the butcher. Beyond the shops was a gateway on the right into fields where the Fairs and Circuses took place.

The road continued towards Radlett with a few houses along the way, in one of which lived Carl Brisson the singer, actor. Mrs Pritchard remembers often meeting him when he was walking his dogs. Past the houses was a water splash, or ford, later bridged over, spoiling much of the fun enjoyed here by the younger generation.

Mrs Pritchard remarks, "I have to say that it seemed to me the village was divided into two in a sense. There were the people who lived in the village i.e. Theobalds Road area, (the original village centre) Glenhaven Avenue who had their groups and our end, Clarendon Road, Maldon Road, Shenley Road also had our own groups. The children for instance played in their own roads naturally and apart from school and church 'do's we didn't mix geographically. There were of course the friendships that developed that passed those boundaries and kept the village integrated. I had friends in Clarendon and Malden Roads, but I also had friends in Furzehill Road and Drayton Road. That's how things were then."

Being a small community (about 3000 population) everybody knew everyone else and all joined in the fetes, bazaars and other organised community gatherings.

The Watersplash, Theobold Road, Boreham Wood

In the early 1920s there was only one doctor in the village, Doctor Martin who lived in Allum Lane, some way from the main area of Boreham Wood. Mrs Pritchard recalls having to walk there to get help when her little sister was ill with a high fever. Her sister had developed Scarlet Fever.

Shenley Road was the main shopping area for the village and supplied a reasonable variety of shops for a smallish village. Up the slight hill near to Station Road and on the same side was Cole the Chemist, then came the wine shop. Next to this was a Newsagent shop which also served as a post office before the new post office was built on the other side of the street further down the hill; Grooms the men's outfitters, and after that Alliston's Elstree radio service where radio batteries could be recharged. By 1935 Boreham Wood had three banks almost opposite one another, the National Provincial by Alliston's and Barclays beside the Crown Hotel. The third bank was on the corner of Station Road, but I do not remember the name. Between the National Provincial Bank and the next group of shops was an open piece of land and some houses. Wilkins shoe shop was next and a few years later Mrs Chessell's children's clothes and wool shop opened beside Wilkins. There was possibly an estate agent or betting shop next, that seemed to me to have an air of mystery about it, probably because my family never entered there. All these shops were well back from the main road, leaving a wide pavement area before meeting the opening to Drayton Road.

On the other side of Drayton Road was another private house before coming to Hunt's the butcher. This shop was later taken over by Mr Young. Beside Hunt's was a house whose occupants ran a dolls' hospital. Most dolls in the 1930s had china heads, easily broken. More than one of my poor dolls had to go there to be repaired. Next to the dolls' hospital was the sweet and toy shop of the Misses Byers sisters. My sister remembers that the Misses Byers gave sweets to children who saved silver paper for them. Mr. Cherry the Cobbler was next door. On the corner of Furzehill road was a shop selling oil and candles. This later became a cycle shop. The Baptist Church stood on the opposite corner of Furzehill Road after a piece of open land surrounded by a hedge. The road continued up a rise and down towards the Church of England, All Saints' Church where there were a number of semi-detached cottages, the one nearest to the church being Beatie's the photographer.

Elstree, Station Road, Boreham Wood

Beside the church was the old vicarage, (now replaced by a modern house for the benefit of the vicar and his family) and the church hall. There was then an open space on both sides of Cardinal Avenue, before coming to the next group of shops. On one side of Whitehouse Avenue, the next road along the main street, was a fish shop, (Bonds), a greengrocer (Garrard's) and Bob

Freestone the baker. On the other side was the group of shops in which my father had his Newsagent business. This was made up of a corner shop wine merchant off-license; Mr. Cleaver the grocer or Down's shop; Eve, the Hairdresser; The Library (our shop), and the Grosvenor Restaurant. From there on it was film studios all the way from Shenley Road to Elstree Way, except for Pickford's removal company a short distance up the Elstree Way, but I do not remember when they first appeared, possibly not until just after the war.

Going up Shenley Road towards the railway station, on the other side; the Red Lion Public house was built in the first part of the 1930s and in the second half of the 1930s Eldon Avenue developed. Even later in the 1930s some shops between Eldon Avenue and Grosvenor Road, including another newsagent appeared. Bob Freestone's brother had a bakery at the end of Grosvenor Road and later built a shop named the Dutch Oven on the corner. There was also a dress shop run by the Misses Sampson. No further buildings faced Shenley Road until one came to the corner of Clarendon Road where stood Catchpoles Elm Farm Dairy. Hedges Farm was previously in this area, but had gone before 1935 although I remember my parents referring to Mr and Mrs Hedges by name. Cutting across Clarendon Road was Essex Road leading to the Ideal Film Studios. Apart from a couple of houses there was an empty space here where on November 5th the local boys built a large bonfire. Children made Guys with old clothes stuffed with straw with a painted mask for a face. These they took into the main street in an old barrow usually made from a wooden box on old pram wheels and implored passers by to give 'a penny for the Guy'. These Guys were later burnt upon the bonfire while parents gave a display of fireworks, each family contributing for the benefit and entertainment of all.

From Clarendon Road as far as Central Garage were private dwellings, terrace cottages, two of them housing a doctor and dentist's surgeries. Doctor Winter arriving some time in the late 1930s. Coal deliveries had to be taken through the houses, as there were no back entrances. Beside Central Garage was the entrance to Keystone's Stocking Factory. On the other side of the entrance to Keystone's was Hanson's sweet shop (previously Starkie's); Read's Greengrocer and then Robert's Grocer were next beside Hanson's, Tucker's the Draper and then Clinton, men's hairdresser with his red and white striped barber's pole protruding from above the shop doorway. A double fronted house later became the Electricity Showroom. The Co-op store came next with a small passage between them and the Electricity offices. Then came Tom Wingate's open fronted general store, closed at the end of the day with a green metal roller blind. One then came to the entrance of Wellington and Ward's film factory that made roll films for the more modern cameras of the time. Later they became Dufay Films. A brook ran here which appeared again half way down Clarendon Road by an entrance to the stocking factory and then ran behind the houses in Grosvenor Road. A great place for collecting frog spawn!

The Post Office then a few more shops among them Pentecost, greengrocer and florist (this later became Payne's); Carpenter's dairy, and Bob Freestone, baker on the corner of Glenhaven Avenue. Across Glenhaven Avenue one came to C. Pressey, draper, haberdasher and wools; Hastwell's Ironmongers; King's fish shop; Barclay's Bank and the Crown Hotel.

We were very fortunate in being surrounded by much pleasant countryside. Beyond the film studios, the Red Lion and the cinema, Shenley Road continued as a country lane curving its way past a few council houses and long hedges full of blackberries in September, on its way to Green Street and the village of Shenley. It was a lovely walk or cycle ride that we often made when exploring our environment. Potters Lane winding uphill leading to Well End was another enjoyable country walk or ride. Scratch Woods, approached via Furzehill Road was entered by a tall metal gate on Barnet Lane, the road leading to Elstree village. This was another favourite walking or play area for young people in a time when parents did not have to fear for our safety. It was also a good blackberrying area, giving a delicious addition to the family apple pies. We were able to reach these woods without needing to walk along any main roads, by taking the footpath by the film studios to the top of Bullhead Road, to make our way through fields via footpaths to come out at the top of Furzehill Road just above the 'Home and Rest for Horses'. From there it was a short walk across Barnet Lane to the entrance of the woods. Prince, our dog enjoyed running free to explore all the exciting scents and sounds around him while we equally enjoyed our games of hide and seek. Our childhood was blessed in the fact that we had so many fields, woods, ponds and other country places where we were free to explore and play.

Although on my last visit to Borehamwood I noticed that the old entrance to Scratch Woods still remains, many other areas of our childhood playgrounds such as the bluebell woods and fields have disappeared. These have been replaced by housing estates and schools, as has the area where the fairs and circuses were held.

In Shenley Road, if one looks above the new shop fronts it is possible to see the remnants of some of the original buildings, a stark contrast to the altered fronts on the lower street level. Where Keystones Stocking Factory and Dufay Films once stood their place is now taken by a very large and modern shopping complex stretching behind the main street all the way from Clarendon Road to the old Post Office. The old Red Lion Public House on the corner of Eldon Avenue has been turned into McDonalds beef burger drive in restaurant and beside it where the cinema once stood; large office blocks take its place. The War Memorial has been moved from its original position outside the Crown Hotel near the railway station, to this area close to the beginning of Elstree Way. Along Shenley Road a little beyond the new office blocks, the old Roman Catholic Church still stands, but is joined by its younger replacement.

Returning towards the main village, now town centre, Clarendon Road, Essex Road and Maldon Road remain much the same apart from the rows of cars parked outside the houses. Few cars would have been seen in the 1920s or 1930s for the occupants of the cottage terrace homes would have been most unlikely to have afforded such a luxury. The entrance to the old Rock Studios from Clarendon Road is still there, although the studios have now become the BBC TV studios producing the TV 'soap' shows such as 'East Enders' plus documentaries and comedy programmes. Opposite Clarendon Road on the other side of Shenley Road the old Church Hall has become Borehamwood Village Hall, but apart from the sign and colour (it is now a dark red instead of green) looks much as I remember it.

Some of the other studio buildings on Shenley Road are still producing films, renting the properties from the local authority, so keeping the industry alive, but it is hardly the hive of activity we knew in the thirties. The 'right of way' path (through the grounds where the facades of film sets were built), leading to a stile and exit at the top of Hillside Avenue and Bullhead Road, has been built over by industrial buildings and what appears to be a multi-storey car park, although at the time I could see very few cars making use of it. The rest of the path although retaining its wire fencing remains, but is unusable as access to Shenley Road has been cut off.

Grosvenor Road where my old home still stands was easily recognisable, but I was sad to see that all the Spring flowering Almond and Cherry trees which had lined the road had gone. As had the tall old oak trees we used to climb, one of which stood outside a neighbouring house two houses further down the road.

As I walked down Grosvenor Road, the names of many of the inhabitants came flooding back to me. The Binnoths, a couple from Switzerland and their son and daughter; the Hills with their daughter, my friend Peggy and her younger brother Billy; and after them in the same house the Goddards. Poor Mr Goddard who suffered from lung cancer and whose coughing we could hear before he gained his final release; the family of the RAC man who we saw dressed in his grey/blue uniform to go out on patrol with his motor bike and sidecar; the Rushtons who lived in one of the bungalows; the Innocenti family, our immediate neighbours whose young daughters I took out in their pram and who became two of my bridesmaids at my wedding. Their father was a member of an Italian family who had settled in the district some years before. The Armours with their two sons who were our playmates and later a daughter; the Heathcotes whose Sunday joint our dog Prince stole one day; the Bakers, Mr Baker a veteran of the Royal Flying Corps of the first World War; the Knights, mother, father and twin sons, pals of mine, whose father was Scott Saunders a well known comedian of stage and radio and whose mother was in many films. From the corner house, first the Carols, friends of my parents and their son and later the Jones and their son. In between times houses were rented by people in the film industry on a short term basis, actors and technicians as the industry required. Of the houses and bungalows there was little change, but in what used to be the Dutch Oven Bakery on the corner of Grosvenor Road and Shenley Road, there were marked alterations. The Horses and stables had gone, the building amended to become an Italian Restaurant. The bright greeny/blue roof tiles of the 1930s, had been replaced by those of the more traditional reddish brown colour. The adjoining dress shop remained, but no longer sold dresses, it was instead an estate agents office.

There were also changes to the recreation ground at the end of Grosvenor Road where we had played our games of cricket and football. A rather ugly brick building stood in a corner of the ground where once the children's round-about had been. It had been built towards the end of the 1939-45 war, or just after the end of hostilities and had served as a health centre where young mothers took their babies to be weighed and checked. It then became a centre for Workers Educational Association classes and a First Aid Post. Now I found it boarded up and neglected. Much of the rest of the recreation ground had been made into a garden protected by hedging where seats provided opportunities for quiet contemplation and no ball games were allowed. One corner of the ground had been reserved for the pleasure of younger children. This contained the Monkey Ladder (possibly the same one from which I fell), a see-saw and two swings all painted the same dark green colour I remember from my young days there.

In Theobald Street alongside the railway more old cottages were being demolished and replaced by other buildings. From the rundown appearance of other old shops alongside the Wellington Pub where Bob Freestone, Tompkins, Bonds and Rastwell once sold their various wares, it seemed that they too would be deemed for demolition thus removing almost all the last vestiges of the original character of the old village.

A short distance further down Theobald Street or Radlett Road as we more often called it, was Red Road a small tree lined road of private houses for the more wealthy members of the local population, which runs alongside the railway line leading to Radlett and St. Albans. The planked bridge across the line, from where we watched the steam trains chuffing under us and waved to the engine drivers, had been replaced by a much wider and more substantial brick structure. It was no longer possible to see over its taller walls the now electrified, trains rushing along below.

However, the park on the other side of the bridge remained open to all those who wished to walk through the wide area of grassland and still looked much as I remembered apart from the extending golf course encroaching on one side of its boundary, outlined by a number of stakes. Judging by the unfortunate mess left within the entrance area, the park is much used by dog owners walking their pets, who seem to ignore the 'poop' bin put close by for their use.

Allum Lane is still one of the more attractive areas of Borehamwood, although strictly speaking, being on the other side of the railway bridge from town, occupants of the houses there probably consider themselves part of Elstree, as the station is known as Elstree Station. Rising fairly steeply uphill, Allum Lane is lined with beautiful horse chestnut trees, grown even larger over the years than I remembered them as a child, when even then they seemed huge to me. On this return visit the light was shimmering gently through the branches in the Autumn sun, bringing out the glorious glowing colours of the changing leaves, whilst our feet rustled through those already fallen, reminding me of the family walks up here with my brother, sister, and parents to collect the shiny, round mahogany coloured conkers, broken away from their prickly green cases to lie among the fallen leaves at the base of the tree. It is obviously a custom still maintained by the present generation of children.

A few of the more substantial houses remain one of which is signified by the history written on its wall. It informs passers by "THIS BUILDING WAS BEGUN 1789. THE GROUND EXTENDING 9INCHES EASTWARD FROM THIS QUOIN IS THE BUILDING BELONGING TO WILLIAM PUTLAND". William Putland was obviously keen to claim every inch of his land. The building on which the writing appears was originally the coach house for the CLOCK HOUSE a large house built for the above William Putland. Two other houses stood where Barham Avenue is now. One was Barham House and the other Hillside. Barham House, in 1754-76 was occupied by the writer and traveller Edward Wortley-Montagu. Both Barham House and Hillside were demolished in1932. The old Coach House was made into two dwellings in 1951.

The old Manor House opposite the station still stands and was to become a community centre I believe, but there are many more new detached homes that have been built in the grounds of the old buildings. Halfway up the hill Barham Avenue was considered to be a 'select' area in my young days and is still a privately maintained road, although it has been extended in the form of a crescent to join up with the main road again further down the hill. A short distance above Barham Avenue, I noticed a pleasant looking path through a wooded area. This led out towards the golf course running behind Barham Avenue and joining up with the park we had approached from Red Road. On the brow of the hill in Allum Lane, the Villa Capri, Richard Tauber's house used to stand. I remember it as a white painted house in typical 1920s-30s fashion. It has gone along with many others, but Richard Tauber is remembered in the name given to a new close of houses on the opposite side of the road, Tauber Close.

On the summit of the hill stands Nicoll Farm and the pigsty where our Sunday walks culminated. For it was here we leaned over the wall to talk to the pigs and indulge in a little pig back scratching they so enjoyed. Sadly, although all the old buildings remained it is no longer a working farm and there were no pigs to welcome our attentions. The sty building was there, but overgrown with weeds, no longer of use to the present owners it seems.

It was good to see that Boreham Wood was one of the lucky towns to survive the Dr. Beechham 'cut' and succeeding economic drives and retained its railway station. A useful commuter area it has a direct service to London, Kings Cross and St.Pancras. One change I noticed, the entrance to the station is now from the Borehamwood side of the bridge and not the Elstree side as I remembered. A little closer for the town's people, a little further for those coming from Elstree.

Deacons Hill is beside the Elstree side of the station and a short walk up the hill brought me in view of my old kindergarten school. A private house now, but still recognisable as the two teacher school I had attended, run by Miss Windsor and Miss Shelton. Both teachers strict but fair in their treatment of children, where the worst punishment was a rap across the knuckles with a ruler if one was really naughty, usually only suffered by the boys. I doubt whether any parent complained about that.

Another hill road, Furzehill, runs from the centre of the town towards Barnet and again has managed to retain a few of its original buildings. It is the site of the new Baptist Church, replacing the one of which my family were members, that stood on the corner of Furzehill and Shenley Road. Brownlow and Drayton are small roads joining with Furzehill. They have some of the remaining old cottages fronted by small strips of garden. They are interspersed with a few modern small houses. The Elstree and Boreham wood

Museum and the Borehamwood Times Newspaper are now situated in Drayton Road.

Furzehill School remains in its same position, but is a much larger building than the original premises, taking up more of the playground with classrooms. As a teenager I played here in a netball team with a local league. Furzehill retains the leafy appearance of the country road I recalled, although there were groups of new housing where once had been fields. Over the brow of the hill and on the down slope, used to be the 'Home and Rest for Horses' another favourite place to visit on our walks, where old, or poorly treated animals could enjoy a peaceful retirement grazing in the fields and being housed in specially built stables, cared for by loving hands. It was a happy afternoon for we children, stroking their soft muzzles and feeding them handfuls of grass or pieces of apple. Another housing estate has taken their place, but the memory of the horses home has been kept in the names of the roads, each road being named after different breeds of horses e.g. Perecheron Way, Palomino Drive etc.

More than fifty years have passed since I was a resident of Boreham Wood and that is a long time in our short span of life. Many say you should never go back, however, old memories and curiosity won the day when I began to write of the 1920s and 1930s period of this century. Life and technology move at such a pace that change is inevitable and much of what we knew and often enjoyed has disappeared never to return. Perhaps some of our descendants may one day enquire out of curiosity "I wonder what it was like before . . . ?" Maybe this book will give a little clue to the answer of that question.

Before leaving the town I was speaking to a lady in the pine furniture shop between Furzehill and Drayton Roads. She told me that she can always identify the long term residents of Borehamwood, as ignoring the large growth of the New Town, they still referred to it as 'the village', but for me sadly, I found that little of the character or atmosphere of the old village remained.

When I recalled the memory of the temptation of the chocolate elephant I never thought it would lead me to so many more memories of this time between the two world wars. It has been a fascinating journey for me. Perhaps it will add a spark to the memories of others!

SHENLEY ROAD NORTH SIDE

1 Crown Hotel
2 Barclays Bank
3 Fish Shop
4 Ironmonger (H.Hastwell)
5 Draper (C. Pressey)
6 Baker (Bob Freestone)
7 Theobald Farm Dairy (Carpenter)
8 Florist & Greengrocer (Pentecost later S.H. Payne)
9 & Post Office
10 (built here late 1930s-40s)
11 'Poplars' Large House & Garden
12 T. Wingate General Store No.49
13 Shop
14 Shop
15 Shop
16 Shop
17 Co-op

55 Electricity Showroom
56 Barber (A. Clinton)
57 Draper (E. Tucker)
58 Greengrocer (Robert or Read)
59 Sweets (Starkes later Hanson)
60 Central Garage
61 Dentist (L. Isbill)
62 Doctor Winter
63 Elm Farm Dairy (Wm. Burrows later L. Cook)

SHENLEY ROAD SOUTH SIDE

38 Westminster Bank
39 Station Parade Chemist (Cole, B.W. Rugg or R. MacNaughton)
40 Off Licence
41 Men's Outfitters (Groom)
42 Post Office, Newsagent (Mrs A.M. Kidwell)
43 Radio Shop (H. Alliston)
44 National Provincial Bank
45 Shoe Shop (Wilkins)
46 Wools, Baby Wear (Chessell)
47 ? Betting Shop, Estate ?
48 House
49 House, Dolls Hospital
50 Butcher (S. Hunt)
51 Sweets (Misses Byers)
52 Cobbler (F. Cherry)
53 Grocer (Kilby?)
54 Cycle Shop (previously oil & candles)

64 Photographer (L. Beattie)
65 Optician (Wright & Mills)
66 ? previously Hedges Farm?
67 Dutch Oven Bakery (Freestone)
68 Fishmonger (Bond) Studio Parade, 132 Shenley Road
69 Butcher (Warner) 9 Studio Parade
70 Greengrocer (F. Archer) Garrard
71 Baker (Bob Freestone) 7 Studio Parade
72 Osbornes Off Licence 6 Studio Parade, Shenley Road
73 Grocer (J. Downe, Mr. Cleaver)
74 Grocer (later part sweet shop)
75 Hairdresser Eve, 4 Studio Parade, 144 Shenley Road
76 Newsagent (The Library, R. Acason) 3 Studio Parade, 146 Shenley Road
77 Restaurant, The Grosvenor (Mrs. C. Mann) 1 & 2 Studio Parade, 148 Shenley Road

THEOBALD STREET

18 Butcher (Tompkinson)
19 Hardware (Rastall)
20 Baker (Bob Freestone)
21 Fishmonger (Bonds)
22 Wellington Public House (A.G.R. Sutton)
23 Blacksmith
24 Working Men's Club
25 Cottage
26 Cottage
27 Cottage
28 Cottage
29 Cottage
30 Cottage
31 Mission Room
32 Field (where fair and circus held)
36 Upholsterer (G. Braithwaite)
37 Undertaker (Nelson Staples No.6)

Also in Theobald Street there was Percy Blazier an outfitter, a garage, Roberts Cartage Contractor.

In Station Yard Lockharts Coal Merchant

All saints Church, (1910) Vicar from 1917 Rev. H. Curgenen, then Rev. W. Maddock, 1937

Baptist Free Church, (1909) Rev. A. Small then Rev. A. H.. Waugh

Roman Catholic Curch in Shenley Road beyond Cinema (not shown)

Sion Convent in Theobald Street (not shown)